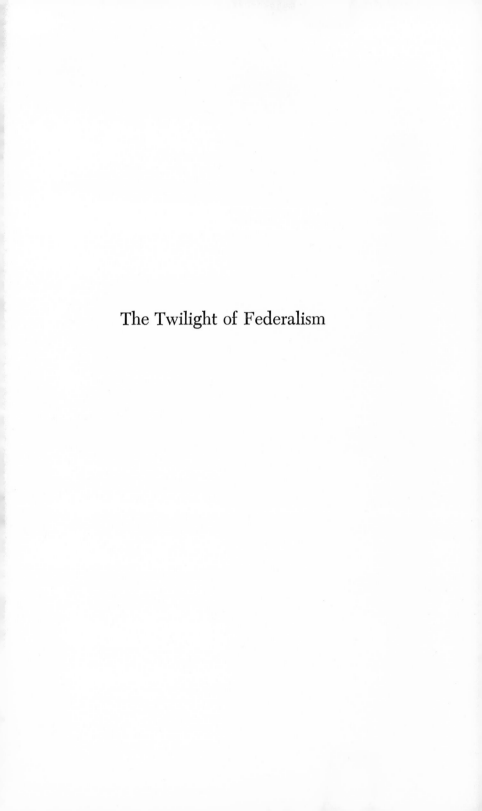

The Twilight of Federalism

THE TWILIGHT OF FEDERALISM

THE DISINTEGRATION OF THE FEDERALIST PARTY
1815-1830

BY SHAW LIVERMORE, JR.

PRINCETON, NEW JERSEY

PRINCETON UNIVERSITY PRESS

1962

FOR MY

MOTHER AND FATHER

PREFACE

PORTRAYALS OF POLITICAL CURRENTS in popular histories of the United States often include the view that the Federalist party was destroyed about the year 1815, leaving the national political field entirely to the party of Thomas Jefferson. Federalists, according to this view, simply departed the political scene. Then for several years an absence of clear-cut issues and a system of party discipline known as King Caucus maintained one-party government until the explosion of 1824. By that time many Jeffersonians had discovered that false and dangerous ideas had come to erode the old and pure Republican virtues. These new ideas were suspiciously similar to those of long-dead Federalism. When Andrew Jackson came forward in 1828 to cleanse the house of democracy he and his followers discovered that their enemy was a party composed of mysteriously revivified Federalists and a corps of Republicans which had been infected by Hamiltonian ideas to a degree beyond the curative powers of General Jackson. Whiggery, for all practical purposes, was simply Federalism called by another name. Daniel Webster and his fellow Federalists had succeeded in creating a new national party in order to fight the old battles once again.

This view is, of course, too simple and sharp-edged for scholars, although it is fair to say that parts of it remain attractive to them. Some argue that a touch of Federalism was what the country needed after years of drift under James Monroe. The curious part of the argument, however (and one that is widely accepted), is that Federalism and Federalists were destroyed by 1816, only to reappear years later. We are asked to believe that the carefully wrought and persuasive doctrines of Federalism ceased to be the rallying cry of a national political party, and especially that thousands of

vii

Federalists, young and old, slunk off to a land of Nod, stayed there for several years, and then decided to come back. Once back they found their way easily into political life, indeed they put a dreadful scare into the ranks of Republicans, who in turn found a redoubtable champion just in time to save the day. The sophisticated might point out that what really happened was that Republicans had taken unto themselves the Federalist program in the years following the war, only to find out later that they had made a lamentable mistake. But because they waited so long to discover the error of their ways, only stern measures, again under Jackson, could restore the essence of Republicanism. Once again, however, the role of Federalists as individuals remains curiously blurred.

The following pages represent an effort to find out what happened to Federalists during the years between Madison's and Jackson's administrations. This effort proceeded from the assumption that Federalists simply could not have vanished after the Hartford Convention, that they did not abruptly depart the political scene in all but a few out-of-the-way local areas. Only once in our national history has one of the two major political parties passed out of existence without another present to take its place at once. Thus this period offers a unique opportunity to study both the leaders and the followers of a dead party. This study proceeded too from a guess that Federalists probably affected, perhaps in a major way, the peculiarly artificial course of one-party government, the continued use of the caucus system long after any real threat of a national Federalist challenge had disappeared, the unique presidential campaign of 1824, and finally the re-emergence of a two-party system.

A search of the sources reveals that Federalists certainly did not leave the American political arena at the end of Madison's second term. True, most of them were angry and confused upon seeing their party driven to irretrievable defeat, but they maintained a burning interest in political affairs.

After the Republicans had adopted much of the Federalist program of public policy the most important question for Federalists as individuals became that of re-entering public life. Thousands of ambitious Federalists found unbearable their effective proscription from public office. Federalists had always believed themselves especially suited by birth and training to rule over others. Their desire for office was further heightened by the fact that American society in their time offered few institutional channels through which men who fancied themselves superior to others could find public acceptance of their self-assumed superiority. No clearly defined social classes existed, no great hereditary fortunes had been accumulated, and no semi-public posts in the military or ecclesiastical superstructures were open only to certain established families. Thus many Federalists were inordinately eager to obtain public office. To get office demanded that they pay close attention to public affairs.

Republicans, for many reasons, were just as eager to keep Federalists out of government. They knew perfectly well that divisions within their own party would tempt Federalists to offer their votes to one faction or another in exchange for public offices. This fact inevitably affected the endless political jockeying that characterized the breakdown of a monolithic Republican party. Federalists counted heavily in many political crises as they scrambled to break down the proscription system. They tied themselves to each of the many factions that arose in state and nation, until in 1828 there were probably as many men who had once acted with the Federalist party in Jackson's corner as in Adams'. At least in terms of personnel there had been a genuine realignment of parties. The following chapters are largely an account of this phenomenon.

One or two other comments are in order. Because this study is focused upon Federalists in New England and the middle states no effort is made to characterize southern Federalism or the course of those few Federalists in the trans-Appalachian states. One would presume that similar motivations and actions obtained for Federalists outside the Northeast, but it must for the moment remain presumption. The term *Republican* has been used throughout to denote the party of Jefferson, although many Republicans preferred to be called Democrats. Federalists almost always called their opponents Democrats. The hopeless task of deciding when a Federalist became a former Federalist has been side-stepped by avoiding qualifying adjectives.

The author wishes to thank the many librarians and curators of manuscript collections who have furthered his researches. He hopes too that Merle Curti can understand something of his gratitude for the keen criticism, unfailing patience, and bright inspiration that have nourished this work.

CONTENTS

The Twilight of Federalism

CHAPTER I

Peace Brings Little Comfort

═══

NEWS OF PEACE reached New York on Saturday, the ninth of February, 1815. A grateful populace celebrated far into the night, then streamed into churches the next day to hear sermons thanking God for his rich blessings. The war was over and, for the moment, domestic quarrels gave way to profound relief. Twenty years of painfully bitter partisan jarrings between Federalists and Jeffersonian Republicans had preceded that first Sabbath of peace in almost three years. The surcease was brief. A respected newspaper claimed on Monday that the people did not inquire about the terms of the peace, for they were "sick at heart . . . of a war that threatened to wring from them the remaining means of subsistence, and of which they could see neither the object nor the end."[1] The editor, William Coleman, who had been picked by Alexander Hamilton to edit the *New York Post*, thus kept aloft the tattered Federalist ensign he had helped guard through long years of defeat and frustration.

The achievements of Federalist rule under Washington and Adams had been spectacular. Just as spectacular, perhaps, was the decline of Federalist strength after the "Revolution of 1800." The presidential election that year had been a titanic one, hard fought and closely contested. Yet in 1804 the Federalist campaign against Jefferson was as desultory as the succeeding one when Madison was first elected. Federalists, with deep misgivings, had decided in 1812 to support a dissident Republican, but the same dismal results followed. The battle of 1800 had been fought with vigor and numbers; those afterwards seemed to reflect a party hopelessly in decline and without spirit. What had happened?

[1] *New York Post*, February 11, 1815.

3

To most Federalists the crisis arose from the heresies that first had overwhelmed the French monarchy and then, in their view, had become the tools of cynical American demagogues. Senseless destruction of traditional institutions like religion, government by the rich and able, agencies for preserving domestic law and order as well as for warding off foreign enemies, and accepted rules governing relations between classes—all this was to Federalists implicit in the hateful word *democracy*. The most damnable sin for a politician was flattery of the people, telling the unfit that they were able to govern themselves. It would unhinge an orderly society, and this precisely was what Federalists expected of Jeffersonianism with its intellectual freight of government by the many, free thought, and ill-concealed license. Was it not natural that the Jeffersonians would set up a cry to make suffrage open to every man whether or not he could demonstrate even a small measure of responsibility? Federalism was the creed of those nourished on the experience of colonial America or contemporary England; it grappled with and then was overwhelmed by those who understood that the nineteenth century was to be the century of democracy and individualism and that America would be its harbinger.

Federalism was the political expression of those who sought security and self-fulfillment in an ordered, structured social system. In this view, life's perils could be met only by men and women acting in concert, deriving strength from others about them and in turn lending their own talents and obedience to the whole. The very essence of civilization was a carefully wrought social fabric, a fabric that was delicate in the extreme, reflecting as it did a careful balancing of the capacities and ambitions of men on the one hand with traditions, opportunities, and dangers on the other. For survival and happiness men must recognize the hostility of nature and the power of religious precepts regarding man's sinfulness. To cope with them demanded that each person recognize his inability to face such perils alone; instead, he must do for the whole society what he could best do and accept gratefully from the whole what it believed his due. Such a conception rested upon an understanding that men's abilities were markedly diverse and that society itself was an entity separate from the individuals who composed it. This idea, of course, was an old one. Organic or anthropomorphic conceptions of society had been set forth by innumerable political philosophers since antiquity and had formed the basis for seventeenth- and eighteenth-century English society from which most Americans had come. Through the colonial period it had been the prevailing view of society though the materials for revolt from it built up steadily.

Between about 1775 and 1825 the prevailing attitude of Americans toward their society changed drastically toward the distinctive individualism which Tocqueville has described so dramatically. Jeffersonianism became the political vehicle for this change and, because a basic reorientation occurred in American society, Federalism was simply swept from the field. Never again would a major political party rest upon the old attachment to an organic society. Federalism shone forth brilliantly in the 1790's, partly because of a few dominating leaders and the remarkable acceptance of the Constitution, but its foundation as a political party, belief in an integrated, functional society, fast slipped away. It could not hope to remain a majority party however many thousands of devoted partisans remained to regret the new order of things. Jefferson's party, which had first formed as a center of opposition to certain Federalist policies, soon became the political expression of those who believed that Americans were destined to find ultimate happiness and fulfillment in themselves, in their own endeavors, and their own resources. Men were going out from society, convinced that it had stultified instead of developed, corrupted instead of ennobled. Self-reliance, fulsome dreams of men sucking out of nature its true bounty, and

5

boundless optimism characterized these Americans who joined under Jefferson's standard. To splinter society and release the individual was their aim. America the fruitful, Americans the finders of grace within themselves—these would be the cement which bound together the new society.[2]

Such a view helps to dispel the confusion that has come often from interpolating from its leadership the nature of the Federalist party as a party. The party's candidates were successful in hundreds of elections held on the state and local levels. These elections simply could not be won by the votes of only the rich, the well-born, and the educated, in spite of the fact that suffrage restrictions existed in most of the states. Recent scholarship has indicated that these restrictions did not confine the electorate to such a narrow basis as has been thought by some.[3] What is more to the point is that many people did not bother to vote or they voted for men who were used to governing along accepted lines. Federalism clearly had a solid appeal that extended well below the upper ranks of society even though it is true that once Jefferson's party had made its vision of the future clear to all Americans and had effectively organized these followers, this appeal was not sufficient to form a national majority.

The functional society had deeper roots in some parts of the country than others. In general it persisted longest in areas that had been fully settled before the Revolution, areas such as Connecticut, the land of "steady habits," much of southeastern Pennsylvania, and the Valley of Virginia. Often the distinctive role of religious leaders (Connecticut) or the

[2] The view of Federalism marked out in these two paragraphs was suggested by the interpretation of American social history presented by Rowland Berthoff in his brilliant article, "The American Social Order: A Conservative Hypothesis," *American Historical Review*, LXV (April 1960), 495-514.

[3] See, for example, Robert E. Brown, *Middle-Class Democracy and the Revolution in Massachusetts, 1691-1780* (Ithaca, N.Y., 1955); and Chilton Williamson, *American Suffrage from Property to Democracy, 1760-1860* (Princeton, N.J., 1960), 20-61.

existence of tightly knit European communities (the Pennsylvania Dutch) reinforced this respect for a functional society. Such places were likely to have a relatively small net increase in population, usually indicating that people were emigrating but few were coming in to settle. Those who went out, unless they went in substantial groups such as certain New England settlements in Ohio, were generally attracted to the Jeffersonian party. This large-scale moving away from society thus contributed to the social disorganization that marked the 1820's and 1830's, a trend which was further hastened by industrialism with its attendant urbanization.

The characteristic Federalist understanding of political leadership lends further weight to this general view of the different bases upon which our first two major parties rested. Again and again Federalists stressed the importance of highly skilled leaders, who could be drawn from only a small segment of society. While Jeffersonians increasingly tended to emphasize rotation in office and the binding nature of instruction of U.S. senators and representatives by state legislatures, Federalists insisted upon the value of experience and independence. The function of governing was, in the Federalist view, to be understood and practiced by the few, just as watchmaking or blacksmithing. Contrary to the general case in Europe, no narrow ruling class had emerged in the American colonies, but there had been a general acceptance of the fact that political leaders would be drawn from a distinct layer of society. Drawing from this tradition, Jefferson labored to develop a theory of a natural aristocracy, but by championing the destruction of old social forms and bonds he inexorably laid the groundwork for the familiar Jacksonian belief in government by the people, as well as of and for them. Where Federalists proudly claimed that their party was led by men of wealth and talents, Jeffersonians soon made the claim a term of derision; what warrant was there for this outmoded practice when men had now seen that they could face

7

life's perils by themselves? One man was as good and capable as another if he but applied himself.

Even in their days of triumph and glory the Federalists had begun to suffer from a curiously enervating melancholy. The personality of Fisher Ames strikingly personified this mood. Ames was a brilliant young Federalist politician from Massachusetts who rose to leadership of Federalist forces in Congress during the late 1790's. At times he seemed to have a Rasputin-like effect upon his colleagues as he sketched violent word-pictures of Jacobins—the followers of Robespierre and Danton—rapidly turning America into a vast pest-hole. Some said the doleful prophecies of this brooding, tragic figure hung over the Federalist house forever afterward. Indeed, visions of the right-thinking being cut down by myrmidons, men seduced by claims that the few should no longer shape the destiny of the many, seemingly transfixed the Federalist psyche well before the climactic struggle of 1800. After that year it appeared that some Federalists even hoped secretly that the ignorant would soon debase society completely; then everyone could see that the prophecy had come to pass. The Federalist struggle to preserve their world was seriously compromised by a kind of death-wish, a feeling that the bell had tolled.

One also finds the cause of Federalism's decline in antiquated and inept political techniques. From the lack of systematic proselyting, to badly defined lines of command, and on to the inclinations of Federalist leaders to be prima donnas and indulge in raucous public quarrels with their comrades, the record is one of almost uniformly bad management. Federalist leaders, for the most part, seemed to assume a communion of interest among their followers and fellow leaders that did not require attention to party organization and control from legislative halls down to the humblest supporter. The indispensable organizers, the smoothers, the fixers, the disciplinarians, and the publicists were largely missing from the Federalist ranks. Jeffersonian leaders, on the other hand, used infinite finesse in carefully worded party platforms at the state and local levels, statements of principles that would appeal widely by blurring internal quarrels and striking at the enemy's weaknesses. The legislative caucus, whereby party leaders could squabble in private and then present closed ranks when voting for the record or presenting candidates for office, was quickly developed by the Jeffersonians into an unusually effective device, one that demanded a variety of ways by which secondary party leaders could be disciplined. Rarely did a Federalist leader realize that these political devices were part of a whole which could not be effected piecemeal. For Republicans they had flowed naturally from a sensitive appraisal of an electorate which increasingly rejected any notion that some men were destined to rule. Among men who had come to make political judgments for themselves, entirely new political techniques were required to develop governing majorities.

That America would survive the triumph of Jeffersonianism was of course irrelevant to Federalists whose vital years were spent glorying in the golden years before 1800 and then languishing in anger when they were swept out of national office, never to return. Federalists were extremely proud of their accomplishments. They believed they had turned the new Constitution into a viable instrument of government, secured the nation's finances, founded a sound military force, gained the respect of foreign nations, and restored confidence among the doers and builders, the men who would turn America's potential riches into real wealth. These were indeed formidable achievements in twelve years. Small wonder that Federalists gaped in disbelief when the voters shunned them to follow a man who damned so many of these policies, who announced no coherent economic, diplomatic, or defense policies of his own, and who instead talked vaguely about the glories of being a small farmer or about the general rights of man. Genuine incredulity and frustration mixed with a long-standing abhorrence of democracy-mongering generated a prodigious wrath. The Federalists, overwhelmed by despair, sullenly flung curses at their antagonists, their own number, and at the air they breathed.

Stunned by their defeat and by the manifest popularity of Jefferson, many Federalists simply lapsed into waspish parochialism. Others tried hard to blunt the developing lines of Republican policy. They vigorously opposed the purchase of Louisiana, avowedly on constitutional grounds, but most of them probably sensed that little help to Federalism would come from this huge addition of lands in the West. Later, when Republicans refused to recharter the national bank in 1811, Federalists feared that the great fiscal structure reared by Hamilton was being wrecked. Few seemed aware how little Federalist legislation was actually swept away in these years. Most of the time the major issue was the Republican embargo policy. While opposing military intervention in the Napoleonic wars, Federalists insisted that American merchants and seamen had a right to trade with whomever they wished. The government, in their view, was bound to protect that commerce by diplomatic and, if necessary, military means, rather than by forbidding American ships and goods to leave the country. Above all, Federalists demanded that a more powerful military and naval establishment be set up at once.

After three years of intricate twistings, the Madison administration finally chose war. Federalists as a body had contested this path, and they continued to condemn the war after it had begun. As military defeats followed one upon the other and the public debt began to swell, Federalists sharpened their attacks upon Madison and his political friends. Because few Americans had more than a fuzzy idea how the war had come about or what would be gained by it, grumbling increased in many areas, countered only in part by sentiments of inchoate patriotism. Federalists smelled political gains; indeed at the fall elections in 1814 they suddenly broke their skein of political losses and made sharp advances. More than a third of the members of both houses in the next Congress would be Federalists. All of the New England states were safely in their hands, together with Maryland and Delaware. Federalists elected a third of New York's lower house, had just short of a majority in New Jersey's legislature and about 30 per cent of Pennsylvania's two houses. The solid bank of Republicans in Pennsylvania's congressional delegation was broken up by the election of five Federalists. Outside the New England and middle states, however, Federalist prospects did not brighten noticeably. "Mr. Madison's War" was still generally popular in the South and West, in spite of lively Federalist minorities in Virginia and the Carolinas. Some Federalist newspapers were still published in Kentucky and Ohio, but their readers were few in number.

Federalist dreams of a continuing resurgence were shattered, however, by three events that followed hard upon each other. The infamous Hartford Convention met on December 15, 1814, the peace treaty at Ghent was signed Christmas eve, and General Jackson's army leveled Pakenham's forces at New Orleans on January 8. Accumulated vexations, perhaps topped by a marauding British expedition sent to the Maine coast, prompted New England Federalist leaders to meet in Hartford during the bleakest hours of the war for the purpose of agreeing upon formal grievances and remedies to be tendered the national government. Although relative moderates controlled the convention, the circumstances, together with the long list of demands that touched the fundamental nature of the union, convinced many that the delegates were threatening secession. Such a threat made during war was easily equated with treason. Federalist leaders and editors strove to allay such fears, but at the same time a majority of Federalists in New England and the middle states

11

appear to have believed that the convention's proposals were good ones, and, above all, that the delegates had a perfect right to meet and petition the federal government. Within a few weeks, however, it was clear that the political effects were crushing. Republican spokesmen quickly made the convention an opprobrious epithet that was good currency for years. Embittered Federalists never could appreciate the exquisite irony in the fact that the convention's report was made many days after the peace treaty was signed, but before news of it reached America.

The same lag in news that was so unkind to Federalists delivered to the Republicans a glittering military victory and a new leader. Even William Coleman could do little else but rejoice over the victory at New Orleans. Americans, he wrote extravagantly, "hold their soil too sacred to be polluted by any hostile foot whatever, and animated with one spirit, they will rush forward with or without arms in their hands, to repel the ruthless invader."[4] After carefully congratulating New York and Boston merchants on the saving of millions of dollars in cotton stored at New Orleans, Coleman curtly declared that Madison's administration was not "entitled to the least share of the honor attending this very brilliant affair, or to partake in the smallest of the glory acquired."[5]

Jackson's victory brightened the otherwise indifferent military chapter of the war. Yet Federalists pounced upon the peace treaty to support their view that the war itself had been wicked. Coleman predicted before its terms were known that not one of the avowed objects of the war would be gained by it. Rather was the war in his view simply a maneuver to insure Madison's re-election in 1812.[6] The orator at the annual celebration of the Washington Benevolent Society in

---

[4] *New York Post*, February 6, 1815. The phrase "with or without arms" was a sarcastic reference to the story that Kentucky militiamen were not supplied with arms when they arrived at New Orleans.

[5] *Ibid.*, February 7, 1815.

[6] *Ibid.*, February 11, 1815.

Philadelphia (in modern parlance, a Federalist front organization) believed the treaty "exposed the motives which caused
the late war [and] exhibited the indecision, depravity, and
absence of all the requisites for government in our rulers."
A youthful Federalist blandly described this speech as "decidedly federal, but not abusive."[7] When the treaty was presented to the Senate, the most prominent Federalist in that
body, Rufus King of New York, used biting satire in review-
ing "the great blessings of the present war." A gallery observer wrote a friend: "Every sentence was Cantharides to
the already blistered feelings of the administration." He noted
too that no one rose to answer King.[8] The vigor of Federalist
attacks upon the treaty reflected both their genuine anger
at a war which had gained no appreciable concessions from
the British and their frustration upon losing the political
fruits that may have been theirs had the war gone on its
burdensome and indecisive way.

The war over, Republicans began to talk, cautiously at
first then with less restraint, about the honor Americans had
earned from the war. The claims of honor grew more ornate
at about the same rate as did Republican accusations of dis-
loyalty, a circumstance that further roiled Federalists and led
them to couple increasingly contemptuous sneers at the war's
course with overly sanguine expectations that continued high
taxes would help them politically. Coleman merrily reminded
his readers in March that one hundred and fifty millions remained to be collected to cover the costs of the war.[9] Later
in the year, after Federalists made telling gains in New York
state elections (it appeared they would capture the lower
house), one of Daniel Webster's friends exulted: *The People
are not Fools; Taxes will tell: we shall seize the reins*—Gold

[7] J. C. Biddle to W. M. Meredith, February 23, 1815, Meredith
Mss, PHS. Abbreviations of depositories are explained in the Bibli-
ography.
[8] *New York Post*, February 20, 1815.
[9] *Ibid.*, March 23, 1815.

is the God of the American people: the purse strings are their political religion which connect their heart with their Idol; no party can prophane [*sic*] Them, & live."[10] Other Federalists, however, realized that the Republican themes of honor and patriotism went deep into the hearts of American searching for self-respect and solace after the tremors of war; they wanted to believe their efforts had been noble and effective. Republicans obliged with soothing words in contrast to the continued carping that came from Federalist spokesmen. "I fear Democracy," lamented one stern Connecticut patriarch, "will have a long reign with an increased and triumphant majority."[11] Such prescience proceeded not only from gauging the effectiveness of Republican versions of the war but also from the increasingly fundamental changes in Republican policy at Washington.

Although changes had occurred during the war itself, the first comprehensive statement of a new Republican direction came with President Madison's recommendations that accompanied the peace treaty he submitted to the Senate in February. Foremost among them was a request for the maintenance of an adequate regular military and naval force in peacetime. Further, he asked that Congress take suitable measures for proper harbor defense, for the cultivation of the military art, and for adding a measure of discipline to the "distinguished bravery" of the militia. Madison did not stop there. He also suggested a system of direct internal taxation, advocated higher salaries for public officers, and made an eloquent appeal for assistance to manufacturers.[12] Madison's firm sponsorship of a new national bank drew special attention from Federalist observers. The rancorous Republican opposition to rechartering the first bank in 1811 was still fresh in their minds when

[10] J. Purdy to D. Webster, May 5, 1815, Webster Mss, LC.
[11] E. Baldwin to R. S. Baldwin, February 20, 1815, Baldwin Mss, YL.
[12] *New York Post*, February 23, 1815.

administration leaders proposed a second bank in the 1814-15 session. Bickering over details killed it then, but the proposal was quickly revived. A Federalist wag described the turn of events thus: "They are now, good souls, heartily in love with a national bank. A lover never sighed half so much for his absent fair-one, as they have within the year for the establishment of a bank."[13] Most of Madison's proposals, of course, were good Federalist doctrine for which the originators had been relentlessly attacked in recent years.

The breathtaking scope of the Republican *volte-face* astonished and delighted most Federalists. Coleman was glad to see Republicans had been "compelled to confess" their past errors by making such an "exchange of Jeffersonian policy for federalism."[14] When Madison reiterated his proposals in a presidential message later in the year, a Connecticut Federalist affixed his imprimatur by primly suggesting that the president had been obliged to adopt Federalist measures in order "to obtain the good opinion of the more enlightened part of the community."[15] The crusty governor of Connecticut, John Cotton Smith, saw the change as the sole consolation growing out the war. "*The Administration,*" he wrote a friend, "*have fought themselves completely on to federal ground.*"[16] Coming closest to an official pronouncement of Federalist views was a resolution passed by the Federalist-controlled state senate of Massachusetts. That august body declared itself pleased by the administration's disposition "to resort to the principles and systems, which characterized the happiest periods our country has enjoyed, since the adoption of the Constitution." The senators were particularly pleased by the measures designed to rest the country's security upon

[13] *Boston Palladium*, November 10, 1815.

[14] *New York Post*, February 23, 1815.

[15] S. W. Johnson to D. Daggett, December 12, 1815, Daggett Mss, YL.

[16] Smith to D. Daggett, December 16, 1815, H. E. Smith Mss, NYHS.

a competent and well-instructed military force rather than "on a mere love of justice."[17]

This form of gentle sarcasm increasingly gave way to more pungent commentaries. Federalist presses, for example, added their own amens to excerpts from John Randolph's long speech needling the administration in February 1816. With crackling wit Randolph, a nominal Republican though truly a party unto himself, compared the past views of Republican greats to present government policies, which he labelled "old Federalism, vamped up into something bearing the superficial appearance of Republicanism."[18] Sheer expediency was the charge, and Federalists delighted in embroidering it endlessly. Stirring attacks in old Republican newspapers upon internal taxes, peacetime armies, and the unconstitutionality of national banks were set down beside current pronouncements of Republican leaders and stitched together with ironic ridicule. The evidence was crushing, so crushing that some Federalists believed their opponents were going too far. Venerable Gouverneur Morris wrote his good friend Rufus King in 1816 that "the Party now in Power seems disposed to do all that federal men ever wished and will, I fear, do more than is good to strengthen and consolidate the federal government."[19] The Federalist *Connecticut Mirror* observed that the only opposition in Congress by Federalists arose from their desire to restrain the majority "from carrying their measures to a length far beyond what was ever contemplated by the federal administration."[20]

One issue, in particular, evoked Federalist misgivings. That was tariff protection for manufacturers. Although Alexander Hamilton had strongly supported such a policy, the Federalist party as a whole was still too deeply committed

---

[17] *Boston Palladium*, June 14, 1816.

[18] *Annals of the Congress of the United States. Fourteenth Congress, First Session* (Washington, D.C., 1854), 685.

[19] Morris to King, January 6, 1816, King Mss, NYHS.

[20] February 24, 1816.

to commercial interests to take up the cause. During the embargo and war years Republicans had tried increasingly to encourage home manufactures, and after the war Madison led a large segment of his party in advocating protection. Throughout New England and the middle states Republican leaders posed as the true protectors of suffering manufacturers, and Henry Clay's charge that Federalists were deaf to the pleas of ironmongers and textile makers was echoed in Republican politicial addresses and pamphlets.[21] The tariff issue was effective in these years just after the war, a fact attested to by the continuous expressions of compassion for the manufacturer's problems that flowed from Federalist pens. Yet few Federalists were to be found who would actually support increases in tariff schedules. Some were content to prate of men "prematurely forced" into the manufacturing business by "a course of silly democratic experiments."[22] That Federalists were leery of tariffs was convincingly demonstrated in Congress when two Philadelphia Federalists who led the House fight to retain double duties on imports past the expiration date in June 1815 found themselves deserted by every other Federalist member.[23]

The lack of agreement among Federalists upon the merits of measures sometimes thought to suit their views was reflected in other debates and votes in Congress, although one must remember that a generous amount of normal political jockeying also intruded. Federalists in both houses made strenuous efforts to amend the national bank bill to lessen the government's voice in its affairs. On the final Senate vote, seven Federalists opposed the bank bill, two voted for it, and one did not vote.[24] The ten Federalist senators split evenly over a bill to appropriate money for internal improvements

[21] See the *Boston Palladium*, March 18, 26, June 28, 1816, for examples of the Republican charges.
[22] *Ibid.*, February 27, 1816.
[23] *Annals of Congress*, 458.
[24] *Boston Palladium*, April 9, 1816.

and Federalists divided 42-8 against a House measure to retain the tax on bank notes and refined sugar.[25] A more characteristic vote came on an amendment to the Indiana Enabling Bill. Senator Goldsborough, a Maryland Federalist, moved to cut out the suffrage restrictions in elections for delegates to the constitutional convention in the territory. His fine speech in praise of democratic virtues apparently did not move his Federalist colleagues; two voted nay and seven did not vote at all, though the record shows that these seven gentlemen had attended the session earlier that afternoon.[26] Goldsborough's resolution was defeated by Republican votes, however, and the Federalist *Boston Palladium* noted darkly that it was "NEGATIVED in a body where the DEMOCRATS are the majority!"[27]

Congressional action on a revenue bill revealed another dimension of Federalist behavior. In 1816 the Republican leadership proposed a substantial cut in the levy of direct internal taxation, but most Federalists in both houses spoke in favor of complete repeal in spite of the fact that Federalists had traditionally recommended this form of taxation. At length, Alexander Hanson, a wholly dedicated but erratic Maryland Federalist, rose to chide his friends. First he noticed the number of Republicans who, during the debate, had defended the principle of direct taxation. "The honorable gentlemen," Hanson said, "not only profess themselves converts to the principles of Washington and federalism, but to my great joy they are engaged in reducing them to practice." He then implored his Federalist colleagues to maintain the "same steadiness and uniformity of conduct" that they had in previous years, because the honored tenets of Federalism should always have "consistency at least to recommend them." But years of political defeat had apparently ravaged those princi-

[25] *Annals of Congress*, 162, 321.
[26] *Ibid.*, 224.
[27] June 28, 1816.

ples that Hanson believed had once been pure.[28] Only 10
Federalists joined Hanson, while 41 voted for complete repeal
of all direct taxes. Senate Federalists were even more determined to reap the expected political rewards by standing for
lower taxes; not one supported the Republican bill.[29] Such
actions did little to sustain Federalist claims, long and loudly
expressed, to being the party of fiscal responsibility.

Madison's last annual message, in December 1816, carried
the reversal of traditional Republican policy even further. He
asked for the exercise of existing powers, "and where necessary, of resorting to the prescribed mode of enlarging them,"
to bring about a "comprehensive system of roads and canals."
Beyond this Madison wanted an alteration of the Federal
judiciary along lines Federalists had proposed during the
later 1790's, and the establishment of a national university
at Washington.[30] The message provoked another flurry of
Federalist comment to the effect that Republicans were fast
becoming better Federalists than Hamilton himself. The editor
of the *Baltimore Federal Republican* pronounced flatly that
his political opponents had become "proselytes to our doctrines." Democracy herself, he added, had written "with her
own hand the word FALSEHOOD on all the charges which
she has brought against the federal party."[31]

The trouble was that Republicans would never agree that
they had erred in the past. Sometimes they would hint vaguely
that times had changed, but that was all. "Let them have the
magnanimity to acknowledge it," one Federalist blustered, "and
we will as generously forgive the ten thousand blunders &
crimes they have committed."[32] From one of the few Federalist
newspapers in the West came further angry words. "And
yet," wrote the editor of the *Western Monitor*, published at

[28] *Annals of Congress*, 909-10.
[29] *Ibid.*, 160, 166.
[30] *Boston Palladium*, December 13, 1816.   [31] January 3, 1817.
[32] J. C. Smith to D. Daggett, December 16, 1815, H. E. Smith Mss,
NYHS.

Lexington, Kentucky, "the men who have *uniformly* supported these measures are vilified and abused as enemies of their country! 'Oh shame, where is thy blush!' "[33] Three months later the same editor, by way of bringing up short those Federalists who would praise Republicans for their reversals, wished it recalled clearly that "these very men are now in one breath recommending the measures they formerly abused, and in the next, vilifying the men who taught them those measures. They do not even acknowledge that they have changed their ground."[34] A Connecticut man saw the Republican shift as "delusive and hollow-hearted—calculated only to seduce and destroy."[35]

Ample evidence exists that Republicans still profoundly distrusted Federalists after the war, a distrust that goes far to explain why the followers of Jefferson would not admit publicly past "errors" and join their opponents in a new atmosphere of mutual confession and affection. One Pennsylvania Republican recalled in later years that the only Federalists in Congress who seemed genuinely happy that the war had ended were two representatives from Connecticut and Virginia.[36] John Quincy Adams, his feelings sharpened by harsh personal experience, often mused over those characteristics which another Republican termed the "malignant Spirit of Federalists." Adams believed New England Federalists incorrigible "because their errors are errors of principle, and because they are honest in the belief that all of the wisdom of the nation is in their heads, and all of its virtues in their hearts. They have erected their whole political system upon the perverted axiom that a part is greater than the whole." As the Federalists declined further into a minority, they would, continued Adams, "fall into hypochondriac fits, and fancy the

[33] Reprinted in the *Boston Palladium*, February 23, 1816.
[34] Reprinted in *ibid.*, May 10, 1816.
[35] *Connecticut Mirror*, April 22, 1816.
[36] Philip S. Klein, ed., "Memoirs of a Senator from Pennsylvania," *The Pennsylvania Magazine of History and Biography*, LXII (1938), 379.

world is coming to an end for want of putting its trust in them."[37]

This current of hostility was reflected more vividly in a letter from a Long Islander to a New York congressman: "It is really delightful to see how cordially you progress with Timothy Pickering & Co.—I have no doubt but many good democrats among you begin to believe, the federalists are under strong convictions, and will soon be converted, & sue for admission into our political church. If such be the case I shall believe the millenium has already begun, and that the lamb and the Tyger are about to lie down together. It is perhaps more probably that this calm is portentious of a storm, the young John Bulls who controul for the federal multitude are not disposed to give up contention for the Ship, they will sooner sink her. They will never consent to live under a democracy, especially the New Englanders. I spent a few weeks last summer in Connecticut, among my early friends. The Prince Regent can boast of no such faithful devoted subjects in England, or even Scotland. Their slangwangers and convention men, have washed them up to such a degree of idolitrous veneration for the royal family & Castlereagh & Co. & all their great men in Church & State, that they would think it the greatest honor to be - - - - - - upon by them, why not as well as a Hottentot Groom & bride at their nuptials?"[38] The same correspondent later warned his friend that Republicans must stand solidly behind Monroe for the presidential nomination in 1816 because the Federalists still had political pretentions.[39] His warning was echoed by one of Monroe's confidants who, after discreet talks with Federalist friends, reported: "I now learn you may expect a deadly opposition from the Federal party, which is not altogether what I ex-

[37] Adams to W. Eustis, January 13, 1817, W. C. Ford, ed., *Writings of John Quincy Adams* (7 vols.; N.Y., 1913-17), VI, 138.
[38] E. Sage to J. W. Taylor, January 27, 1816, Taylor Mss, NYHS.
[39] Sage to Taylor, March 7, 1816, Taylor Mss, NYHS.

pected."[40] This widespread belief among Republicans that Federalists still thirsted for power served to heighten their general animosity.

Besides political power, Republicans also feared that Federalists would try to grasp further economic power. Much of this fear centered about the new bank, which Republicans had supported with ambivalent feelings. During debate on the bank issue a former governor of New York warned his congressman that the Federalists were "combining their monied men for the purpose of monopolizing all the salable stock of the U.S. Bank, should one be established. . . . If they raise the necessary funds, I think it will be difficult to defeat their object."[41] Another New Yorker found on the list of tentative directors of the bank, the names of Robert Lenox and Archibald Gracie, whom he described as "two violent scotch federalists, who would gladly banish the Republican Party to Botany Bay, if they had the power."[42] The famous Baltimore editor, Hezekiah Niles, believed the bank would "present a *mighty machine* in the hands of our enemies who will monopolize it, by some means or other. . . . Its whole benefit will immediately go into the hands of the *worst cursers of the people*, the harpies ever ready to prey upon the labor of society, [and] diet on the spoils of the poor & needy."[43]

It appeared that some Federalists did in fact see benefit in the bank. For instance, a young Baltimorean, Jonathan Meredith, wrote a Philadelphia relative that he, Meredith, would be made president of the Baltimore branch if the relative

[40] J. E. Mercer to Monroe, January 18, 1816, Monroe Mss, NYPL.

[41] M. Lewis to J. W. Taylor, December 22, 1815, Taylor Mss, NYHS.

[42] J. Barker to J. W. Taylor, February 17, 1815, Taylor Mss, NYHS.

[43] Niles to W. Darlington, March 1, 1816, Darlington Mss, LC. Later, when the bill had passed, Niles wrote Darlington that the bank would be "the tomb of republicanism, at least in the cities and towns." Niles to Darlington, April 5, 1816. Henry Clay made much the same prediction in a private letter. Clay to W. Jones, January 8, 1817, Jones Mss, PHS.

would use his political influence to obtain for a friend the agency for accepting subscriptions to the new bank.[44] Senator Daggett of Connecticut tried to have the branch in that state moved from New Haven to Middletown, where Daggett and his Federalist friends would presumably have more influence.[45] Republicans, accordingly, were extremely careful in making arrangements. At the election for directors 10 Republicans and 10 Federalists were chosen, but since President Madison appointed 5 additional directors to represent the government his party had effective command over the bank's affairs.[46]

Thus, although Federalists had not made a serious bid for the presidency since 1800, an accumulation of deep-seated animosities mixed with genuine fears that Federalists were still dangerous led Republicans after the war to continue a concerted policy of excluding Federalists from public life. Proscription from office, a goal Jefferson had savored and recommended to his successors, cut deep into Federalist hearts. Republicans made it their principal weapon for combatting the enemy's bid for political power. During the war, some Republicans had been disposed to relent in order to gain a measure of national unity, but afterward proscription was resumed by Republican administrations on every governmental level. They continued it, with some exceptions, until Jackson's presidency. No single theme or policy provoked such a steady and angry stream of denunciation from Federalists as did proscription. From public speech, newspaper editorial, and private correspondence came a mountain of evidence that the policy was starkly effective and that, for a party which believed itself peculiarly fitted to govern, being kept from public office was exquisitely punishing. To an

[44] J. Meredith to W. Meredith, December 31, 1815, Meredith Mss, PHS.

[45] Daggett to A. Dallas, November 9, 1816, Dallas Mss, PHS.

[46] There are tens of references to this Republican concern about the political affiliations of the bank's directors in the papers of Congressman J. W. Taylor, Taylor Mss, NYHS.

extent not heretofore widely appreciated, proscription was the rock upon which Federalist thought and action was shaped during these years. The celebrated Jacksonian policy of banishing one's opponents from appointive office was not new; it obviously came directly out of the experience of many years in which Republican politicians had combatted Federalists by excluding them from office on any level they could. If one agrees that the so-called spoils system deeply affected the developing American party structure, he must search for its roots in the pre-Jacksonian era.

The stiffening attitude of Republicans after the war was noted at once by Coleman's *New York Post*. Through the spring of 1815 its columns were sprinkled with notices of removals from office. From the recorder in New York City to the warden of the state prison, from health officers to port wardens, the Republican state organization doggedly sought out every state appointee who could be classed as a Federalist and replaced him with a deserving Republican. An Albany Federalist complained that the Republicans did not think of "conciliation" any more as appointee after another was summarily removed.[47] One of Coleman's confidential correspondents remarked bitterly that the Republicans were "manifesting their respect for the Federalists of this state, and their entire confidence in their talents and political virtues by hurling them from office without distinction or the pretext of fault." As did most Federalists, this correspondent attributed the "whole miserable business" to Thomas Jefferson.[48] A Connecticut Federalist used harsh words in considering the name "Republican Party," which in his mind answered a valuable purpose "in excluding from office the best talents in our country, while the present occupants bask in presidential patronage, and swim on the surface."[49]

[47] E. Baldwin to H. S. Baldwin, February 20, 1815, Baldwin Mss, YL.
[48] *New York Post*, August 20, 1816.
[49] *Connecticut Mirror*, February 24, 1816.

The one area in which Republicans occasionally appointed Federalists was the judiciary. Why this happened is difficult to determine from comments made at the time, and especially puzzling because Republicans so often resented important judicial decisions. The most frequent point made at the time was simply that the best lawyers were Federalists. In New Hampshire, for instance, Governor Plumer, an ex-Federalist but by 1816 a firm Republican, decided reluctantly and against the advice of many supporters that he should offer a few high judicial posts to prominent Federalists. To complicate Plumer's plight, several of these men curtly refused to serve, one going so far as to nail Plumer's letter to the door of a local grog shop.[50] The *Boston Palladium* was delighted with Plumer's troubles and happily reprinted complaints by Republicans on the Governor's Council that Plumer had given serious offense by making such offers to Federalists.[51]

Although some Federalists were too proud to accept appointments from a Republican, especially when there was still a hope that Federalists might return to power via the ballot, others found suitable reasons why they could do so. A son of Rufus King, perhaps the most influential Federalist in the country, had begun the practice of law in Chillicothe, Ohio, where he soon gained the esteem of the governor. The latter offered to appoint young King his military aide, but there was a hurdle. "My politics," King wrote his father, "are in his way—I might be a Rep^e if I could turn to his hand—that is he w^d use his influence—but it won't do now, the Sovereign w^d accuse him of turning federalist."[52] Harrison Gray Otis, leader of the Hartford Convention, aroused the suspicions of fellow Federalists by making it known that he was available to "help" Madison's administration. In a chatty

[50] W. Plumer to J. Mason, November 25, 1816, Plumer Letterbook, LC.
[51] December 27, 1816.
[52] E. King to King, June 13, 1816, King Mss, NYHS.

letter to Secretary of the Treasury Dallas, Otis wrote that he had some slight reservations about the national bank proposal, but on the whole he favored it. Otis assured Dallas that although he had no "favors or employment to solicit," he would be flattered if he could be "in any way instrumental in facilitating the commencement of operations of the Bank."[53] Mr. Otis could hardly be accused of lacking the art of gentlemanly indirection.

[53] Otis to A. Dallas, March 22, 1816, Dallas Mss, PHS.

CHAPTER II

Blasted Election Hopes

WHILE SOME FEDERALISTS were looking for scraps from the executive table, the great majority preferred victory at the polls. They counted on several factors. The lack of British concessions in the peace treaty and the heavy national debt that remained to be paid were thought by Federalists to be uppermost in the public mind; at the same time, memories of Hartford and New Orleans were, by some prestidigitation, believed to be dimming. The most probable Republican candidate, James Monroe, was assumed by most Federalists to be a lusterless man who would bring little personal support into the election; in fact he would likely alienate further northern Republican leaders, who were already chafing under the so-called Virginia influence. In addition, Federalists hoped that the country would see the utter bankruptcy of Republican policy revealed clearly in the startling reverses recommended by Madison and partly carried out by the Republican Congress.

Federalists were cheered too in knowing that they had a leader who commanded wide respect among followers of the party. He was Rufus King of New York.[1] First rising to political prominence in Massachusetts, King moved to New York City, where a favorable marriage had planted him solidly in the uppermost ranks of society. This circumstance was believed by some to account for an austere haughtiness which plagued King just as it did the Adamses. For more than three decades King's principal interest was politics. He worked diligently at his trade, corresponded widely, and under

[1] Even before the war was over a Federalist ticket was being discussed at Washington that coupled King with Langdon Cheves of South Carolina. The latter was a Republican, then speaker of the House, who had opposed some of the administration's programs. *New York Post*, February 9, 1815.

Alexander Hamilton's tutelage was readily accepted into the most private councils of the party. His position was further cemented when Hamilton asked him to act as a second for his duel with Aaron Burr in 1804. As had most Federalists, King stubbornly opposed Madison's diplomatic maneuvers before the war, although during it he voted in Congress for supplies and made generous loans to the New York City Defense Fund. Some of his friends were affronted for the moment by these latter actions, but at war's end few challenged his Federalist purity. Although Rufus King had many talents, he was never more than a secondary leader. Most conspicuously he lacked breadth of view, imagination, and the vital power to inspire others. Seemingly imprisoned within his own dignity, King rarely charmed the occasional visitor nor did he have the resources with which to attract a wide network of loyal lieutenants. Respect and admiration came to him from many quarters, expressions of personal attachment and feeling from few.

The greatest leaders of Federalism had left the political scene well before 1815. The loss of Washington's Olympian presence was followed almost at once by John Adams' political retirement in 1801 and Hamilton's death in 1804. Had Daniel Webster been born earlier he would have been counted among this group, but the second rank of leaders, men like Charles Pinckney, Harrison Gray Otis, and Rufus King, did not have the force of personality and achievement that could extend out beyond their local areas and pull the party together. Competition for prestige within the party remained intense, yet it was a competition that had increasingly little relevance to the needs of a lasting national party. The glittering speech or the ornamented pamphlet were too often regarded as adequate credentials for position among party leaders. Mournful nostalgia and empty indictments of change were too often preferred to new policies or practical suggestions for winning elections. Good family connections seemed to count for more than hard work in local constituencies. In short, the standards for leadership, like so many aspects of the Federalist party, were attuned to a style of political conduct that was increasingly ineffective in a changing society.

Similarly archaic was the internal organization of the party, a factor mentioned earlier. In a few areas Federalists did succeed in building political machinery which could reward and punish lesser leaders, compromise intra-party disputes, and nominate candidates who would enjoy the widest party support. Federalists in Boston and Philadelphia were particularly advanced in this respect, and among the smaller cities the Federalist organization in Lancaster, Pennsylvania, was most prominent. Beyond these instances Federalists were modestly successful in a few rural districts such as a number of the Hudson River counties and, in the years just before the War of 1812, several Maryland counties. Such exceptions, however, do not alter the fact that, compared to the relatively sophisticated Republican machines which existed in most states by 1816, Federalists lagged well behind in meeting new political needs. They neither dispensed patronage with a careful eye to party necessity nor subsidized indispensable party newspapers. One searches in vain for evidence that Federalists looked after another staple of political success, the systematic printing and distribution of pamphlets and broadsides. Even in the thick of elections Federalists largely neglected such rudiments of coordinated campaigning as taking voters to the polls. Equally startling is the fact that, in spite of repeated complaints that Federalists comprised the party of wealth, few charges ever appeared in Republican newspapers accusing them of using undue sums to pay workers, print literature, or "jolly up" receptive voters.

Beyond state lines the Federalist party had no formal organization. Even within regions like New England where Federalist strength was great, communication among party leaders was not systematic. Plans for the Hartford Convention, for example, were made on an *ad hoc* basis rather than as a result of continuing negotiation. Liaison between Federalist leaders in the North and South utterly collapsed during the first three Republican administrations and was not repaired afterward. During the congressional session of 1815-16 many Federalists were at the capital, but one finds no evidence that efforts were made then to decide upon a distinctive program of party proposals or to make plans for the presidential campaign of 1816. This contrasts sharply with the pattern by which the Republican party had taken shape during the 1790's, a pattern marked by patient discussion and planning among congressmen at Washington.[2] No action was taken to coordinate the actions of Federalists in the state legislatures, a detail to which Republicans paid constant attention. Moreover, no Federalist national committee or secretariat existed, formal or informal, nor did any individual Federalists take it upon themselves to act as a clearing house for the exchange of information or to travel about regularly seeing local leaders. Federalists, then, were for the most part unable to fashion the political techniques that were to become standard for major parties in the nineteenth century. To find the reasons for this inability, one must again go back to the fact that Federalists subscribed to a different understanding of man's relationship to his society.

The ragged Federalist organization and Rufus King's lack of commanding stature led some Federalists to look about for other ways to beat Monroe. Alexander Hanson, whose Baltimore newspaper office had been wrecked by a Republican mob during the war, wrote his friend Robert Goodloe Harper that adverse state returns in 1815 had wrecked King's prospects. He suggested that the Federalists again take up DeWitt Clinton as they had in 1812.[3] This same idea had occurred

[2] See Noble E. Cunningham, Jr., *The Jeffersonian Republicans: The Formation of Party Organization, 1789-1801* (Chapel Hill, N.C., 1957).

[3] Hanson to Harper, September 22, 1815, Maxcy Mss, LC.

to other Federalists, but a New York leader announced that Clinton was "so perfectly torpid that nothing can be done by or for him."[4] At the beginning of 1816 Federalist hopes rose momentarily on the expectation that William Crawford might run against Monroe as an independent Republican. Monroe was duly warned that the Federalists hoped "to produce a competition & in that contest to aid the weakest side."[5] Federalist editors suddenly discovered that Mr. Crawford had many heretofore hidden virtues. The *Raleigh* (N.C.) *Minerva* noted hopefully that many North Carolina Republicans intended to support Crawford come what may, and a Philadelphia newspaper advised Crawford's friends that if they would take up a Federalist for his running mate the ticket could well succeed.[6] This wild hope vanished when Crawford dutifully obeyed the Republican caucus decision. Federalists settled back in support of King. John Adams had earlier forecast to a friend that the Federalists would "still hold up their Pretentions and nominate their Men, however desperate their prospect may be."[7]

If there was any one event that ruined Federalist chances for the presidency it was the spring election for governor in New York state. One Federalist explained: "The present appears to me to be a crisis with us. If we cannot get command of this State, we cannot expect to have any effectual agency in the presidential election. If we cannot make any impression upon the presidential election, this time, I see no hope for the future."[8] Rufus King agreed reluctantly to be the Federalist candidate after a stream of letters from friends who saw him as the only rallying point within the party. In legislative elec-

---

[4] W. W. Van Ness to Solomon Van Rennselaer, October 17, 1815, Catharina V. R. Bonney, *A Legacy of Historical Gleanings* (2 vols.; Albany, 1875), I, 326.

[5] J. E. Mercer to Monroe, January 18, 1816, Monroe Mss, NYPL.

[6] Both reprinted in the *Boston Palladium*, April 2, 1816.

[7] Adams to T. McKean, November 26, 1815, McKean Mss, PHS.

[8] T. Dwight to R. King, February 10, 1816, King Mss, NYHS.

tions the previous year Federalists had done well. In fact they had been prevented from naming the all-important Council of Appointment only by an outright fraud engineered by Martin Van Buren.[9] Federalists entered into the 1816 fray with considerable energy. Coleman asked for "one great, unanimous exertion . . . to show we are duly impressed with the value of the great occasion which is now offered to reunite and reanimate the party." The party, he continued, "is now called upon to play for her last stake, *to put her life upon the die*," and he closed his stirring editorial with the battle-cry: "Come on then—shoulder to shoulder—heads up—charge!"[10]

The campaign raged furiously for more than two months. Federalists held meeting after meeting, and their speeches and addresses covered the whole range of issues between the parties. Heavy taxation, a depreciated currency, excessive government expenditures, the "Fellow's steal," the "malignant Virginia influence," and alleged bungling during the war were all raked from every side. Federalists argued that King reflected all the virtues, all the wisdom, and all the experience, whereas his opponent, Daniel Tompkins, was pictured as a thieving incompetent. The Federalist surge, however, caused the Republicans to unite against the common enemy. King's chances for the presidency all but vanished when he went down in defeat, 45,412 to 38,647. He had received a respectable 46 per cent of the total vote evenly distributed throughout the state—even in the western district King had slightly less than 44 per cent of the vote. Republicans were quick to point out that property requirements, which applied only to voters for gubernatorial and state senatorial candidates, had aided King considerably. For example, in New York County King

---

[9] Henry Fellows, a Federalist, was disqualified for election as assemblyman because of an outrageous technicality. The Council of Appointment, which filled most appointed state offices, was elected by a joint ballot in the state legislature. Federalists commonly referred to the incident as "the Fellows steal."

[10] *New York Post*, March 13, 1816.

won by a vote of 1,926 to 1,861, though the combined vote for assemblymen was 5,912 to 4,809 in favor of the Republicans. The disparity in Federalist votes, however, does cast doubt upon the charge that all Federalists were rich men.

State elections elsewhere brought Federalists little encouragement. Federalist majorities in Connecticut were cut sharply, primarily because of a religious dispute. New Hampshire Federalists were defeated in a close vote, and their gubernatorial candidate in Rhode Island won by only 372 votes. Republicans crushed their opponents in Vermont, where Federalists had won all the House seats in 1814. Pennsylvania Federalists held their own. They retained control of Philadelphia, won about 40 per cent of the legislative contests, and elected 6 of Pennsylvania's 23 House seats. A substantial victory cheered Maryland Federalists. There, continued legislative control and a majority of the state's congressional delegation were both assured in a hard-fought contest. Federalist editors were heartened by reports that in Ohio and North Carolina two nominal Federalists had replaced Republican incumbents in the House of Representatives. The net result of this showing, however, did little to raise Federalist hopes for the presidency.

An illuminating comment on the Federalist dilemma in 1816 is recorded in a private circular sent to Federalist leaders in other states by two Philadelphia Federalists. Written in August, the circular bewailed the fact that there were no suitable means of communication among Federalist leaders, and then it addressed several inquiries concerning the impending election. Would it be wise to support Federalist candidates? Or should they support a minority Republican slate wherever and whenever one was set up? The authors acknowledged that the late hour and the New York election "would seem to forbid a hope that we could succeed in any candidate of our own," but not to hold up candidates would reveal weakness and would further lessen discipline within the party. Yet if Federalist candidates were supported the Republicans would be spurred to greater efforts.[11] The problem seemed to defy solution.

As it happened, Federalists in the various states pursued different paths at the fall election. In Massachusetts, Connecticut, and Delaware, where presidential electors were selected by state legislatures firmly controlled by Federalists, the electors voted for King. The Federalist minority in New York's legislature cast its votes for Federalist electors, while in New Jersey and Rhode Island the Federalists did not put a separate slate before the voters. Federalist electors were defeated in New Hampshire but no Federalist slate was nominated in Pennsylvania. Many Philadelphia Federalists instead voted for an independent Republican ticket, though the Republican defection was purely local. In Maryland district elections Federalists elected four of their own men but three of these electors did not attend the Electoral College meeting.

Monroe's sweeping victory led Federalists to seek explanations. Some blamed local Federalist politicians for not making the necessary exertions on election days during 1815 and the spring of 1816. Others isolated Republican sharp dealings such as the Fellows affair and gerrymandering in Pennsylvania. A few even blamed Matthew Carey's widely read *Olive Branch*. Professedly a conciliatory book, old guard Federalists regarded it as a "virulent Party Work . . . deadly hostile to every hope of conciliation," and particularly vicious because of the "disguise of the title." It appeared to them that Carey had couched his criticism of Republican shortcomings in terms of apologies whereas those of Federalists were stated as charges.[12] To the more perceptive, however, one factor loomed large. That was the tendency of many Federalist leaders to pursue a "soft" line in the hope of splitting the dominant party.

[11] Printed in *Penn. Mag. of Hist. and Biog.*, VI (1882), 247-49.
[12] R. H. Y. Goldsborough to M. Carey, January 6, 1817, and W. Tudor to M. Carey, December 26, 1820, Gardiner Collection, PHS.

An astute Boston Republican, George Erving, summarized in 1816 the shift in Federalist demeanor. He noted in a letter to Monroe that although the political principles of the Federalists had undergone no real change, "yet certainly the exterior character of these gentlemen's deportment is altogether moderate." Erving accounted for the hints of repentance for their wartime behavior in terms of the Federalist realization that those extreme measures had disorganized their ranks. "It is the force of circumstance," he wrote, "which had produced a temporary calm; they have to take a new departure under the great disadvantage of having lost the confidence of their followers." Erving further reported that a prominent Boston Federalist had, in private conversation, expressed his conviction "that the southern and western influence must rule the country," and that there was, consequently, little hope for the Federalist party.[13]

The awkward militia claim was perhaps a more specific motive for the noticeably moderate conduct of Massachusetts Federalists. During the war Governor Strong had refused to place the state militia under national command, but afterward the legislature felt the state should be reimbursed in the same manner as the other states. Federalist members from Massachusetts displayed unusual geniality toward their opponents in Congress, and Timothy Pickering wrote home in April 1816 that there had happily been an abatement of party feeling. "By allowing more time," he continued, "it may perhaps entirely subside, and members may probably come together at the next session, with dispositions more favourable to our claim, than exist at the present moment."[14] Bay State Federalists widely proclaimed that their gubernatorial candidate, John Brooks, intended to follow a policy of "moderation and candour towards his opponents."[15]

[13] Erving to Monroe, January 25, 1816, Monroe Mss, NYPL.
[14] Pickering to J. H. Peirce, April 15, 1816, Pickering Mss, MHS.
[15] *Boston Palladium*, February 6, 1816.

Failure to capitalize upon the political gains made during the war led inevitably to discord within the Federalist ranks. Quarreling and backbiting were not new postwar phenomena among the Federalists, but they seemed to increase in frequency and intensity as the future of the party darkened. Even during the war Federalist leaders had contended with recusants. "The merchants," Jeremiah Mason wrote a Boston friend, "are of all classes of society the least apt to make a manly opposition. They have never acted with any concert, and have always in the end quietly submitted. Gain is their great object. They will never enter into a contest with the Government in which no money can be made."[16] Pecuniary dishonesty, or rumors of it, also led to recriminations. Referring to a scandal over alleged bribery in obtaining a bank charter just before the war, a New Yorker wrote Rufus King: "There is such a cloud over the characters of several gentlemen, who may be considered as the leaders of the party in this State, that I have long feared that the most respectable men of the community would withdraw in disgust from taking any interest in our politics."[17] King later the same year credited a story that several Maryland Federalists had been bribed to vote for certain legislation. "This is the degradation," he confided to his friend Christopher Gore of Boston, "and depreciation of our Party, which had in its ranks too many who in nothing of worth differ from our opponents."[18]

The Compensation Bill of 1816, raising congressmen's salaries, had caused many anxious moments among Federalists as well as Republicans. Daniel Webster upbraided the Massachusetts legislature for condemning Federalists who

[16] Mason to J. Appleton, December 21, 1813, G. S. Hilliard, ed., *Memoir and Correspondence of Jeremiah Mason* (Cambridge, Mass., 1873), 70.

[17] D. B. Ogden to King, February 17, 1816, Charles R. King, ed., *The Life and Correspondence of Rufus King* (6 vols.; New York, 1898), v, 514.

[18] King to Gore, November 5, 1816, *ibid.*, vi, 34.

voted for the bill. "When her Federal members," Webster charged, "who come here to be kicked, and stoned, and abused in her behalf, think proper to raise their compensation . . . she denounces them, man by man, without exception. No respect for talents, services, character, or feelings, restrains her from joining with the lowest democracy in its loudest cry."[19] But a ranking New York Federalist, James Emott, upbraided the Federalists in Congress, "who insist so strongly in having . . . another swill at the treasury though they may talk of the dignity of self-respect, and refer to their character to repel any imputation of improper motives." Emott felt that defense was deemed by the country "too short and too thin."[20] His correspondent, Rufus King, had voted against the bill, causing Republicans to hint darkly that he had done so only to curry favor in his campaign for the governor's chair. Timothy Pickering, who occasioned much unrest among his Federalist constituents by his affirmative vote, remarked candidly in a House debate that many Federalists had condemned the bill in order "to turn the tables on their opponents."[21]

Alexander Hanson's laments further illustrate the currents of dissent. After the war he announced to Robert Goodloe Harper that he intended in his newspaper to "write down that mean servile temporizing spirit which has spread so much since June 1812" and to castigate many leading Baltimore Federalists.[22] Harper counselled Hanson to be more gentle. "They no doubt have their faults," Harper agreed, "but they have much merit too, and I do not believe the lash to be the best means of correcting them. Be firm and lofty in opinion and conduct, but gentle and indulgent with your friends."[23]

[19] Webster to W. Sullivan, January 2, 1816, Fletcher Webster, ed., *The Writings and Speeches of Daniel Webster* (18 vols.; Boston, 1903), XVII, 255-56.
[20] Emott to R. King, December 28, 1816, King, *King*, VI, 41.
[21] *Boston Palladium*, January 28, 1817.
[22] Hanson to Harper, September 22, 1815, Maxcy Mss, LC.
[23] Harper to Hanson, September 28, 1815, *ibid*.

Early in 1816 Hanson wrote William Coleman that certain
Federalist leaders, Webster and Mason among them, were
trying to ruin him, deprive him of his standing, and obscure
his name. Coleman asked King to write a soothing letter.[24]
That same year, Hanson, with overtones of incipient paranoia,
wrote Harper that he had "been discarded by the party, for-
mally and officially at Annapolis thro' the intrigues of Taney
& Dorsey."[25] Roger Taney later recalled that he had been
disgusted by the wartime conduct of the "Eastern Federalists,"
with whom Hanson had been linked.[26]

Many Federalists became so disenthralled with the party
that they left it and joined the opposition. Their motives were
varied. Some had an honest disagreement with policy, and
others were obviously attracted to the Republicans because
the shift would enhance their prospects of office and distinction. Whatever the reasons, their apostasy caused deep-felt
grief in Federalist ranks and was the subject of innumerable
conversations, letters, and newspaper comments. One grizzled
veteran of Pennsylvania Federalism, Samuel Sitgreaves, confessed to Timothy Pickering that he felt "many, very many,
Occasions of Discontent and Distrust at the Conduct of those
who still assume the Name of Federalists—sickened by the
frequent Instances of total Defection of Men of high Standing
amongst them—and foreseeing, in the Restlessness and Im-
patience and Equivocation of others, the repeated Occurrence
of similar Apostasies—I have lost all Confidence in the Integrity of Man."[27]

William Coleman, in his *New York Post*, detailed the
melancholy story of defection. The names of Ambrose Spencer,
who had "so dishonorably" apostatized, Walter Bowne, a

[24] Hanson to Coleman, July 7, 1816, and Coleman to King, July
19, 1816, King Mss, NYHS.
[25] Hanson to Harper, October 14, 1816, Harper Mss, LC.
[26] Samuel Tyler, *Memoir of Roger Brooke Taney, LL.D.* (Baltimore
1872), 159-60.
[27] Sitgreaves to Pickering, April 18, 1816, Pickering Mss, MHS.

wealthy New York banker, and Jonathan Dayton of New Jersey, who had once acted with the Federalists but was now "king of the Democrats," were ticked off in the columns of the *Post*. When King lost his election in 1816, Coleman blamed it on unsuspected traitors and renegades from Federalism, all summarized in the phrase: "Apostates, Coodies, and Drunkards." Coodies, Coleman explained, were Federalists who had fled the party for base motives and not from any honorable change of sentiment.[28]

The Federal Republican Young Men of New York met in 1816 and took note of the sad turn. It was among the younger Federalists that apostasy was most frequent. "It is with sincere regret," the convention resolved, "that we have recently witnessed some most unworthy examples of defection and apostasy in men who we had ever been accustomed to respect . . . however . . . we are not disheartened by desertions which increase our purity more than they diminish our strength; and . . . we have no wish to retain in the circle of our friends, whether political or social, any person who is capable of finding in the power, the pleasures or the emoluments of office, an adequate compensation for the loss of his integrity."[29] The resolution's sharp tenor indicates the bitterness and frustration that Federalists experienced in effecting the "purification" of their party. That apostasy had its rewards was evident from the numbers of former Federalists, particularly in New England, who had gained the confidence of Republicans and thereby stood to share in the spoils. John Quincy Adams was soon to be appointed secretary of state and John Holmes of Massachusetts, who, in the scathing words of the *Connecticut Mirror*, had "made a great noise in that State, as apostates are very prone to do to ingratiate themselves with the Chiefs of their new faith," was the recipient of an important administration appointment.[30]

[28] *New York Post*, April 12, 1816. See the *Post* generally for the months of March and April.
[29] *Ibid.*, April 20, 26, 1816.   [30] March 8, 1816.

In the gubernatorial elections in 1816 former Federalists were running on the Republican ticket in Massachusetts, Connecticut, and New Hampshire. This phenomenon aroused much comment and sarcasm on the part of Federalists. Behold the Republicans, cried the *Boston Palladium*, who have fought hard, but just as they "are about to grasp the fruits of the contest, in step a few deserters from Federalism and gather the harvest."[31] The *Salem Gazette* explained that the nomination of Franklin Dexter, eulogist of the revered Fisher Ames, offered another opportunity for the Republicans "of gratuitously displaying their obsequiousness and slavishness of temper, by giving their votes to a man who holds them in utter contempt, and who, whenever they approach him as their *master*, wagging their tails and ready to fawn, cringe, and lick his hand, spurns them from his presence with a kick, and sends them away yelping." The *Gazette* went on: "The democrats, from their eagerness to catch at and promote apostates, seem to esteem themselves no higher than Lascars and Seapoys, who are always *officered* by the *Company's European Servants*."[32] "WHO WILL TRUST A TRAITOR?" demanded the *Connecticut Mirror*, "WHO WILL PLACE THE LEAST CONFIDENCE IN A DESERTER? Such men are corrupted before they are drawn off from the friends. . . . Apostasy from political orthodoxy, is as closely allied to treason, as religious apostasy is to heresy."[33] The famed Federalist ability for billingsgate never found a more suitable subject than apostasy.

The figure of Oliver Wolcott, nominated for governor by Connecticut Republicans in 1816, was particularly infuriating to the Federalists. Sitgreaves of Pennsylvania mournfully acknowledged that Wolcott "had descended from the proud Eminence in which He Stood," but a Connecticut Federalist

[31] March 26, 1816.
[32] Reprinted in the *New York Post*, April 20, 1816.
[33] February 26, 1816.

disdainfully reported that Wolcott's nomination would "receive no federal support," and that Wolcott himself had no expectation of winning.[34] Those who hoped that Wolcott was not serious about his candidacy could not have been aware of a letter he wrote to Matthew Carey during the war. Wolcott wrote: "I have for nearly ten years, witnessed with grief, indignation and despondency, the successful perversion of the principles of the Federal Party, to purposes diametrically opposed to those of its Founders. . . . I perceive the contrast between what Federalism, *was* and *now is*, as distinctly as you do. . . . The distinct avowal of these determinations has subjected me to inconveniences, which I could not have anticipated. Combinations have been formed to destroy my Character, Credit and Property. I presume they have not been attended, with all the success, which was expected by their Contrivers; but they have deprived me of much of that Society and Comfort, which I feel a consciousness of having merited from my Country. . . . I make these observations that you may know my sentiments & situation: I am certain that a great number of respectable Men think as I do; but I am surprised to find so little independence, in the avowal of them."[35]

As Federalists surveyed the Republican hegemony and what to them was a disastrous turn of fortune since 1800, they sought explanations and a bit of solace in their conceptions of the average man's nature, a conception they compared invidiously to that of the ideal "Federalist man." Jeremiah Mason wrote his wife from Washington during the war that she would find it difficult "to conceive the degree of wickedness and total depravity to which our great men here have arrived," though perhaps not impossible since she was liberally aided "by certain theological opinions somewhat unfavorable to

[34] S. Sitgreaves to T. Pickering, April 18, 1816, Pickering Mss, MHS; J. Gould to D. Daggett, April 3, 1816, Daggett Mss, YL.
[35] Wolcott to Carey, December 16, 1814, Gardiner Collection, PHS.

human nature."[36] Rufus King called upon Edmund Burke as authority for the principle that men who possessed unlimited and discretionary power tending to their own advantage will always abuse it, and since it was plain that the administration during and after the war possessed such power, "we are not to expect a miraculous interposition to alter the laws of nature."[37]

In Federalist eyes, perhaps the most despicable characteristic of the Republicans was pandering to the low-born. It was the age-old complaint against patent demagoguery. Mason believed that the administrations of Jefferson and Madison had found favor with the public solely by "courting their prejudices and worst passions," and he was not certain that "our people are so much more enlightened and virtuous than the rest of mankind."[38] After his defeat in 1816 King recalled Aristotle's dictum that in a democracy "the first imposition . . . is to flatter the people" with violence the inevitable result.[39] Old Timothy Dwight found the chief cause of all contemporary wickedness in the continual spread of French philosophy, which, in departing from sound logic and good sense, was designed to "amuse, perplex, and beguile," and was addressed "not to men of learning and understanding . . . but to the ignorant, unthinking and vulgar. It is directed, not to the understanding even of these; but to their weaknesses, prejudices, and passions."[40] About the worst thing that could be said of a law was that it had, according to Federalists, "fallen a victim to popular excitement, and . . . may be considered as an attempt to propitiate the sovereign people, and compromise with their jealousies."[41] But Federalist men were made of sterner stuff.

[36] Mason to his wife, January 29, 1814, Hilliard, *Mason*, 82.
[37] King to J. Mason, November 22, 1815, *ibid.*, 122.
[38] Mason to J. Appleton, March 27, 1814, *ibid.*, 90.
[39] King to C. Gore, May 8, 1816, King, *King*, v, 534.
[40] Timothy Dwight, *Travels in New-England and New-York* (4 vols.; New Haven, Conn., 1821-22), IV, 374.
[41] *Boston Palladium*, January 14, 1817.

"I meet also here," Joseph Hopkinson of Philadelphia wrote from Washington, "with great satisfaction, many national Federalists, among leading men, too; who think, speak and will act on great national grounds, and with a single view to the real greatness and prosperity of the country." Hopkinson, who was carrying on the tradition of a politically prominent family, added that it was agreeable so to find other men like himself, particularly since "an effort will probably be made by Federalists of a more fiery temperament to chill us into a different discipline . . . but you know I am not one to be commanded in this way."[42] When in 1816 it was the general Federalist position in Congress to tread softly, in order to placate the voters, Hopkinson was considered, next to John Randolph, "the most severe oppositionist."[43] Such strength of character was shared by Rufus King. In a reflective mood, albeit a melancholy one as he could see only darkness in the future, King asserted that it "would be most unworthy to affect to have changed our Opinions—I would not suffer the self Humiliation & Reproaches of the Changelings I could name, for the highest Offices, & applauses, that could be given them."[44]

This conception of a growing sea of darkness surrounding a few islands of virtue led many Federalists to foresee the demise of their party. An embittered veteran from Connecticut decided that "This American world was made for Democracy," and Christopher Gore, a former Massachusetts governor, believed that a time of crisis had arrived, one that left him "both alarmed & mortified at the precarious Tenure on which we hold our Liberty & Property, not to speak of the Honour & Character of the Country."[45] Crushed by his own

[42] Hopkinson to his wife, Burton A. Konkle, *Joseph Hopkinson* (Philadelphia, 1931), 177-78.
[43] *Boston Palladium*, April 12, 1816.
[44] King to C. Gore, May 15, 1816, King, *King*, v, 535.
[45] T. R. Gold to D. Daggett, May 13, 1816, Daggett Mss, YL; and Gore to R. King, June 14, 1816, King, *King*, vi, 26.

defeat in 1816, Rufus King argued that "Federalism would and should pursue its own natural Course—Federalists of our age must be content with the past."[46] Jeremiah Mason predicted that on the national level Federalism would "soon become extinct."[47] Some at least wanted to make a fight. "For Honor's sake," one exclaimed, "let us die like men. If the Federal cause is to be abandoned, let it be done with a grace; let us retreat from the battle ground, in such order, that our enemies shall not insult us with their triumphs."[48] This pessimism, though widespread, was not representative of all Federalist opinion, and a few partisans believed that the nation would soon tire of Republican excesses, their deceptions, and their "deeply rooted and widely extended animosities."[49]

A larger number, however, saw some hope for Federalists under the administration of a new Republican president, James Monroe. Early in 1816 two Connecticut Federalists agreed that a lessening of party tension offered promise. They believed that "a new president of honourable views . . . from whatever party he might be elected" could hasten the day when "the principles of federalism . . . would regenerate the administration."[50] Some individual Federalists saw in this possible lessening of party tension a chance to return from the wilderness of proscription and obtain appointments under a new president. Just after Monroe's election Gore reported from Massachusetts that Harrison Gray Otis and Thomas Perkins were about to leave for Washington. Their purpose was said to be "mere pleasure," but gossip had it that "many of their Intimates will not be disappointed if other Views are indulged." Lest this appear mysterious Gore quickly added with his characteristic wit that "the Want of their Services

[46] King to C. Gore, May 15, 1816, King, *King*, v, 535.
[47] Mason to C. Gore, December 30, 1816, Hilliard, *Mason*, 148.
[48] M. Hatch to D. Daggett, February 18, 1817, Daggett Mss, YL.
[49] W. Coxe to D. Daggett, February 12, 1816, *ibid.*
[50] R. M. Sherman to D. Daggett, February 9, 1816, *ibid.*

is not felt now, and craving appetites of those who have always been Friends are more numerous than Mr. M. can gratify."[51] The place-hunting trip of Otis and Perkins, however, could not compare with the audacity of a young Boston Federalist, William Tudor, Jr.

Tudor baldly suggested to the president-elect that he abandon the Republican party in New England and take up the Federalists as his principal political support in that area. Extravagant praise for Monroe was followed by the recommendation that in pursuit of "general and liberal interests" it would be wise to end the long warfare between the administration and New England. The hardy population and great monied capital of the region would be useful in case of emergency. Tudor then noted that there was among Federalists "a disposition to conciliation," and that he had heard many "respectable" men voice their belief in Monroe's "magnanimity & generous feelings." The Republicans, on the other hand, were an "utterly contemptible" faction whose baseness Monroe could not possibly comprehend, though perhaps he could make some estimate from "the specimens" he had seen at Washington. In spite of being fed for years on administration pap they were still "a cringing and subservient" lot who would betray Monroe at the first opportunity. Tudor admitted that Federalists had acted badly on occasion, but this was to be explained by the fact that "not one solitary instance can be found of any one holding the slightest employ under the National government . . . not even a tide waiter or postmaster." The Federalists, therefore, had had to act in self-defense for "the security of property & every other right."

In the year 1817, Tudor continued, Federalists were tired of the struggle and they looked with favor upon the new policies at Washington. If Monroe were to protest that Jefferson strongly advised that the parties be kept about equal in

---

[51] Gore to R. King, December 25, 1816, King Mss, NYHS.

New England, Tudor pointed out that Monroe would "still have a party against you, which is now for you." Finally, Tudor reminded his correspondent that he, Tudor, was a well educated and intelligent fellow, deeply interested in the public service. He would be happy to be one of Monroe's chosen instruments in effecting the new policy.[52] One does not know whether to be more amazed at Tudor's bravado or his estimate of Monroe's intelligence and gullibility.

As Monroe's inauguration came and passed, anxious eyes and ears awaited the first indication of his intended course. Federalist hearts beat faster as they contemplated possible glories awaiting them under the administration of a man whom most of them despised as weak, vacillating, and without discernible talents.

[52] Tudor to Monroe, February 22, 1817, Monroe Mss, NYPL. See also, William Tudor, Jr., *Letters on the Eastern States* (Boston 1821), 44-52. In this work, first published in 1819, Tudor still maintained that his proposal to Monroe would have been feasible.

CHAPTER III

The Era of Good Feelings

———

B EFORE HIS INAUGURATION Monroe pondered the difficult problem of the Federalists. He received conflicting advice from many quarters, but in his usual fashion he decided to proceed cautiously. Monroe would hold out a tentative hand of friendship to the Federalists while at the same time recognizing the valid claims of the Republican "family." In his inaugural address the president noticed approvingly that the passions of party had meliorated and that American society was really "one great family with a common interest." In veiled terms he acknowledged that experience had brought about some important changes in Republican policy and that it would be the object of his "constant and zealous exertions" to promote further the "harmony" among Republicans and Federalists although always "in accord with the principles of our Republican government."[1] Many Federalists saw in these cautious words cause for encouragement.

The reasons for Monroe's visit to the "disaffected" New England states are not clear. Knowing Federalists were inclined to believe that it was the result of a discreet visit by Daniel Webster in which Webster told the president-elect that he would find a warm welcome in the Federalist strongholds.[2] With the announced purpose of making an unofficial tour of military establishments Monroe set out for Baltimore. It quickly became apparent that the nation would regard the tour as an official goodwill visit. Federalist editors carefully scanned civic addresses directed to Monroe and especially his responses to them. They were looking for hints of a disposition to treat Federalists in a "liberal" manner. In Baltimore

[1] *New York Evening Post*, March 8, 1817.
[2] George T. Curtis, *Life of Daniel Webster* (2 vols.; New York, 1870), I, 161.

Monroe again congratulated the country on "the increased harmony of public opinion," and in Philadelphia he announced that he intended to "promote tranquillity."[3] When he moved into New England, the Federalist welcoming committees framed their addresses more pointedly. New Londoners hopefully noticed that "a spirit of mutual charity and forbearance nationally prevails,"[4] while in Boston the committee trusted that Monroe's visit would enable him "to apply in practice . . . those principles of an elevated and impartial policy, which you have been pleased to promulgate as the basis of your intended administration." Monroe dodged this opening and contented himself with affirming his high opinion of George Washington.[5] On the whole, Monroe answered with innocuous affirmations of his desire to promote harmony. Federalist editors, however, often tried to read much more into them.

In all but one of the cities Monroe visited there was only one welcoming committee. At Boston the Republican minority in the legislature felt compelled to make a separate address, an unexpected occurrence that obviously rattled the Virginian. Monroe asserted in a labored answer that bringing about a "union of the community" was one of his main duties and that his conduct would be "invariably directed to that end." Compounding the chagrin of the Republican group, Monroe stated that in order to accomplish such a desirable end, he would "be careful to avoid such measures, as may, by any possibility, sacrifice it."[6] William Coleman, who had not found it within himself to join the general Federalist chorus of praise for Monroe, pricked up his ears at this event. Was this a rebuff to Monroe's own party?[7]

Most of the Federalists on Monroe's itinerary went to considerable lengths to appear friendly, hospitable, and reconciled.

[3] *Boston Palladium*, June 10, 1817.
[4] Address of Welcome, New London, in Monroe Mss, NYPL.
[5] *Boston Palladium*, July 25, 1817.
[6] *Ibid.*, July 25, 1817.
[7] *New York Post*, July 30, 1817.

They arranged elaborate receptions and took great pleasure in inviting him to their homes. Among others Monroe visited the Boston homes of Thomas H. Perkins, Theodore Lyman, H. G. Otis, and George Sullivan. The Republican *Boston Patriot* was a mite unhappy that the Federalists appeared to monopolize the president's visit, but the editor beamed when Monroe also visited the homes of George Blake, General Dearborn, and William Gray. The *Patriot* noted with pride that the latter gentleman was the possessor of a "princely fortune."[8] Some smaller New England towns which were controlled politically by the Republicans delegated a prominent and wealthy Federalist to convey the official welcome and entertain Monroe in his home.[9] There was pathos in this. Republicans obviously wanted to impress the chief executive, but to do so they had to call upon the hated Federalists to find a house suitable for entertaining a president.

Republican editors in other parts of the country expressed apprehension when they received reports of Monroe's reception. This delighted the Federalists. What was exceptional about Federalist behavior? "It is amusing," the *Connecticut Mirror* observed, "to see how disappointed and chagrined a certain class of men are, because President Monroe . . . has been treated with great politeness and civility by the Federalists."[10] The *Baltimore Federal Republican* commented that it was sorry to see that some Republicans had voiced doubts about the patriotism of their own president. Did they question whether Monroe was a gentleman because Federalists treated him as one?[11] The Republican criticism continued, causing the *Connecticut Mirror* to strike back in language that shed light upon the persistent Republican distrust of Federalists. The Republicans, wrote the *Mirror* editor: ". . . are not so much wounded at the conduct of the Federalists, as they are

[8] Reprinted in the *Boston Palladium*, July 8, 1817.
[9] *Ibid.*, July 29, 1817.
[10] July 17, 1817.
[11] August 15, 1817.

at the marked attention and respect which the President bestows on the Federalists. That he should treat *them* with so much civility, apparently prefer their society, and resort to them for information, rather than associate with democrats, is cutting to the quick—this is too much for their feelings of democracy to endure. The president is doubtless a man of discernment, and has so much self-respect, as to take special care, what company he keeps. Were he to associate, only, with our New-England democrats, while in this section of our country, what a pitiful opinion would he form of the character and people of New-England. . . ."[12] Bantering with Republicans was not, however, the principal interest of Federalists. They were more concerned about the prospect that Monroe would see fit to invite Federalists into his administration.

A Boston Federalist was overjoyed at the reception given to Monroe and especially at Monroe's apparent reciprocation of the felicities. "They have," he wrote, "as it were, shaken hands and become reconciled, and have tacitly agreed to bury all past misunderstanding in oblivion. . . . In this situation, neither is at liberty to retract without dishonor or deservedly incurring disgrace. . . ."[13] This unique application of the covenant concept should necessarily lead to appointments. A few weeks later another observer noted that the time had come "in which the inquiry relative to the appointment to office . . . [was] 'is he capable, is he honest?' " "All men of respectable characters," he continued, "are equally entitled to be appointed to those offices for which they may be suitably qualified," and he hoped that the day would soon come when talented men were appointed to office instead of "illiterate men . . . who have little to recommend them except party virulence."[14]

[12] August 18, 1817.
[13] *Boston Palladium*, July 15, 1817.
[14] *Ibid.*, August 5, 1817.

Reminiscent of the plan William Tudor, Jr., had sent Monroe earlier in the year, a more subtle Federalist, George Sullivan, suggested a course that he believed would enhance Monroe's strength as president. Sullivan began his appeal with glowing tales of Federalist enthrallment with Monroe, but then warned him that many New England Republicans and some unspecified "old federal leaders" really did not appreciate Monroe's merits. Beyond New England there were crafty Republicans who were plotting Monroe's downfall, such men as Clay, Clinton and Crawford. The way to foil all these forces was to "let down" the New England Republicans by not appointing them to major offices. Monroe could then render the old Federal leaders harmless by precluding them from consistent opposition. "The federal leaders," he wrote, "have carefully reserved to themselves in all their addresses the opportunity of dissenting to your course of administration, until you give them some pledge that they will be received into your counsels. If a pledge of this sort could be found satisfactory to the mass of the federal party in New England without compromitting yourself with your friends or engaging yourself to take old enemies into your counsels, you might preclude the latter from all opposition & eventually despoil them of all influence. Such a pledge is in your power to give."[15]

Sullivan knew the man who could accomplish all these aims. That man was his good friend Daniel Webster, who would make Monroe an admirable attorney general. "His admission to your counsels," Sullivan continued, "would be a sufficient pledge to the *mass* of federalists and their leaders could ask no more—His popularity with the republicans everywhere, would exclude all jealousy of federal influence," and Monroe's administration would then "rest secure against the violence of almost any faction." Webster, Sullivan added,

[15] Sullivan to Monroe, July 10, 1817, Monroe Mss, NYPL.

was disposed to support Monroe, but he could not "consistently institute such support till you have given some pledge of intention to bring in the federalists. That pledge given to himself will of course obviate all difficulty on his part."[16] This carefully written proposal was of course rejected by Monroe, but at least it was slightly more subtle than many others sent Monroe by job-seeking Federalists.[17]

The overtures made by Federalists toward Monroe were further described in the correspondence of Federalist leaders. When Monroe was in Boston, King wrote that there "would doubtless be performed some works of supererogation" on the part of the Federalists there, but they should not place too much reliance "upon the efficacy of these over zealous Deeds." King acknowledged that there were "more than one or two Aspirants, carefully watching and weighing all that occurs, or is omitted in the Course of this presidential journey."[18] Old Christopher Gore reported to King that before Monroe arrived in Boston, H. G. Otis and Federalist editor Benjamin Russell were "exerting every Being & Thing to testify the Respect of the Cradle of Liberty & its rebellious Sons for the Chief of the Nation."[19] Gore had heard of George Sullivan's efforts to "sell" Webster to Monroe, and when Monroe appointed William Wirt his attorney general, Gore wrote sarcastically that Boston had been shown "on what Basis his Federalism, or Attachment to old Principles rests— and how easily they may be set aside."[20] Hanson icily reported at the beginning of the new session of Congress "that the Yankee members who have come on do not appear to have

[16] *Ibid.*

[17] See, for example, E. St.L. Livermore to Monroe, September 11, 1817, and W. Tudor, Sr. to Monroe, July 11, 1817, Monroe Mss, LC; or Richard Derby to Monroe, November 9, 1817, and A. Hamilton to Monroe, September 4, 1818, Monroe Mss, NYPL.

[18] King to J. Mason, July 4, 1817, King Mss, NYHS.

[19] Gore to King, June 17, July 12, 1817, *ibid.*

[20] Gore to R. King, November 23, 1817, *ibid.*

fattened much upon the 'soft corn' Mr. Monroe gave them when he was *touring*."[21]

Jeremiah Mason had also heard of the efforts to convince Monroe that he should bring Webster into his cabinet, but by early 1818 Mason agreed that "the Federalists have nothing to expect in the way of appointments to office from the present administration." He believed, however, that immediate appointments should not be the only reason for Federalists cozying up to Monroe. Mason realized that there was a growing element of opposition to Monroe within his own party and that Monroe must have been aware of this when he went to New England. If the Federalist leaders there would give up all semblance of an opposition and especially give up hope of trying to get the militia claim paid through a policy of sycophancy, they would have "an extremely favorable opportunity." Mason further confided to Daniel Webster: "If New England were in unison with the Government—every emigrant from New England would yet add to their respectability by their junction with us— Those people are settled in Ohio generally, & in Louisiana, Alabama, Mississippi & Indiana—all of whom are favorable to the admin[n] & all of whom are directly interested in our Country & acquiring very great influence in their own, & all these men are desirous of having us a rallying point, & will oppose the present growing Opposition—They are united to us by *interest* & *Will*, & they want only to know that we can & are disposed to have our share in the National Councils— I now ask you, my friend, whether we had not better take this ground, or remain where we now are without the least influence or share in the Union. . . . The present policy of Monroe, is substantially Washington's policy, & if New England is with him, her position will be immediately an erect one, & her influence powerful.[22] Mason was a shrewd political

21 Hanson to R. King, November 23, 1817, *ibid.*
22 Mason to C. Gore, March 5, 1818, Hilliard, *Mason*, 197.

observer. In this letter he adumbrated one of the political bases of the National Republican and Whig parties.

Monroe himself wrote at length of his private impressions upon leaving New England. Stung by the criticism of Republican editors, especially Thomas Ritchie in Richmond, his letter was essentially defensive though occasionally he attacked his critics. Monroe again asserted that he firmly intended to bring about a union of all Americans on strict Republican principles and that he had been careful not to alienate either Republicans or those Federalists who sincerely wanted to make amends for their bad behavior during the war. He carefully stated that "a premature favour, of any leading federalist," would tend to defeat his object, for it would excite "the resentment of the republicans," at the same time that it "cemented the federalists who would infer that it proceeded from fear of them as a party." Monroe reviewed his visits to the private homes of Federalists and insisted that he was only being courteous while at the same time giving the Federalists every opportunity to swing over graciously to the Republican standard.[23] The long letter showed a perplexing mixture of political naïveté and astuteness.

Republicans had mixed feelings about the tour. Madison, for example, perceived that Monroe had given Federalist leaders the opportunity to "return to the national family." The Federalists, by their cordial reception, had made verbal commitments that would prevent them from resuming an opposition without a "public demonstration, that their conversion was inspired by the mere hope of sharing in the loaves and fishes."[24] A Philadelphia Republican congratulated Monroe on his tour and noted that the Federalists and both Republican factions in that city all regarded Monroe as "the model of their magistrate."[25] Many Republicans, however,

[23] Monroe to an unknown correspondent (probably George Hay), August 5, 1817, Monroe Mss, NYPL.

[24] Madison to Monroe, August 22, 1817, Monroe Mss, LC.

[25] C. J. Ingersoll to Monroe, September 7, 1817, Ingersoll Mss, NYHS.

never forgave Monroe for his visit and his demonstrations of friendship to Federalists. That rabid Yankee Republican, Nathaniel Ames, could not transcend his consuming hatred for Federalists. He noted archly that the Federalists "seem now slinking back, trying to recover their lost influence, and are loud and forward to do more than all Democrats to honor the President on his arrival at Boston."[26] William Plumer, Jr., recalled in later years that many Republican war-horses privately congratulated him on his father's lone dissenting electoral vote in 1820, some of them specifically mentioning the "Northern Tour."[27]

Republican suspicions were further aroused when the Federalists indicated they intended to continue their new friendship with Monroe. Federalist toasts at Independence Day celebrations in 1817 were full of praise, many directed to the symbolism of the "comrade-in-arms" relationship between Colonel Monroe and General Brooks, the Federalist governor of Massachusetts.[28] Federalists generally approved of Monroe's message in December 1817, one editor being particularly pleased because the message lacked "metaphorical and philosophic distinctions" and was distinctly similar to "a merchant's letter of advice to his agents and supercargoes."[29] Another expressed with satisfaction his belief that Monroe was truly committed to the implementation of Federal policy and that Federalists were "not so very anxious to preserve the name, if they are assured of the thing."[30] When Henry Clay, during the Congressional session of 1817-18, made a veiled attack upon Monroe the Federalists rose, almost as a body, to his defense. "The federalists," a New Hampshire

[26] Charles Warren, *Jacobin and Junto or Early American Politics as Viewed in the Diary of Dr. Nathaniel Ames 1758-1822* (Cambridge, 1931), 322.

[27] William Plumer, Jr., *Life of William Plumer* (Boston, 1857), 495.

[28] *Connecticut Mirror*, July 14, 1817.

[29] *Ibid.*, December 15, 1817.

[30] *Baltimore Federal Republican*, March 6, 1818.

Republican mourned, "vote in concert and always with the administration. I fear they will cling to the President until they sink him to the earth."[31]

That most Federalists were generally pleased with the policy pursued by Monroe and the Republican majority is clear. As the *Baltimore Federal Republican* put it: "The nearer the Democratic administration and party come up to the old federal principles and measures, the better they act and the more we prosper—That is the reason that every body is contented with President Monroe's administration, which is in system and effect strictly federal."[32] A year later the same paper playfully charged that the Republicans seemed to be on the verge of spiriting away George Washington from the Federalists. The editor wished the Republicans to know that George undeniably belonged to the Federalists, "though we readily admit, that considering the time that has elapsed since the intrusion and joint-occupancy, an inceptive right may have accrued to our adversaries."[33] When Henry Clay in a tariff debate argued that he would be happy to see an excise tax put on whiskey, some Federalists believed that the millennium had come.[34] A combination of wishful thinking and discernment moved a Boston Federalist to observe that, although the Federalist party could have been revived during and after the war, "it was much better, that the party which had displaced it, and which had the popular prejudice in its favor, should gradually assume its principles, which were the original principles of our government." The Republicans, for example, had strengthened the navy, whereas in the hands of the Federalists, "suspicion would have watched every step."[35]

The pages of Federalist newspapers during Monroe's first administration were literally filled with appeals to fellow

[31] S. Hale to W. Plumer, March 22, 1818, Plumer Mss, LC.
[32] June 25, 1819.   [33] June 2, 1820.
[34] *Baltimore Federal Republican*, July 11, 1820.
[35] Tudor, *Letters on the Eastern States*, 51-52.

Federalists, the Republicans, and independent voters for a cease-fire in the battle of parties. Some were pleading, some overbearing, and others accompanied by columns of historical and reflective reasoning. Coleman in 1817 reprinted an editorial from the *Ohio Federalist* wherein the editor renounced further partisanship, "so thoroughly am I convinced of the evil, and so heartily am I tired of the strife."[36] The *New Haven Journal* hoped the Fifteenth Congress would "pursue the examples of their predecessors in the Fourteenth Congress, discard the spirit of party, and unite harmoniously in the promotion of the great interests of the country."[37] A Rhode-Islander asked fellow Federalists: "Are we in opposition to an anti-commercial, anti-naval administration? or, are we at war with a mere shadow, the unsubstantial spectre of our former enemy?"[38] The world, wrote a New York man, was "experiencing a complete revolution in commercial concerns, that materially affects the interests of agriculture and the mechanic arts, having not the least affinity with the politics of this country." The terms *Republican* and *Federalist* were thus "obsolete."[39]

Two new Federalist newspapers began publication, the announced object of which was to submerge party animosities in the interest of national objectives. The *New York American* was founded in 1819 by a group of young Federalist litterateurs and lawyers under the influence of Josiah Ogden Hoffman. Johnston Verplanck, Hugh Maxwell, and two sons of Alexander Hamilton were the first editors, though later Charles King, the senator's son, came to be the principal editor. The paper was begun as a voice for those Federalists who disliked DeWitt Clinton, but the prepublication proposals well illustrate the new national line adopted by many Federalists. The young editors wrote: "Exclusively American,

[36] *New York Post*, August 5, 1817.
[37] Reprinted in the *Connecticut Mirror*, November 24, 1817.
[38] *Rhode-Island American* (Providence), December 3, 1818.
[39] *New York American*, July 24, 1819.

their aim will be to support the character, and to promote the interests of the country, without reference to the present nominal distinctions of party. Federal in their attachment to the Union, and those principles on which it is grounded; republican in their veneration for all the institutions of their native land; and democratic in their deference to the will of the people, among whom they are proud to be included. . . . We mean the people *shall* be our rulers. . . . We know no distinctions of class that entitles any men to the title of *public men*; and if there be any such, we are too democratic to acquiesce in so aristocratic an assumption of rank. Our aim is to level all obnoxious distinctions."[40]

The next year Robert Walsh began publishing in Philadelphia his *National Gazette*, which announced a similar position to that of the *American*. "We are Federal only in reference to the Constitution of the United States," Walsh argued, "and Democratic or Republican relatively to the character of our American institutions."[41] Both papers soon came to enjoy a well-deserved reputation for their literateness and "meatiness," though they could not shake off the imputation of Federalism. They remain, however, valuable sources of expression for that body of Federalists, principally, the younger ones, who wanted to bring about a new alignment of political forces in the country.

For various reasons Federalists during these years were quick to praise those Republicans who appeared conciliatory or who were important enough to flatter. The *Exeter* (N.H.) *Watchman* lauded John Randolph for a speech in which he praised Pickering and Hamilton, and it commended John Calhoun and some other southern Republicans for their "elevated, and independent politics."[42] These same men were described by a Hartford printer as "real representatives of the

[40] Reprinted in *ibid.*, March 3, 1819.
[41] *Philadelphia National Gazette*, October 11, 1820.
[42] Reprinted in the *Boston Palladium*, April 15, 1817.

nation, rather than bigotted and fiery partisans."[43] A speech by the governor of Kentucky decrying violent partisanship quickly went the rounds of the Federalist presses. In the glow of Monroe's recent visit, prominent Boston Federalists, H. G. Otis and Judge Parker among them, were careful to attend a bi-partisan dinner in honor of the apostate, John Quincy Adams, upon his return from Europe in 1817.[44] The virulent *Connecticut Mirror* found it meet to commend Governor Wolcott's inaugural address, which pleaded for a "spirit of conciliation," and the editor later praised Smith Thompson of New York, upon his appointment to the cabinet, for not having intervened directly in New York's political squabbles.[45] Federalist editors were peculiarly sensitive to suggestions by Republican officials that they intended to be more "liberal" in their appointment policies. Thus editors everywhere rushed to congratulate Governor Heister of Pennsylvania when he declared in 1820 that he was disposed to select men without distinction of party.[46]

Federalists could not, of course, maintain a common front of acquiescence and good humor. An acquired querulousness and fresh memories of bitter partisanship forbade it. The most irritating provocation was continuing proscription from office. Moreover, remembrances of past glories and occasional compulsive yearnings to reassert their purity led Federalists to fling out against the new order in flurries of ill-temper that were often fanned by Republican taunts or impending local elections. An added goad was the fact that most Federalists boggled at one or another postwar administration policy.

In spite of constant rebuffs, Federalist leaders persisted in the belief that somehow they could wangle an appointment.

---

[43] Reprinted in the *Boston Palladium*, July 18, 1817.

[44] *Boston Palladium*, August 19, 1817.

[45] October 13, 1817; November 23, 1818.

[46] See, for example, the *Baltimore Federal Republican*, December 29, 1820.

The number of those thirsting for jobs was considerable and their techniques were many and varied. Nathaniel Pendleton, one of Hamilton's seconds in his fatal duel, appears to have spent countless hours trying to get a district judgeship in New York. He wrote letter after letter to prominent Republicans asking their support and insisted that New York Federalists were disposed to support the administration though some felt it would be unwise to continue such a course if the exclusion policy persisted. Pendleton's appointment would be just the thing to assure continued Federalist support.[47] These efforts were unrewarded just as the "hint" Joseph Hopkinson received in 1819 turned to dross. Webster had been excited at Hopkinson's prospect, and when it did not materialize he spent years trying to get a federal appointment for his friend.[48]

Federalist complaints about proscription were endless and peevish. The *Raleigh Minerva* observed gravely that the appointment of James Bayard in 1814 had been the only major exception to the exclusion policy,[49] and the *Baltimore Federal Republican* primly saw "no reason" why the Federalists should continue to be pariahs.[50] Banishment from office was to the editor of the *Connecticut Mirror* the "subject of deepest regret." He hoped his Republican friends would therefore excuse the Federalists "for the little exultation we have manifested upon the *effects* of the triumph of *federal principles* over the miserable crooked policy of the democrats."[51] This same theme evoked acrid eloquence from another veteran. He complained that after the Republicans had "patched up the rended and abused garments of Federalism to hide their nakedness,

[47] See draft letters to J. Q. Adams, January 8, 1818, S. Thompson, March 5, 1819, and W. Johnson, September 14, 1819, Pendleton Mss, NYHS.
[48] D. Webster to J. Hopkinson, March 22, 1819, Webster, *Webster*, XVII, 46-47.
[49] Reprinted in the *Connecticut Mirror*, July 21, 1817.
[50] May 25, 1819.
[51] October 19, 1818.

they will with all the impudence of the plagiarist, declare them to constitute the genuine garb of Democracy."[52]

The flavor of periodic Federalist protestations of purity can be sampled in *Baltimore Federal Republican* editorials. The editor welcomed a new partner with the prediction that the cause he "had ever maintained shall still be vindicated," and that true Federalists, then excluded from public confidence, could alone devise "the means of restoring to this suffering, this bleeding country, its character, its wealth, and its happiness." Earlier, the same editor solemnly assured his readers: "We were born federalists—we have lived, and we will die federalists—we will, to our last breath, uphold the cause of federalism, against the world, if it be necessary."[53] Such demonstrations of loyalty were more common when a Federalist editor, after having written for months that in respect to national issues the Federalists wished to allay party animosities, attempted to spur Federalist voters to action in a state election. The dilemma was maddening.

Certain provocations from their opponents were more than Federalists could stand. The continuing exploitation of the Hartford Convention theme evoked splenetic responses. A favorite retort was to enumerate the "heroes of Bladensburgh," who "cowardlike, fled from the face of a comparatively insignificant force, and stamped upon our history the foulest blot that ever disgraced a nation's character."[54] William Coleman still brooded about the continued popularity of Carey's *Olive Branch*, which he termed "one of the most insidious publications that has appeared in this country."[55] And the prominent feting of old Charles Carroll, the signer, at a Baltimore Independence Day celebration recalled for Robert Walsh the days when Republicans stigmatized Carroll as a "hoary headed aristocrat, a tory, and covered him with all the op-

[52] *Baltimore Federal Republican*, September 28, 1819.
[53] *Ibid.*, April 4, 1820, March 12, 1819.
[54] *Connecticut Mirror*, December 29, 1817.
[55] *New York Post*, March 13, 1817.

probrious epithets usually applied to conspicuous members of the Federal Party."⁵⁶ Federalist members in the Congress were ever on guard to answer Republican taunts. Thus a Federalist Congressman reported gleefully to a friend that he had administered a stinging reproof to a Republican who had abused Gouverneur Morris "and many other federalists of that day . . . in the grossest manner."⁵⁷ The galleries were treated to such spectacles as the Federalists senators standing as one to oppose a measure to compensate all persons who had been fined under the 1798 Sedition Law,⁵⁸ and Harrison Gray Otis pouring out his wrath upon the head of Georgia's Senator Forsyth when the latter attacked the war-time record of Massachusetts.⁵⁹

Such provocations caused the Federalists considerable mental anguish, because pride conflicted with an acknowledged course of political expediency. Nowhere was this better demonstrated than in the public debate over Andrew Jackson's Florida campaign in 1818. Most Federalists greeted the news of Jackson's exploits with charges of despotism, but many toned down their criticism when it appeared the Republicans tended to regard the affair as a party matter. A Long Islander wrote jauntily that the "Hartford Convention folks appear determined to hang Jackson," an observation partially borne out by the fact that most Federalists in Congress voted for censure, though they were joined by several Republicans.⁶⁰ By the early months of 1819, however, the Federalist attack abated, and the *Boston Palladium* protested that the attack upon Jackson had been genuinely bipartisan.⁶¹ The opinion of the Republican *National Intelligencer* that party feelings had not entered into the debate was eagerly seized upon by

---

⁵⁶ *Philadelphia National Gazette*, July 8, 1820.
⁵⁷ H. R. Storrs to M. Miller, December 6, 1818, Storrs Mss, NYHS.
⁵⁸ *Niles Weekly Register*, December 12, 1818.
⁵⁹ *Boston Palladium*, March 9, 1819.
⁶⁰ Ebenezer Sage to J. W. Taylor, January 9, 1819, Taylor Mss, NYHS.
⁶¹ February 2, 1819.

Federalists.[62] These second thoughts about Jackson were not confined to newspapers. Robert Walsh wrote his friend Senator Daggett of Connecticut that he was glad the matter had been disposed of since he had always thought Jackson's conduct "susceptible of vindication."[63]

The attitudes of William Coleman and his hero, Rufus King, were striking. Coleman abused Jackson when the issue first arose, but then began to find occasions upon which to laud him. He approved of Jackson's action in not accepting a public demonstration in Washington and his toast favoring a cessation of party animosity at a Nashville dinner.[64] This conduct can be explained in part by an extraordinary letter Coleman sent King in February, 1819. Coleman wrote: "I see by the last papers from Washington that the debate on the Seminole War is to be renewed in the Senate. *Cui Bono*? I am sorry for it. I deprecate it as an event the most unfortunate that could happen just at this time. It would blast hopes that are yet entertained by the federalists here & at Albany, & towards realizing which every exertion has been made & now is making. I cannot but express a wish that other subjects may take the place of it. In spite of all we can say, it is made the criterion of attachment to the government, here, by both factions of the democratic party & prudence makes us bend before the storm, at least, in some measure. You will see by my article of this evening how far, & how far only, I have thought it discreet to go."[65]

King's behavior was exceedingly moderate. To the surprise of many it was he who presented to the Senate Jackson's remonstrance against the Senate report on his actions during the Seminole War. Jonathan Roberts was not alone in presuming that King's actions were more than tangentially con-

[62] *New York Post*, January 27, 1819.
[63] Walsh to Daggett, February 10, 1819, Daggett Mss, YL.
[64] *New York Post*, February 3, July 3, 1819.
[65] Coleman to King, February 22, 1819, King Mss, NYHS.

nected with his effort to secure re-election from a Republican legislature in New York.[66]

Federalists also treated the national bank with circumspection after the scandals that came to light in late 1818. The bank was in serious trouble, yet during the congressional inquiry that followed it became clear that a majority of the Republicans wished to continue the institution. Even Spencer Roane, the high-priest of Jeffersonianism, confessed his belief that if it were then eliminated, "a great and general distress would pervade all classes, the agriculturists as much as any."[67] Federalists did not approve of Republicans as bank directors and managers, but they were careful to couple criticism of mismanagement with affirmations of the bank's general usefulness. There is evidence that continued Republican support for the bank depended in part upon maintenance of Republican majorities or at least an equal voice on the boards of directors both of the parent bank and the branches. A Baltimore Republican wrote Nicholas Biddle in 1820: "I now wish you to attend to this election, as you know that the Republicans are one short of their number, and the necessity of giving us our Share of the Direction, as we do hold more than the half of the Stock, and it having been Policy to divide the two Parties, in the direction, Since the Bank was Established."[68] The political status of monied men was not lightly regarded.

The other principal economic issue debated during this period was that of domestic manufactures. Federalist opinion continued mixed though it seems clear that a substantial majority of Federalists did not approve of further assistance from the government. Indeed it was the Republicans who took the lead in pressing for aid. The 1817 meeting of the American Society for the Encouragement of American Manufactures

[66] Klein, "Memoirs of a Senator," 403-05.
[67] Roane to J. Barbour, February 26, 1819, Barbour Mss, NYPL.
[68] J. McKim, Jr., to Biddle, January 8, 1820, Reginald McGrane, ed., *The Correspondence of Nicholas Biddle Dealing with National Affairs: 1807-1844* (Boston and New York, 1919), 13.

inducted such worthies as Jefferson, Madison, and Monroe, and all replied with sympathetic words.[69] At so-called domestic manufactures meetings in Philadelphia and New York, politically prominent Republicans heavily outnumbered Federalist leaders.[70] Republican orators and editors continued to argue that the manufacturer and the factory-hand must look to Republicans for assistance because the Federalists as a party were opposed to the tariff. This charge was nominally disputed by Federalist editors, but the number of their newspapers that favored higher tariffs was heavily outweighed by those which became increasingly hostile.

This distinctive pattern of Federalist behavior caused much uneasiness among Jeffersonians. Recollections of past Federalist indignities did not die quickly. A New Hampshire Republican hoped that the hatchet would be buried deep enough "to conceal the handle," but many memories were yet filled with vivid images of the black cockade.[71] A stalwart New Yorker still believed that New England was ripe for "monarchist trappings," as demonstrated by the fact that "the presbyterian Clergy of the blue light order, have already pronounced the Prince Regent & the Autocrat of the Russias to be the purest saints in the Christian world, because they belong to the Bible Society."[72] Major Noah, a staunch Republican editor, was not impressed by Federalist professions of friendship. "Cunning fellows as they are," he charged, "they fight most obstinately against republicans, but, when egregiously beat, they cry out 'come let's be friends, and share your dinner with us.' When did Federalist ever give us a crumb?"[73]

Republicans were also concerned because they believed their party had been corrupted by Federalism. "The people

[69] *Boston Palladium*, June 17, 1817.
[70] See lists of delegates in *ibid.*, August 27, November 30, and December 10, 1819.
[71] H. W. Gordon to W. Plumer, August 22, 1817, Plumer Mss, LC.
[72] E. Sage to J. W. Taylor, March 15, 1818, Taylor Mss, NYHS.
[73] *National Advocate* (New York), November 14, 1820.

are looking about," one wrote, "to find out what has become of federalism, & not being able to see or hear anything of it, have concluded it is dead, honest souls! They have not yet discovered that Democracy, weary of wrangling, has taken federalism to wife upon condition she should wear the breeches." He believed that the Democracy had been going downhill steadily since the first administration of Jefferson and that Monroe was even more guilty than Madison in neglecting the true friends who "made him what he is."[74] When James Barbour of Virginia observed in the Senate that Federalism was dead, David Daggett arose to observe that "federalism was not *dead*, but sleeping—that its spirit had *transmigrated* to other bodies." Barbour answered with "great severity," but a Republican senator, James Wilson, noted that "there was too much truth in what Mr. Daggett said, and it was evidently felt very sensibly by many of the Republicans." Wilson feared that "unprincipled men among the Republicans" would be increasingly tempted to combine with the Federalists to "gratify their ambition."[75]

Partisan Republicans feared that the Federalist policy of renouncing formal opposition while at the same time attacking the caucus and proscription would soon weaken the dominant party. A Massachusetts pamphleteer warned his fellow Republicans in 1817 that "however smooth may be their professions," when the Federalist leaders preached "peace, and harmony, and conciliation," their real object remained the same.[76] The low estate of the Federalist party and its apparent disposition to support Monroe could not, in William Crawford's estimation, "fail to relax the bonds by which the Republican party has been hitherto held together," and if they persisted until the latent schisms among Republicans matured, the

[74] E. Sage to J. W. Taylor, January 18, 1818, Taylor Mss, NYHS.
[75] Wilson to W. Darlington, February 8, 1818, Darlington Mss, LC.
[76] *Royalty of Federalism! Read, Try, Decide, on the Charge of Washington, That Leading Federalists Are to Monarchy Devoted* (Boston, [1817?]), 16.

future of the party would be in jeopardy.[77] Martin Van Buren remarked that the Federalists had always "been desirous to bring every usage or plan designed to secure party unity into disrepute with the people," and insofar as they were successful the Federalists were benefited. He believed that such disciplinary measures were peculiarly necessary to the Republicans, a fact that in his seasoned judgment reflected a basic difference in the nature of the two parties. Although individual Federalists could act upon a semi-mystical, intuitive understanding of their common interest, Republicans had to depend upon leadership and organization.[78]

This hostility toward and fear of the Federalists on the one hand, and a belief that the Federalists were doomed on the other, led to an ambivalence within the Republican party. Unwavering Republican papers like the *Philadelphia Franklin Gazette* and the *Portland Argus* could say kind things about Rufus King in 1819,[79] but a year later Benjamin Crowninshield of Massachusetts was railing against Federalist "aristocrats" for seeking to make property holdings a basis for state senate representation.[80] Jefferson was writing his friends glowing reports in 1818 that the utter demise of the Federalist party was near,[81] but in Boston the Republicans still would not participate in a joint celebration of Independence Day.[82] John Quincy Adams firmly believed that the Federalists would continue to decline, but his diary in these years is filled with suspicions about individual Federalists.[83]

[77] Crawford to A. Gallatin, March 12, 1817, Henry Adams, ed., *The Writings of Albert Gallatin* (3 vols.; Philadelphia, 1879), II, 27.

[78] Martin Van Buren, *Inquiry into the Origin and Course of Political Parties in the United States* (New York, 1867), 5-6.

[79] Reprinted in the *Baltimore Federal Republican*, April 6, May 28, 1819.

[80] *Boston Palladium*, December 26, 1820.

[81] Jefferson to A. Gallatin, February 15, 1818, Adams, *Gallatin*, II, 57.

[82] *Boston Palladium*, June 30, 1820.

[83] See, for example, the entries for November 27, 1818 and December 17, 1818, Charles F. Adams, ed., *Memoirs of John Quincy Adams*,

Such fears and doubts led Republicans to continue the policy of proscription. An editorial in the *Boston Patriot* provides a profound insight into the Republican rationale for this course. "We have already suggested," it read: "that open faithful and fearless devotion to the republican cause; to the views, wishes, and interest of the great body of the people, was, in our opinion, the high road to every office in the gift of the government of the U. States. To aim at affording equal protection to all, is an object purely patriotick. It deserves and will receive the gratitude of the people and of the government. The friendship or recommendation of any of the men who during the war, enlisted against their country, cannot, at headquarters, have the least favourable influence. . . . Arouse, Republicans, to a sense of your own worth. Your sufferings for your country, your fearless, faithful devotion to its good, have entitled you to the highest estimation of the people and government. Respect yourselves. Protect one another: cast off your timidity. If you require encouragement, protection and support, you can look for them with confidence both to the government and people of the Union. . . . While you thus highly esteem your own worth, and acquire a power important beyond calculation; and while you use that power not only to protect your friends, never exert it for purposes of revenge or oppression. Be liberal, but be liberal as men who hold and intend to hold the power."[84]

This view is a remarkably different one from that which Federalists held in regard to the meaning and importance of public office.

Comprising Portions of His Diary from 1795 to 1848 (12 vols.; Philadelphia, 1872-78), IV, 182-83, 193-94.

[84] Reprinted in the *Worcester* (Mass.) *National Aegis*, December 2, 1818.

CHAPTER IV

Defeat in the States

=====

T<small>HE</small> <small>RELATIONSHIPS</small> between the parties on the state and local level were often markedly different from those in the national arena. While professing general satisfaction with Monroe's administration, the Federalists in the New England and middle states continued an active and frequently bitter contest for political influence. The Federalists were severely hampered by the necessity for seeking distinctions between the national Republican party and the state or local organizations, a necessity that led to tortured and implausible rationalizations. From state to state Federalist politicians had to adjust their techniques to the relative strength of the two parties and the internal structure of the Republican organization. The fast-moving events in New York state merit particular attention.

A Republican faction led by DeWitt Clinton had become dominant by 1817. Martin Van Buren was from the first apprehensive that Clinton would not treat the Democracy with respect, suspicions that increased when the Federalists did not run a gubernatorial candidate of their own against Clinton. Just the year before, Rufus King had led a vigorous Federalist campaign. Other Republicans shared Van Buren's fears. "How goes the Election your way?" one asked sarcastically. "All harmony and union in our quarter—a *very* millennium—the Lamb & the Lion—will soon feed at the same Stall & we think we may safely give adders & Rattlesnakes for play things to our Children—seeing that we are all federalists & all Republicans—oh! what happy times are at hand."[1] The split between the Republican factions widened during 1817 and the follow-

<hr/>

[1] R. M. Williams to John Townsend, May 14, 1817, Townsend Mss, NYPL.

ing year. As all-out war became inevitable, it dawned upon Federalists that decisive power lay in their hands.[2] This was confirmed when Governor Clinton, perceiving that Van Buren was slowly winning the intra-party struggle, discreetly put out feelers for Federalist support.

A violent eruption followed swiftly. Federalists in the Assembly and Senate threw their support in early 1819 behind Clinton's choice for speaker of the Assembly and his nominees for the all-important Council of Appointment. The support was conclusive. Van Buren's men, dubbed "Bucktails," then had solid evidence that an "unholy alliance" existed, and thereafter they made this the chief campaign issue in all their struggles with Clinton. This same act occasioned a flurry of Federalist soul-searching. The future of Federalism and of individual Federalists was the central question, not the merits of the two Republican factions. Because the Federalist standard commanded the allegiance of more than a third of the electorate, its lodgment profoundly affected state politics for years afterward.

Bucktails at once sensed the political implications of Clinton's flirtation and budding romance with the Federalists. Smith Thompson, the secretary of the navy, wrote Van Buren: "The great object you ought to keep in view is to avoid, the least semblance of an understanding or bargain with the

[2] See, for example, William Coleman to Morris Miller, June 20, 1819, Coleman Mss, NYHS. In this letter Coleman reported that he intended to meet soon with a group of anti-Clinton Republicans. He planned to impress upon them the advisability of securing the consent of Smith Thompson, the secretary of the navy, to run against Clinton the next year. "If we cannot have Thompson," Coleman continued, "we shall I presume be driven to take Yates, & I cannot say my hopes would be sanguine [Yates was another Republican leader]. But *Thompson can be had*, if he can be made to believe he will have the support of the great majority of the federalists: this I say with some confidence. Next to a nomination, let us obtain the declarations & where it is practicable the commitments of federalists in every part of the State, particularly the western part." For some reason many Federalists believed that Thompson was a pliable sort of fellow. See, however, his letter to Van Buren later in this chapter.

70

federalists—That is the rock on which Mr. C. is to split, and give him no chance for an offset against you. There is no doubt I presume from what I hear fall from Mr. King's friends here, that if you would make him Senator, You could have the Council. Altho personally I have a very high respect for Mr. K. and do not believe his reappointment would set unpleasantly on the friends of the administration here, yet the great fear to be apprehended, is the political effect it would have in our State—It would disarm you of the most powerful argument you now have against your adversaries—Federal aid—Federal coalition—You must not think me insensitive, to the situation of my friends in office—You may suffer a short time—But I am persuaded it will ultimately redound not only to your honor, and the general good, but I hope and trust to your personal benefit."[3] A year later when the Clinton-Federalist alliance had hardened, Thompson wrote: "But you must calculate to the fight over again with the Federalists with the accessions of the Clintonians to their ranks. Mr. Clinton has to all intents & purposes thrown himself politically into the arms of the federalists."[4]

Van Buren could agree with Thompson that the Bucktails must hang the Federalist albatross around Clinton's neck, but he thought he could lure just enough Federalist votes away from the governor to defeat him in the election of 1820. Major Noah reported confidently from New York that the Federalists "want their Mayor, Recorder & a few others to be preserved which if it could be done they would go Heart & hand with us."[5] Several prominent Federalists had already declared for the Bucktails, but Van Buren's master stroke was deciding to support Rufus King's bid for another term in the United States Senate. To convince other Bucktail leaders that this would be wise was one of the most difficult political chores

---

[3] Thompson to Van Buren, January 23, 1819, Van Buren Mss, LC.
[4] Thompson to Van Buren, January 23, 1820, *ibid.*
[5] M. M. Noah to Van Buren, July 13, 1819, *ibid.*

71

the Red Fox ever undertook. He made a brilliant speech, heavily underlining King's support for the war and for Monroe's administration. This together with persuasive private talks convinced most of the Bucktails, though many had severe misgivings. Federalist friends of King were immensely pleased, but they winced when Van Buren announced that the Bucktail candidate for governor would be Daniel Tompkins, a partisan symbol of New York Republicanism. The official campaign address was devoted almost exclusively to the charge that Clinton had committed himself to the Federalists. Room was carefully left, however, for those Federalists who pledged themselves to support Van Buren's forces.[6]

As office-hungry Federalists clambered onto Clinton's machine in droves, the Clintonian Republicans became disquieted. "Almost the only difficulty," a Canandaiguan reported, "is the idea that is gaining ground with many of our old republicans, that the Clintonian is substantially the federal party, under a new guise—This is really the most potent argument that the bucktails can use, and it is the only one, which gains any *proselytes*."[7] The disenchantment of James Tallmadge, a high-ranking Republican leader, was symptomatic of the difficulties Clinton foisted upon his Republican friends. He complained in April 1819 that he was being lambasted by the Federalists for defending Jackson, by Clinton for supporting Monroe, and by Bucktails for being a Clintonian.[8] The governor's appointment of a few prominent Federalists led Tallmadge to ask: "Will the Republican party support a Governor in power that he may make federal appointments?"[9] A year later he was thoroughly soured on Clinton. "He has found it consistent with his ideas of friendship & fidelity," Tallmadge charged, "to assail & persecute me—after having sold me to purchase blue

[6] *Republican Nomination for Governor and Lt. Governor. With an Address to the Electors of the State of New York* (n.p., 1820).

[7] J. Willson to J. Townsend, March 7, 1820, Townsend Mss, NYPL.

[8] Tallmadge to J. W. Taylor, April 4, 1819, Taylor Mss, NYHS.

[9] Tallmadge to J. W. Taylor, July 17, 1819, *ibid.*

lights."[10] Clinton's sponsorship of the canal policy and his obvious administrative abilities, however, kept many wavering Republicans in his camp.

What considerations led Federalists to support or oppose Clinton and some to stay neutral? To those who joined Clinton the main issue was simple and clear. They could, by supporting the weaker Republican faction, force it to consider claims for office and influence. The governor was well aware of this price, but his technique was adroit. For every job he gave to a Federalist he held out the promise of one to several others if they would support him with vigor.[11]

There were other reasons. Clinton personified respectability and dignity, with even a slight touch of the pompous. He was a conspicuous patron of the arts and even fancied himself something of a scientist. Some Federalists doted on "the energetic course he took when mayor of the City of New York to suppress the riots at the time of the Baltimore massacre."[12] Others comforted themselves with the belief that he had left behind "the jacobinism which formerly characterized him," and would now busy himself with "arresting the mad course of democracy."[13] Those Federalists who enlisted firmly in Clinton's cause were inclined to revile such of their colleagues as did not join them. They bandied about such phrases as "malcontent," "disappointed, office-seeking Federalists," and "objects of disgust and contempt."[14] Young Alexander Hamilton was stigmatized by one as "this degenerate son of Gen. H."[15]

[10] Tallmadge to J. W. Taylor, March 2, 1820, *ibid.*
[11] *New York American*, July 3, 21, 1819.
[12] S. E. Baldwin to E. Baldwin, July 24, 1819, Baldwin Mss, YL.
[13] J. Pintard to his daughter, May 2, 1820, Dorothy C. Barck, ed., *Letters from John Pintard to His Daughter Eliza Noel Pintard Davidson* (4 vols.; New York, 1940), I, 287; E. Baldwin to S. E. Baldwin, April 21, 1819, Baldwin Mss, YL.
[14] W. W. Van Ness to Solomon Van Rensselaer, January 18, 1820, Bonney, *Legacy*, 342; J. Pintard to his daughter, April 23, 1819, Barck, *Pintard*, I, 185.
[15] J. Pintard to his daughter, March 15, 1819, *ibid.*, I, 172.

However compelling the reasoning of these Clintonian Federalists, that of Federalists opposed to the governor had much substance. They feared that if Federalists as a body attached themselves to Clinton, the Republicans would desert him and leave the Federalists once again isolated. The short-run prospects might be good, but the hope of integrating themselves into the dominant party would be destroyed. Then too, Federalists remembered that Clinton in 1817 had spoken scornfully of the Federalists when he sought to assure Republicans that he was trustworthy. His famous statement that the Federalists would rather rule in Hell than serve in Heaven still rankled in sensitive memories.[16] Only after it appeared that he was losing ground within the Republican ranks did he suddenly discover that Federalists made excellent administrators. It had an aura of crudeness about it. Clinton's refusal in 1819 to nourish Rufus King's hopes for re-election to the Senate was a particularly sore point. When many Federalists followed the Clintonian Republicans in denying King, those Federalists who remained loyal to King were deeply outraged. They dubbed their miscreant colleagues "the Swiss," and the name soon passed into political jargon of the day. King became a rallying point for anti-Clinton Federalists.

Founded in March 1819, the *New York American* quickly became the organ of these anti-Clinton Federalists. The first issue carried a long open letter to Clinton berating him and the Federalists who supported him. "In short, Sir," the young editors exclaimed, "you first insulted the federal party by unfounded vituperations, as you now do by obsequious blandishments; and it is natural enough, that those who had not the spirit to feel resentment for your injuries, should not have the honesty to resist your temptations."[17] The *American* soon moved from a posture of independence to an *ad hoc* alliance with the Bucktails to bring down Clinton. With sarcasm and

[16] *New York American*, March 3, 1819.
[17] *Ibid.*, March 3, 1819.

74

cutting words the *American* editors relentlessly attacked the Swiss and urged Federalist voters to withdraw their support from Federalist legislative leaders who had been most active in cementing the alliance with Clinton. One of the few Federalists who had resisted voting for Clinton's appointees wrote dramatically: "I have passed the Rubicon, and left the federal party for ever."[18]

Federalists were electrified in April 1820 by the appearance of a public address signed by 51 prominent Federalists. Issued as an election address advocating the election of Daniel Tompkins, this statement pitilessly excoriated those Federalists who supported Clinton. The signers, who included representatives of such prominent families as the Delanceys, Hasbroucks, and Verplancks, characterized themselves as "high-minded" Federalists.[19] The term was picked up at once by Federalist and Clintonian critics as the generic name of the group and was used thereafter with a derisive connotation.

The address was an amazing document. It began by asserting that the Federal party was "broken up and dissolved," not only in the formal party sense, but also in the sense of feelings "of mutual confidence and private regard," which had been perhaps its strongest cement in former years. The acceptance by the national administration of Federalist policy, according to the "High-Minders," left no major principles at issue between the parties. Only interested individuals, "who from party alone have received their influence and consideration in society," would wish to maintain the party name and discipline. The purpose of such individuals could only be to "maintain a corrupt association" in order to acquire patronage and power. The signers then explicitly removed themselves forever from the rolls of the Federalist party. The next section advised readers that the group intended to unite itself "unequivocally and without reserve" to the Republican party. "We make no

[18] J. A. King to C. King, January 4, 1820, King Mss, NYHS.
[19] *New York Post*, April 22, 1820.

conditions," they promised, "we ask for no stipulations—but we will not suffer a superstitious attachment to a name . . . to divide us from those from whom, in principle and feeling, we acknowledge no separation." In curious words for Federalists, the signers paid homage to "the general intelligence and virtue of the people," and bowed "with undissembled respect, to their enlightened will." A stinging attack upon Clinton and his Federalist friends closed the long statement.[20]

The reaction to this address was immediate and clamorous. Coleman was furious at those "who have modestly undertaken to dictate to a large and respectable part of the community, what course they shall pursue."[21] He rejoiced in an answering address by some up-state Federalists who principally attacked the contention that support of Tompkins was necessary in order to demonstrate fealty to the national administration.[22] Federalists in other states, especially in Maryland, were greatly exercised. The two most influential Federalist newspapers in Maryland directed a steady stream of abuse at the dissidents.[23] They bitterly charged that the "corrupt association" sobriquet in effect acknowledged the principal charges levelled at Federalists through the years by Republicans, charges that upright Federalists could never treat with less than contempt. Deep-seated animosities among prideful Federalists boiled up furiously around this sensational address. The controversy sharply highlighted the principal dilemma of postwar Federalism, that of supporting Monroe's administration while trying to oppose Republicans in the states.

Van Buren's relationship with the "High-Minders" was in some ways anomalous. He became, in his words, "more intimate" with them than was the case with most Republicans and quite frankly acknowledged that he was "pleased with their society and with the spirited manner in which they sus-

[20] *Ibid.*, April 22, 1820.
[21] *Ibid.*, April 22, 1820.   [22] *Ibid.*, April 26, 1820.
[23] See particularly the *Baltimore Federal Gazette*, April 27, 1820; and the *Baltimore Federal Republican*, May 2, 9, 1820.

tained their position."[24] This deeply offended less broad-minded Jeffersonians. Yet Van Buren was by no means wide-eyed in their company. An exchange of letters between Van Buren and George Tibbits, a Federalist assemblyman who hinted that he might give Van Buren a crucial vote, amply demonstrated this fact. Van Buren answered Tibbits' first overture with these wise and gentle words: "I have learnt with great pleasure that you have wisely determined hence forward to Identify yourself with the Republicans of the State & Union —As this act is purely spontaneous & wholly uninfluenced by sinister considerations it is a step which I am persuaded you will never have occasion to regret. You may for a season be somewhat annoyed by the aspersions of old *friends* & the jealousies of new friends, but these are of short duration. A man of sense knows they are circumstances which will always exist."[25] When Tibbits had his first pleasant interview with Van Buren, he then sent a note indicating that he had in mind certain conditions regarding appointments. "I thought I had made myself understood by you before," Van Buren answered tartly, "we esteem & respect you & would be happy to see you & your friends in the Republican ranks—where you will be well used, but the idea of making any stipulations to secure the support of Federalists is wholly inadmissible." Van Buren acknowledged that it required manful firmness suddenly to abandon the Federalist party. He then closed with an affirmation of complete trust in Tibbits' motives and worth.[26]

A large number of Federalists were unhappy with both Clinton and Tompkins in this crucial election. William Coleman gave expression to this group. "After much thought, therefore," he wrote privately, "I have determined while things remain as they are, to keep myself equally aloof from both.

[24] John C. Fitzpatrick, ed., "The Autobiography of Martin Van Buren," *Annual Report of the American Historical Association for the Year 1918* (Washington, D.C., 1920), II, 104.
[25] Van Buren to Tibbits, December 28, 1819, Van Buren Mss, LC.
[26] Tibbits to Van Buren, January 9, 1820, Van Buren to Tibbits, January 9, 1820, *ibid.*

'The plague take both your Houses.' "[27] He would have no part of either the Swiss or the High-Minders. Before the election, which Clinton won by a narrow margin, Rufus King made this prophecy: "Great numbers of the Federalists will adhere to Clinton, a minority will unite with the V.P., and a great body of them will take no part."[28] Coleman echoed this calculation and after the election announced proudly that most of the Federalists had stayed home, though more of them would have done so if the anti-Clinton Federalists had kept quiet.[29] It is likely, however, that a majority of all Federalist voters supported Clinton at this election.

The Federalist party in New York was torn asunder by the events of 1819 and 1820. A young Albany lawyer correctly adjudged the situation when he wrote: "Political feelings have recently been unusually acrimonious in this State . . . Federalism in consequence of this state of things has been resuscitated into life and importance, but the uniformity & consistency of its character will be destroyed in the contest."[30] A month later he reported that "the french watch word after their defeat at Waterloo 'Let every man take care of himself' seems to have spread through the ranks of federalism."[31] Individual Federalists, under Clinton's auspices, slipped into political office in significant numbers during this period, but the feast came to an early close. Both wings of the Republican party deeply resented the intrusion. Several of the High-Minders passed permanently into the Bucktail ranks after giving suitable evidence that they were true converts. Clintonian Federalists, for the most part, were never able to shake off the imputation that they were adventurers and they remained "unredeemed." By hammering away at Clinton's alliance the Bucktails gained strength rapidly. They brought

[27] Coleman to J. A. King, February 1, 1820, King Mss, NYHS.
[28] King to M. Van Buren, March 25, 1820, Van Buren Mss, LC.
[29] *New York Post*, May 3, 1820.
[30] E. Baldwin to S. E. Baldwin, March 17, 1819, Baldwin Mss, YL.
[31] E. Baldwin to S. E. Baldwin, April 21, 1819, *ibid.*

about and dominated the constitutional convention held in 1821, the principal purposes of which were to widen the suffrage and eliminate the Council of Appointment. Bucktails had fresh memories of the Federalists who had voted for Clinton and those who had been appointed to office by Clinton's Council of Appointment.

Federalists in the neighboring state of Connecticut were dealt a staggering blow in the spring of 1817 when Oliver Wolcott was elected governor. Old line Republicans and a body of dissident Federalists combined for the victory in a campaign that reeked of religious, patronage and bank controversies. Federalists were appalled at first but they took heart from Wolcott's inaugural address. Speaking of his service in John Adams' administration, he added: "I cannot omit to express the reverence I entertain for those sages, whom no artifices could deceive, no temptations seduce, no dangers intimidate."[32] Yet the toppling of Federalism's long rule was crushing. "In the annals of political warfare, and of jacobinical proscription," one heartbroken Federalist mourned, "the world never saw so fair and spotless a victim as the State of Connecticut offered up as a sacrifice." The first shocked reaction was to hope the ruling coalition would disintegrate quickly.[33]

Wolcott's forces soon demanded a constitutional convention for the principal purpose of extending the suffrage. The Federalists realized they could not make a direct fight for delegates, but they believed enough Federalists would be elected to keep changes in the old order at a minimum. A slim majority of their opponents, however, swept away the hated "stand-up" law, which was almost a caricature of the non-secret ballot, and greatly liberalized voting requirements. One Federalist editor scouted the notion that the "stand-up" law prejudiced

[32] *Connecticut Mirror*, May 19, 1817. See also the *New York Post*, May 6, 1817; and C. Gore to R. King, May 21, 1817, King Mss, NYHS.

[33] E. Baldwin to S. E. Baldwin, November 1, 1817, S. E. Baldwin to E. Baldwin, May 25, 1817, Baldwin Mss, YL.

debtors. "But are all the Democrats debtors," he asked super-ciliously, "and are all the federalists creditors? It is nonsense to pretend that this is the case. Probably some federalists may even be indebted to some democrats."[34] One cannot help but wonder if Federalists looked in the wrong places to account for their many defeats.

After withdrawing opposition for two years, the Federalists decided to contest the spring elections in 1819. They expected good results from the powerful Trumbull Benevolent Society, an association of young Federalists avowedly devoted to elee-mosynary pursuits. "Its real & avowed object is *to do good*," was one wry characterization.[35] Defeat followed again, how-ever, and Federalists looked about for a new technique. They duly noticed that many veteran Republicans were becoming increasingly unhappy with the hunger for office displayed by many late-comers to the ruling party. Accordingly an alliance was formed to contest for seats in the state senate. This so-called Union Republican slate pleaded for an end to party passions and a return to good order.[36] Another defeat con-vinced the still powerful Connecticut Federalists that direct political action and overt alliances were both futile. In the future they would try to work through the majority faction of Republicans. This decision was hastened by the fact that the holocaust which desperate Federalists had predicted after Wolcott's first election had not come about. "When the storm burst upon us," that stern old Federalist, Lyman Beecher, recalled, "indeed, we thought we were dead for a while. But we found we were not dead. Our fears had magnified the danger."[37]

[34] *Connecticut Mirror*, September 1, 1817.
[35] R. S. Baldwin to D. Daggett, January 16, 1819, Daggett Mss, YL.
[36] *The Union Republican Ticket for 1820* (n.p., 1820). See also M. Hatch to D. Daggett, November 12, 1819, Daggett Mss, YL; S. E. Baldwin to E. Baldwin, January 12, 1820, and R. S. Baldwin to E. Baldwin, February 16, 1820, Baldwin Mss, YL.
[37] Charles Beecher, ed., *Autobiography, Correspondence, Etc., of Lyman Beecher, D.D.* (2 vols., New York, 1865), I, 453.

To the north, Massachusetts Federalists were not exposed to the withering experience of their Connecticut colleagues. Governor John Brooks beat back successive Republican challenges with a policy of moderation, smooth and continuous praise of the national administration, and constant reminders of his fine Revolutionary War record. Federalist campaign addresses grew more insipid each year though occasionally a Federalist editor would rake a Republican champion.[38] Massachusetts Federalists were obviously attentive to the experiences of Federalists in other states where open battle more often than not resulted in humiliating defeat.

Contributing to their passive behavior was the desire of Massachusetts Federalists to obtain payment of the knotty militia claim. Most were agreed that this necessitated a consistent policy of peace and harmony toward Republicans. A close friend advised Daniel Webster to impress upon his Boston cronies that the claim would be "settled in Massachusetts & not in Washington."[39] Later the same friend began to believe that Massachusetts should give up the claim. "While the matter remains as it now does," he wrote another Bay Stater, Christopher Gore, "the claims will be a standing bribe to the Federalists to degrade themselves."[40] Gore agreed: "All our Plans & Projects are, at present, of the small and feeble case, we court Democracy & Swear she is kind; at the moment she disregards all our Interests, & treats our Reputation & our Citizens with marked Contumely & Neglect. And this nasty claim for Expenses, during the late war, is at the bottom, & the Motive of many of our Coaxers, not that they much regard the thing itself, but they hope to obtain Popularity with the State for their cunning address in having obtained Payment."[41] Wary Republicans distrusted the gaudy

[38] *Boston Palladium*, March 7, 1817, February 26, 1819, February 15, 1820.
[39] J. Mason to Webster, January 16, 1818, Webster Mss, LC.
[40] Mason to Gore, January 31, 1819, Hilliard, *Mason*, 211.
[41] Gore to R. King, February 24, 1818, King, *King*, VI, 118.

benignity of Massachusetts Federalists. A Long Islander believed "that sooner or later by trick and perseverance their claims will be granted," and another presumed sarcastically that "the expense of the delegates to the Hartford Convention . . . [would] make one item of their Charge."[42] Massachusetts Republicans hinted broadly that if they were elected the Congress would take a new view of the matter.

In the rest of New England, Federalist strength gradually ebbed. New Hampshire Federalists did not run a candidate against Republican Governor Plumer in 1818. "The *leading federalists*," Plumer advised, "are still opposed to the republicans, but they thought opposition would only injure themselves. Tho much of the spirit of party has subsided, it is not extinct, but sleepeth."[43] Dissension between moderate Republicans and those led by the irascible editor, Isaac Hill, prompted the Federalists to run a gubernatorial candidate in 1819, but they lapsed again into relative inactivity the next year. Because New Hampshire Federalists could not find a receptive Republican faction, they retained their organization into the next decade. A Republican governor of the new state of Maine promised he would be "liberal" in his appointments, but tens of Federalists were removed, thus sharpening party lines.[44] As in Maine, Vermont Federalists were a minority, though a change from a general ticket to a district system resulted in the election of three Federalist congressmen in 1820.[45] The balance was closer in Rhode Island where the two parties continued conventional party warfare.

Just as Federalism was an overriding issue in the politics of New York and New England, so too was it ever present in the middle states. From a resounding victory in 1816

[42] E. Sage to J. W. Taylor, February 6, 1818, J. Tayler to J. W. Taylor, January 5, 1819, Taylor Mss, NYHS.
[43] Plumer to J. Q. Adams, March 13, 1818, Plumer Letterbook, LC. See also the *Boston Palladium*, February 26, 1819, and March 21, 1820.
[44] *Ibid.*, March 7, 1820, September 22, 1820.
[45] *Ibid.*, October 31, 1820.

Maryland Federalists witnessed with anguish the steady encroachment of Republicanism in succeeding years. By 1819 the Republicans were able to elect their own governor. The contests in this and the following years were sharp and bitter. Federalist forces were urged on by a group of hard-hitting editors who disdained compromise or retreat. They were plagued, however, by the familiar dilemma of hailing Monroe at the same time they termed state Republicans scoundrels and thieves. After the Republican victory in 1819 the editors feared that the prospect of removal from office would tempt some Federalists to curry favor with the victors. One editor denounced such "milk and water federalism," which indicated "either a weak mind or dishonesty in point of political integrity."[46] Yet as Federalists were removed by the score the list of apostates grew. Federalists girded themselves for a last mighty effort in 1820. Victory barely eluded them. Demoralization followed, signified by the fact that the editors of both Federalist dailies in Baltimore were willing to sue for peace, at least for the present.[47]

One aspect of Maryland Federalism warrants special attention. Although many of its principal leaders were Baltimoreans, the main strength of the party lay in the rural areas. Because Baltimore was one of their strongholds, Republican leaders tried to increase its representation in the state legislature. This situation prompted a country Federalist to ask rhetorically: "Shall I vote for the men who, by effecting the changes, which they have proposed and design, will place the great Agricultural State of Maryland at the feet of the Merchants, the Bank Speculators, the Brokers, the Lottery Officekeepers, the Foreigners, and the MOB OF BALTIMORE? or: Shall I give my support to those, who will maintain, in opposition to them, the honour, the dignity and independence of the CULTIVATORS OF THE SOIL? We would

---

[46] *Baltimore Federal Republican*, December 7, 1819.
[47] *Ibid.*, December 5, 22, 1820; *Baltimore Federal Gazette*, October 10, 1820.

eventually be governed by Baltimore's delegation, backed moreover by the influence which wealth always gives, and aided by deputations of lawyers, and committees from her banks, her various incorporated companies, the city councils, and from interested individuals."[48] This hardy survival of Federalism in older agricultural areas was not only characteristic of Maryland, but of most other states as well. In both the New York and Connecticut constitutional conventions, for example, the principal Federalist objections to a wider suffrage came from rural delegates. One of their chief arguments was that it would hurt the farmer and magnify the influence of the cities and manufacturing interests.

The course of events in Pennsylvania was markedly similar to that in New York. A deep schism had split the democracy into two factions, known as the New School and the Old School. Federalists had allied themselves loosely with the Old School forces, captained by General Heister, in the election of 1817, but the New School men, led by William Findlay, captured the governorship. Enough important Findlayite leaders had broken away by 1819 to make Heister, aided by the bulk of Pennsylvania's Federalists, the favorite in 1820. The New School stump-speakers concentrated their fire upon the Heister-Federalist alliance, but like Van Buren (though with less finesse), they tried to woo some of the Federalists to their side.[49] A rousing campaign was followed by a victory for the Old School.

After the election the New School publicists attacked the Federalists with unbounded fury.[50] Obviously taken aback Heister refused to reward the Federalists as they had expected. Professor Philip Klein has described this colorfully. "The Federalists," he wrote, "who had greeted Heister's election

[48] "Agricola" in the *Baltimore Federal Republican*, September 28, 1819.

[49] See the *Philadelphia Franklin Gazette*, October 6, 1820; and D. Scott to L. Coryell, September 12, 1820, Coryell Mss, PHS.

[50] *Philadelphia Franklin Gazette*, October 20, 31, 1820.

with shouts of pure joy were fairly quivering in anticipation of the political plums that were at last to be dropped into their laps."[51] As in other states, appointment to office was the supreme object of political activity among Pennsylvania Federalists. "Would it be dishonourable," a Federalist editor queried: "to aspire to the station to which our claims entitle us. The *Station* of equal confidence with our fellow citizens. A restoration of equal rights—a participation in public favor —an exemption from the persecution which has too long prevailed, striving to wither our just claims to respect, by insinuations, that we were enemies to our country."[52] The disappointment among Federalists was intense, although they derived some solace from the fact that one of their number was elected speaker of the lower house when neither of the Republican factions could obtain a majority for their man. By committing themselves openly, the Federalists once more isolated themselves. Republican fears and animosities were fanned into open flame during this campaign.

Federalists fared badly in New Jersey during this period, though in the little state of Delaware Federalism remained viable. New Jersey Federalists tried to copy their Pennsylvania brethren by exploiting quarrels within the Republican family but with little success. The state-wide election of 1820 resulted in sweeping Republican gains. James Wilson, a Republican leader, rejoiced in the "mortification" of the Federalists and predicted that only the small agricultural county of Cape May would remain Federalist.[53] Downcast Federalists had to await the Jackson-Adams struggle in the next decade to revive any hopes of influence in New Jersey. Sharp divisions among Delaware Federalists led to the election of a Republican governor in 1820 but the legislature remained safely Federal-

[51] Philip S. Klein, *Pennsylvania Politics: 1817-1832. A Game without Rules* (Philadelphia, 1940), 113-14.
[52] Reprinted from the *Village Record* (Chester, Pa.) in the *Baltimore Federal Republican*, September 29, 1818.
[53] Wilson to W. Darlington, October 23, 1820, Darlington Mss, LC.

ist. By 1824 Delaware could lay claim to being the only Federalist-controlled state in the Union.

Thus the disciples of Washington and Hamilton were forced to function within a bewildering and frustrating milieu. Pride conflicted with expediency; a strong sense of discreteness with the apparent necessity of breaking up the party; and short-run success with the prospect of continuing Republican hostility. Frustration in turn led Federalists to antagonize their opponents needlessly and to squabble among themselves.

Should the party try to stay together or should it be dissolved? Conflicting advice piled up in every quarter. Alexander Hanson of Maryland looked ahead to the selection of Monroe's successor. By remaining united the Federalists would be "in every way qualified to act as the circumstances then existing may require."[54] Jeremiah Mason of New Hampshire, however, pleaded with Webster: "I wish to Heaven you would personally advocate the doctrine of Conciliation, & the necessity of taking a new departure."[55] "A Federalist of the Old School" wrote his local editor: "The doctrine of dissolution has become a fashionable and cant doctrine: But upon what grounds? Was it wisdom to sustain the party when success was hopeless, and its influence a cypher, and now when it stands upon high grounds, and when its principles are acknowledged and adopted, to abandon it? Cannot we as well sustain those principles, and give permanency to them, by remaining true to ourselves, leaving other parties to reject or follow them, as to hastily obliterate the old landmarks of division? Let us as federalists calmly consider it."[56]

Rufus King, however, loftily pronounced that the old parties should be dissolved in the interest of measures that would promote the nation's welfare.[57] The problem was faced directly

[54] Hanson to R. King, March 29, 1817, King Mss, NYHS.
[55] Mason to Webster, January 18, 1818, Webster Mss, LC.
[56] Reprinted from the *Catskill Recorder* in the *New York American*, June 23, 1819.
[57] King to J. Barbour, January 18, 1818, Barbour Mss, NYPL.

by the Federalist presidential electors in 1820. All of them agreed they must vote for Monroe but many could not support Daniel Tompkins for the vice presidency. Webster wanted to avoid the reaction that would follow naming a prominent Federalist, but his Massachusetts colleagues finally decided upon Richard Stockton of New Jersey. The four Delaware electors voted for a local Federalist and one Maryland elector for Robert G. Harper.[58]

Monroe's re-election promised a continuation of existing policies and the further disintegration of the Federalist party. Editors would continue to bicker with each other over "purity of principle," and individual Federalists would go on accusing each other of perfidy and desertion. The onset of the Missouri debates, however, had brightened many eyes. Some Federalists saw an immediate advantage; others a more subtle long-range benefit.

[58] Webster to J. Mason, November 12, 1820, Webster, *Webster*, XVI, 59-60.

87

CHAPTER V

A Beam of Hope from Missouri

HE MOST RECENT extended treatment of the Missouri
Compromise attempts to demonstrate that the Missouri
Question can be largely explained in terms of a Federalist-
Clintonian plot.[1] The author seeks to assemble convincing
evidence that this standard southern charge during the debates
has substance and that certain Federalists had deliberately
precipitated the debate with the hope of again catapulting
themselves into prominence. Professor Moore suggests that
this hope was smashed when the plot was recognized by
northern Republicans. "As soon," he writes, "as a considerable
body of Northern Democrats were convinced that the Federalists and Clintonians were seeking to make political capital out
of the Missouri question, a compromise with the South was
inevitable."[2] This thesis needs modification.

That the Missouri debates were attractive to Federalists
was obvious to most observers. Sharp divisions within the
Republican party always presented a happy challenge to Federalists. If their support were welcomed by one of the Republican factions, they would establish for themselves firm claims
for future preferment. Those Federalists who had been urging
the dissolution of their party quickly realized that the Missouri
debates would make the logic of their position more obvious.
They hoped that a firm alliance between the North and West
to oppose the South would result. This realignment would
necessarily erase the old distinctions and allow Federalists to
contend for favor without the usual stigma. Moreover, the
fact that the debates revolved in part around moral attitudes
provided Federalist orators with an opportunity to practice an

[1] Glover Moore, *The Missouri Controversy 1819-1821* (Lexington,
Ky., 1953).
[2] *Ibid.*, 178.

art at which they were acknowledged masters: that of moral preachment based upon the verities of life. Most northern Federalists, of course, sincerely deplored slavery. It would have been strange if the Federalists had not seized upon the Missouri Question, but this is not to say that the Federalists actually hatched and nurtured the conflict.

When James Tallmadge and John W. Taylor, both New York Republicans, first introduced the subject in 1819, few believed that it would soon become a paramount issue.[3] Powerful forces, however, combined to bring about a crisis. Northern Republicans had long chafed under the "Virginia Influence," which appeared to dominate the party. If Missouri entered the Union with no restriction, the power of the Virginians would, of course, be increased. This all-important political fact became plain to northern Republicans. Most of them were aware, furthermore, that the majority of their constituents would support the effort to restrict slavery. These factors caused most Republican politicians in the North to support restriction not only in 1819 but throughout the controversy. This was true in spite of the fact that they were aware the Federalists would probably benefit from their stand.

"The Missouri question," Van Buren wrote of Rufus King in 1819, "conceals *so far as he is concerned* no plot & he shall give it a true direction."[4] Northern Republicans were under few illusions about the Federalist interest in Missouri, but there was a "true direction." William Plumer of New Hampshire deplored the prospect of a North-South alignment of parties. Yet he wrote his son: "For a member of either house, from a non slave-holding State to tolerate slavery beyond its present limits, is political suicide, & his constituents

[3] Neither Professor Moore nor other investigators have found any evidence that Taylor and Tallmadge, both of whom were at this time associated with the Clintonian faction, had planned their move as part of a grand political design. There is no indication that they consulted either with Clinton or Federalists.

[4] Van Buren to M. M. Noah, December 17, 1819, Van Buren Mss, LC.

ought to limit his public services to his present term."[5] Even
Monroe, who felt certain that the furor over Missouri was
Federalist-inspired, fully recognized the plight of northern
Republicans. Success for the Federalists, he mused after the
compromise had been effected, was prevented only "by the
patriotic devotion of several members in the non slave-holding
states, who preferr'd the sacrifice of themselves at home to
. . . the risk of the Union."[6]

Southern Republicans insisted at every turn that Federalists were the principal *provocateurs*. This charge was just as
often refuted by northern Republicans. "It is well known,"
responded one, "that it originated with Republicans, that it
is supported by the Republicans throughout the free states;
and that the Federalists of the South are its warm opponents."[7]
These facts were incontestable. Hezekiah Niles scoffed at the
charge of Federalism: "This is too small to gull any one."[8]
With his usual suspicion of Federalists, John Quincy Adams
was willing to believe that they had "set on foot" the Missouri
fracas, but he would not agree that the move for restriction
would fail because northern Republicans resented the Federalist intrusion. "The question to the North and in the free
states," he argued, "is merely speculative. The people do not
feel it in their persons or their purses. On the slave side it
comes home to the feelings and interests of every man in
the community."[9]

As southern leaders became more implacable, freely threatening disruption of the party and even the nation, northern
Republican leaders became increasingly apprehensive. Thus,
the 36° 30' provision, which appeared to resolve for the

---

[5] Plumer to W. Plumer, Jr., January 31, 1820, Plumer Letterbook,
LC.

[6] Monroe to G. Hay, May 25, 1821, Monroe Mss, LC.

[7] *Speech of Mr. Plumer, of New Hampshire, on the Missouri Question, Delivered in the House of Representatives of the United States,
February 21, 1820* (n.p., n.d.), 37.

[8] Niles to W. Darlington, January 21, 1820, Darlington Mss, LC.

[9] Adams, *Memoirs*, IV, 518.

moment fears about the intra-party balance of power, was welcomed. These leaders could not, however, publicly express their relief, because the compromise proposals as a whole were not widely acceptable in the North. Those who dreaded the splintering of their party and a possible Federalist renaissance were compelled to find a plausible reason for supporting the compromise. Were not Federalists responsible for their woes? To men hardened in past battles with Hamiltonians the concept of a Federalist plot was certainly a reasonable one. Congressman John Holmes and his colleague Hill, for example, came from the Maine district of Massachusetts, where constituents clamored both for statehood and the curbing of the "slave-power." It was not difficult, nor necessarily hypocritical, for them to enshroud votes for compromise in noisy charges of Federalist perfidy and baseness.[10] Warmth of feeling mercifully softened exaggeration.

The dark shadow of the tariff fell upon the Missouri Question. "We go to all lengths," a Virginian pleaded with a northern friend, "to cherish your manufactures. . . . We foster your manufactures because we rejoice in your prosperity—All we ask in return is to let us alone."[11] Jonathan Mason, a Boston Federalist, carefully noted that, although the North had bombarded Congress with petitions regarding manufactures, there were few, if any, from the South. He thought it odd that northern legislators should antagonize the South, so odd in fact, that Mason, who had alienated his Boston friends by being lukewarm toward both the Missouri and the tariff issues, could readily believe that other Federalists and the Clintonian Republicans must be responsible for the Missouri debates.[12] A letter exchange between Daniel Webster

[10] See Holmes to W. King, December 25, 1819, quoted in Moore, *Missouri Controversy*, 106.

[11] J. Barbour to D. Daggett, December 18, 1819, Daggett Mss, YL.

[12] Mason to W. Eustis, January 29, 1820, Eustis Mss, LC. William Plumer, however, believed that the South would more effectively oppose economic legislation if its strength were increased by the addition of more slave states. Plumer to W. Plumer, Jr., February 28, 1820, Plumer Letterbook, LC.

and Congressman Henry Baldwin of Pittsburgh, a nominal Federalist and fervent protectionist, showed clearly that Baldwin feared southern opposition to economic legislation more than he did slavery in Missouri.[13] He warned a friend of Matthew Carey in December, 1819, that the prospect of new tariff legislation would be dim if the Missouri Question had "the effect of inducing all the members of the Slave-holding States to retaliate upon the rest, for their interferences in a matter in which *they* are deeply interested."[14] A New York friend of Carey exclaimed: "That infernal Missouri Question will defeat us. Our Northern & Eastern Members ought the most of them to have their ears boxed."[15]

Federalist representatives and senators derived deep gratification from their role in the Missouri debates. Senator Mills of Massachusetts reported to his wife: "I have been engaged in this controversy with all my force, and, I assure you it gives me great satisfaction to say, with success. . . . The Southern and Western people here are so little accustomed to be in a minority that they cannot bear defeat with the same patience as those of us who almost every day experience it."[16] Harrison Gray Otis exulted to a friend: "I feel as if I had

[13] Webster to Baldwin, February 15, 1820, Baldwin to Webster, undated, C. H. Van Tyne, ed., *The Letters of Daniel Webster* (N.Y., 1902), 83-4.

[14] C. Raguet to Carey, December 30, 1819, Gardiner Coll., PHS. Carey was perhaps the most effective advocate of the protection policy during these years.

[15] P. Schenck to Carey, February 25, 1820, Gardiner Coll., PHS. The three Republicans, Eddy, Stevens, and Kinsey, who went over to the compromise side just before the crucial House vote, were all deeply interested in tariff legislation. Of the nineteen northern Congressmen who were absent or who voted for compromise, fifteen supported a bill for higher tariffs in April 1820. In addition to Baldwin and Mason, two other Federalists (Henry Storrs of New York and Senator Hunter of Rhode Island) took the compromise side, and both were supporters of higher duties. All other Federalist members from free states voted against compromise.

[16] E. Mills to his wife, February 16, 1819, Henry C. Lodge, ed., "Letters of Hon. Elijah H. Mills," *Proceedings of the Massachusetts Historical Society*, XIX (1881-82), 26.

been working hard again for my old friends and old principles. . . . I have the satisfaction of feeling well upon the occasion, & that is about as much of a reward as any federalist in our Country is entitled to expect."[17]

The more astute among them, however, realized that by taking an active part for restriction they risked defeat of the cause. Otis, for example, realized that Virginia was frightened at the sight of an aroused North, but, he added laconically: "The fear of Federalism and of *Massts* federalism may save her." He counselled his friends to let Republicans lead the way. "Let them be irretrievably committed on the slave question before the fears on this subject become merged in their fears of federalism which are always likely to predominate."[18] Most Federalists, nonetheless, were too deeply committed publicly to attempt any successful under-cover maneuvers when Republican charges of a Federalist plot became more strident. Zeal for distinction and political recognition outweighed the evident necessity for obtaining an object by quiet and subtle means.

Federalists vigorously attacked the argument that they had concocted the Missouri dispute. They pointed out that leading Republicans had joined ardently in the first wave of protest meetings that swept the North in late 1819; that there were not enough Federalists to promote the issue over the wishes of northern Republicans; and that several prominent Federalists had supported the compromise measures. A group in Massachusetts, for example, still thought it vitally important to retain favor with Monroe and the Southerners in the hope their militia claim would be paid.[19] Elsewhere, it was noted that Maryland and Delaware Federalists had generally joined their colleagues south of the Potomac in resisting the restric-

---

[17] Otis to W. Sullivan, February 9, 1820, Otis Mss, NYPL. See also T. Pickering to E. Mills, January 24, 1820, Pickering Mss, MHS, and J. Sergeant to R. Vaux, January 20, 1820, Vaux Mss, PHS.
[18] Otis to W. Sullivan, February 9, 13, 1820, Otis Mss, NYPL.
[19] See C. Gore to R. King, April 18, 1820, King, *King*, VI, 332.

tion move. Federalist editors bitterly resented the effort to once more raise the "federalist bogey," and when confronted with the charge that a Federalist-Clintonian alliance had fomented the Missouri squabble they asked pointedly whether Rufus King and the *New York American*, both ardent restrictionists, could be accused of being in league with Clinton.[20] Again and again they emphasized that Republican legislatures throughout the North had gone on record for restriction, a fact that permitted of no refutation.

During the latter stages of the Missouri debates, the Federalist plot theory was vigorously debated in the northern press. Few Republican readers could have remained ignorant of the evidence summoned up to support this view. Although some Republicans undoubtedly became convinced that the Federalist interest in Missouri was the most important aspect of the issue, many more believed that intra-party and moral considerations transcended the possibility that Federalism would benefit. Republican leaders were warned that they could not dispose of the issue by insisting that it was all a Federalist plot. A perceptive expression of this view appeared in a letter written to the *National Intelligencer* by Joshua Cushman, a prominent Maine Republican. "It is not, sir," he wrote, "the most fortunate for those who are laboring to make an opposition to the further extension of slavery unpopular and odious, by resolving it into a *federal artifice*, to raise the party from its present prostration into power. For it happens to be the fact, that the states the most unequivocally republican are the most decidedly united against this extension. . . . That federalism will ultimately profit by the conflict there can be but little doubt. But it will be in a way very different from that insinuated. The moral sense and political sentiments in the eastern section of the country, recoil from the very idea of slavery. . . . And if the leading republicans, the

[20] See, for example, the *New York Post*, March 4, 1820, and the *Philadelphia National Gazette*, September 2, 1820.

champions of liberty, countenance the atrocity, beyond the original compact, the real friends to humanity and freedom, of every description, forgetting former animosities, will coalesce for the promotion of more benevolent purposes. In the most of the states which contend for restriction, federalist and republican are scarcely known."[21]

If, as Professor Moore suggests, some Federalists believed that the Republican party could be split apart by the Missouri issue or that they, the Federalists, would enjoy a spectacular rise in popularity because of their vigorous sponsorship of restriction, they were disappointed. Professor Moore quite rightly has pointed out that enough northern Republicans voted for compromise to effect it, and that state election returns in northern states during 1820 and 1821 showed no significant Federalist gains.[22] Such goals, however, could only have been entertained by the most sanguine Federalists. More sensible ones hoped to obtain more modest ends from this Republican quarrel. They could try to effect a liaison with one or another Republican faction in the various states and, in another dimension, try to promote the concept of "Northern" princi-ples. By supporting the position of most northern Republican leaders and voters, Federalists hoped to merge old differences into a new political atmosphere, one that promised the hope that Federalists could, as individuals, regain positions of popular acceptance and political preferment.

Representative of this idea of "Northerness," a new phrase slipped into the jargon of the day. This was the phrase: "The Universal Yankee Nation," which denoted the common bonds that supposedly existed among New Englanders and the emigrants from those states who had moved westward. In 1815 a Federalist editor in Boston had tried to see the good aspects of the heavy emigration from his state. "The emi-grants," he remarked, "will inoculate with correct principles

[21] Reprinted in the *New York Post*, February 10, 1821.
[22] Moore, *Missouri Controversy*, 340.

those they may sojurn with. It will be the vaccination of Federalism, annihilating the smallpox of Democracy."[23] Matthew Lyon, of Sedition Law fame, explained to Monroe in 1816 that the people of New England instinctively resented the increase of population in the South and West, although it was "in part derived from their bowels." Lyon reported that he had labored to "reconcile them to their fate" by indicating that there was "no way for them to hold their consequence but to colonize to the West and keep together."[24] Years later, Lyman Beecher, the Connecticut preacher, explained his move to Ohio in terms of "New-Englandizing" the West. "The moral destiny of our nation," he wrote, "and all our institutions and hopes, and the world's hopes, turns on the character of the West."[25] Beecher was primarily engrossed with the West's religious posture, but others had an eye to its political habits.

Robert Walsh in 1822 coined the term, "The Universal Yankee Nation." Answering an appeal made to New England Republicans in behalf of William Crawford, Walsh wrote: "We venture to predict, for their comfort, that . . . [Adams] will be, as he ought to be, the candidate of *all New England* —of the universal Yankee nation wherever dispersed throughout the Union. The Virginia race have unhesitatingly proclaimed and invariably pursued the maxim of being 'true to themselves'—the race of New England cannot be blamed for imitating their example, and are not, we apprehend, quite so purblind as to mistake the source and motives from which proceeds the detraction of Mr. Adams. . . . Every consideration is subordinate to the great distinction between a Southern and an Eastern candidate."[26] The Philadelphian later added that he had devised his phrase after "Mr. Canning's well known 'universal Spanish nation,' " and had meant it to apply

[23] *Boston Palladium*, November 17, 1815.
[24] Lyon to Monroe, March 5, 1816, Monroe Mss, NYPL.
[25] Beecher, *Beecher*, ii, 224.
[26] *Philadelphia National Gazette*, November 6, 1822.

as a counterforce to the Virginians, not as a suggestion that Adams' appeal was less than nation-wide. If the Southerners persisted in objecting to Adams because he lived in New England, then his " 'yankee' brethren everywhere" should fight back.[27]

Soon the phrase cropped up in private letters and the newspapers. Adams, somewhat embarrassed by Walsh's sponsorship, protested: "But your prediction that I should be the choice of the universal Yankee Nation was much hazarded in point of fact, and perhaps questionably in point of principle." He insisted that he had been too long a servant of the whole country to be a favorite of any one section.[28] Surveying the political field in early 1823, Rufus King reflected: "If what Mr. Walsh calls the universal Yankee Nation should unite in . . . [Adams'] favor, it would produce effect, particularly in New York; but the managers will resort to devices to prevent this Union."[29] After 1825, the "Nation" was looked to for support of Adams' re-election. "Depend on it," Webster assured Clay, "the 'Universal Yankee Nation' will give a good account of themselves, from the bottom of Lake Erie to Penobscot River."[30] Another Adams' supporter confidently predicted that the "Nation" would be "moved by the same great moral causes and impulses."[31] Some writers, however, noted that local influences were corrosive. To explain Clay's many followers in western New York, one suggested: "After all, though a portion of 'the universal Yankee nation,' they are *western* in their feelings & interests."[32] Yet most conceded that the concept had substance. Daniel Webster's "Greek campaign" of 1823-24 revealed that his ears were sensitively attuned to the "Nation's" moral sensibilities.

[27] *Ibid.*, November 13, 1822.
[28] Adams to Walsh, November 27, 1822, Ford, *Adams*, VII, 331-32.
[29] King to C. Gore, February 9, 1823, King, *King*, VI, 500.
[30] Webster to Clay, June 2, 1827, Clay Mss, LC.
[31] A. Strong to T. Watkins, May 10, 1827, *ibid.*
[32] H. Wheaton to V. Maxcy, June 19, 1823, Maxcy Mss, LC.

Thrown up by the Greek revolution, the same thick clouds of romanticism that engulfed Shelley and Byron drifted swiftly to American shores. Prominent Republican and Federalist politicians acted in concert at hundreds of public meetings to express appropriately the warm sentiments of their constituents. The ever-alert Daniel Webster, in collaboration with his "Greek expert," Edward Everett, sought about for ways to focalize this popular cause. Accordingly, Webster presented a resolution in Congress asking that Monroe send a commissioner to Greece in order to recommend possible action by the government. Six weeks later, Webster rose in the House of Representatives to render the famous "Greek Address." His felicity of phrase and exegesis of human freedom at once attracted widespread attention. After a flowery debate in Congress, the resolution was allowed to die quietly, although a campaign to collect money and clothing for the valiant Greeks continued.

One of Webster's biographers suggests that his purpose was to provide an issue that would rejuvenate the Federalist party.[33] It would appear that he had more practical aims. Since Monroe had mentioned the Greek revolt in his annual message, Webster carefully stated in his speech that he sought a Congressional expression "responsive to the sentiment of the message, in reference to the sacrifices and sufferings of that heroic people."[34] From Washington, a Massachusetts Republican explained: "Thus you see Mr. W. is not slow in showing his approbation of the policy of the Executive. The federal party is literally merged in this latitude."[35] Webster astutely recognized that the Greek issue had an appeal that transcended party or geography. "If I mistake not," he wrote Everett, "it will, with the country, very much raise the Greek stock. We shall have the nation; and if Mr. Monroe does not

[33] Claude M. Fuess, *Daniel Webster* (2 vols.; Boston, 1930), I, 310-11.
[34] *Philadelphia National Gazette*, December 16, 1823.
[35] T. Fuller to R. Jarvis, December 8, 1823, Jarvis Mss, LC.

do speedily as much as I have suggested, he will soon be obliged to do more."[36] Webster was a trifle too optimistic but Congressional leaders had a difficult task killing his resolution.

The House debate occasioned a curious speech by Henry Clay. He acknowledged that many objections to the resolution had been prompted by its Federalist source. Mr. Clay wished the House to know that this was an unworthy motive, even if Mr. Webster were not the honorable and upright gentleman that he was![37] Federalist editors pounced upon this sally to prove that *some* Republican leaders were willing to abandon unmeaning distinctions.[38] Webster himself was at first startled, then pleased, by the kind words of his fellow member.

Many, including Federalists, were distressed by the resolution's substance. Samuel Breck, a Philadelphia Congressman of impeccable Federalist pedigree, was wholly against it. "I must confess," he confided to a friend, "that I consider the feeling *generally* as artificially got up and destined to be as short lived as it is now violent." He would make no objection to "vehement assurances of sympathy."[39] Robert Walsh and William Coleman applauded Webster handsomely, but they plainly intimated that appropriate sentiments without any commissioners were quite enough.[40] His fellow Federalists were not gifted with Webster's address. He, after all, had led the way by adding just enough controversy to the diffuse and generalized wave of sympathy for the suffering Greeks. A doughty old Albany Republican, however, perceived a certain irony in the resolution. "I read with much pleasure," he announced, "the Elegant speech of Mr. Webster. Altho I

[36] Webster to Everett, January 2, 1824, Webster, *Webster*, XVII, 338.
[37] *Philadelphia National Gazette*, January 27, 1824.
[38] See, for example, Walsh's comments in *ibid.*, January 27, 1824.
[39] Breck to an unknown correspondent, December 27, 1823, Woodhouse Mss, PHS. See also Breck's letter to an unknown correspondent, January 22, 1824, Dreer Coll., PHS.
[40] *Philadelphia National Gazette*, December 23, 1823; *New York Post*, January 30, 1824.

admire his Talents, I could not help feeling astonished that the Representative from a State which in the late glorious & honorable Contest with Great Britain in which we were engaged should by Resolution of their Legislature declare that it was inconsistent for a Moral & Religious people to rejoice at the Successes resulting from Wars & that a Representative from that State should wish the Government to send to a remote part of Europe a person to inquire into the affairs of the people of Greece. The result if adopted might Involve the Religious & Moral people he represents, in a serious and unprofitable Contest, with a foreign and Barbarous Nation."[41] Webster could perhaps overlook such unkindnesses in the general glow of success that attended his "Greek campaign." Nowhere was this more evident than in "the Universal Yankee Nation."

Webster's insistence that new national issues had made old party distinctions an anachronism was echoed by others of the clan. Most of the Federalist newspapers, led by Walsh's *Gazette*, the *New York American*, and the *Portsmouth* (N.H.) *Journal*, persistently embellished this theme in their columns. All advocated the "softening" of party asperity to the end that the moral strength of the community could be concentrated upon pressing national problems. They particularly attacked the caucus system, which they regarded as the principal instrument for artificially maintaining old lines. The editors also lamented the fact that old animosities continued to vitiate personal relationships at a time when most Federalists were generally content with the main lines of Republican policy.

Other Federalist leaders joined in the campaign. Robert Goodloe Harper found many occasions upon which to preach amity and goodwill. In a long series of letters that appeared in Walsh's press, Harper summarized the change of circumstances that had occurred since the war. He claimed to be one of those Federalists who deplored the fact that in many

[41] J. Tayler to J. W. Taylor, April 3, 1824, Taylor Mss, NYHS.

local areas Federalists still maintained a formal opposition. "Such an opposition," he explained, "must tend to prolong and confirm the influence of those, whose claims to public consideration and confidence were felt to require the aid of party spirit and popular prejudice."[42] At this time, Philadelphia boasted the most powerful and efficient Federalist machine anywhere in the country. Harrison Gray Otis privately avowed in 1822 that his principal service to Massachusetts during his current Senate tenure had been "to soften the prejudices and dilute the venom of party feeling . . . as a preliminary to her reconciliation with the other States, and her chance for redeeming any portion of her lost influence."[43] Federalists looked about anxiously for evidences that this new posture was bearing fruit. For Daniel Webster, the outcome of the 1824 New Hampshire elections could only be explained "on the principle of the near approach, or actual arrival, of the 'era of good feeling.' "[44] He was pleased too that many Republicans, including his good friend Judge Story, were helping the good cause by trying to assuage party feelings.[45]

For the most part, Federalists continued their public support of President Monroe. Few Federalist editors surpassed William Coleman in applauding the chief executive's annual messages. Walsh subtly observed that if Monroe had not had the almost undivided support of Federalists in Congress, his administration would have suffered grievously from the factious elements within the dominant party.[46] Christopher Gore advised King that the Massachusetts Federalists still pursued their sycophantic course. "Anything like Disapprobation of Mr. M. or his Cabinet," he reported ruefully, "is not suffered to escape from any Press, or even the smallest Examination of their Measures." That this policy, in his view, had been seem-

[42] *Philadelphia National Gazette*, December 24, 1822.
[43] Otis to W. Sullivan, January 19, 1822, Otis Mss, NYPL.
[44] Webster to E. Webster, undated, Webster, *Webster*, XVII, 346.
[45] See William W. Story, ed., *Life and Letters of Joseph Story* (2 vols.; Boston, 1851), I, 402-03, 424.
[46] *Philadelphia National Gazette*, April 24, 1824.

ingly fruitless, prompted Gore to chide: "It is curious to observe how every one publicly praises the present Chief . . . although to be a Federalist, or to have been of that Party, is a sufficient Reason for Exclusion from Office & Influence."[47]

Occasionally a Federalist editor would rebel against the self-imposed ban on criticism of the amiable president. Frederick Schaeffer, editor of the *Baltimore Federal Republican*, accused Monroe in 1821 of not keeping a careful watch on public funds and of following "the Principle of favoritism" in his appointments.[48] Schaeffer's attack soon waned as other Federalist editors manifested their disapproval of the maverick. The *Philadelphia Union* exclaimed in 1822 that the administration was "fast sinking into contempt by the natural gravitation of its own stupidity." The editor carefully explained, however, that he was not attacking the government's policy, only its deplorable lack of administrative capacity.[49] Thus Federalists continued to have deep-felt reservations about Monroe; few genuinely liked him, but public disapproval was generally taboo.

This policy, to many Republicans, appeared deceptive. Jefferson, who had in 1817 rejoiced at the complete rout of Federalism, was distinctly unhappy about the course of events during the next few years. By 1822 and 1823 he was freely venting his anxieties in letters to many correspondents. "You are told," he wrote Gallatin, "that there are no longer parties among us; that they are all now amalgamated; the lion and the lamb lie down together in peace. Do not believe a word of it. The same parties exist now as ever did." The former president and spiritual adviser to the Republican party speculated that the Federalists had quietly changed their goal from monarchism "to consolidation."[50] In a letter to another friend, Jefferson observed tartly: "The Federalists . . . have given

[47] Gore to King, May 15, 1822, King, *King*, vi, 470-71.
[48] October 19, 1821.
[49] September 24, 1822.
[50] Jefferson to Gallatin, October 29, 1822, Adams, *Gallatin*, ii, 259.

up their name . . . and have taken shelter among us and under
our name, but they have only changed the point of attack."[51]
James Madison was equally apprehensive. He noted with fore-
boding the "great effort being made by the fallen party to
proclaim and eulogize an amalgamation of political sentiments
and views." Actually, Madison argued, the essential difference
between the parties still remained in spite of the fact Republicans had "become reconciled to certain measures which were
prematurely urged upon us by the Federalists." The essential
difference was a disagreement regarding the capacity of the
"people" to govern themselves.[52]

Republican newspapers continued to pepper their columns
with references to the Hartford Convention and "Blue Lights."
They reflected the pervasive feeling that somehow Federalists
were insinuating themselves and their doctrines into the body
politic. An address of a Pennsylvania Republican convention
in 1823 set forth with exhaustive detail the charge that
Federalists had used the amalgamation theme to lull faithful
Republicans into a dangerous lethargy.[53] Walsh's *Gazette* and
the *New York American* were selected as special targets by
those Republicans who distrusted Federalist professions of
"America first, parties second." A New York Republican
attacked the *American* thus: "I confess I view this establishment with much of the same kind of suspicion that old Lacoon
did the far-famed wooden Horse which proved so destructive
to hapless Ilium. That this Paper like the Grecian invention
is pregnant with concealed mischief, and that its conductors
secretly meditate the destruction of the Republican Party,
there can be hardly a doubt. Indeed I have been informed by
a Gentleman, well acquainted with the establishment . . . that
the great object of carrying on the Paper, was to bring back
the People to the doctrines of ultra-federalism, and that the
surest way to accomplish this, was to assume the mask of

[51] Jefferson to S. Smith, August 2, 1823, Smith Mss, LC.
[52] Madison to W. Eustis, May 23, 1823, Madison Mss, LC.
[53] *Philadelphia Union*, March 25, 1823.

Republicanism. . . . Present appearances are somewhat favorable to it."[54]

In spite of the squid-like behavior of many Federalists, most Republicans were conscious of the political gender of public men. Senator Samuel Smith of Maryland, for example, asked Van Buren in 1823 to designate those members of the recently elected New York Congressional delegation who were Federalists.[55] In addition to keeping a close watch on Federalist politicians, Republicans firmly believed that Federalists retained a secret cohesiveness and direction. This was illustrated by a Massachusetts friend's report to John Taylor, an aspirant for the House speakership, that a Bay State Federalist would vote for him, unless there was "a federal motive to do otherwise."[56]

Republicans continued to see in Federalism and Federalists a complex of undesirable characteristics. A writer in the *Portland* (Me.) *Eastern Argus* remarked six particularly offensive qualities. These were: a doubt of the efficacy of Republican government; an attachment to all things British; an elastic view of the implied powers in the Constitution; a depreciation of states rights; a tendency toward extravagancy in expenditures; and a distinctive particularism or parochialism.[57] William Plumer confessed on one occasion that he was thoroughly perplexed by the character of Jeremiah Mason, New Hampshire's most prominent Federalist. "I have met," he wrote, "with but few men in the State, who declaims with more severity against innovations than Mr. Mason, & still fewer who have so many novel projects to effect as he has."[58] Yet another dimension of the Federalist temperament was

[54] J. Campbell to G. Verplanck, February 25, 1823, Verplanck Mss, NYHS.
[55] Smith to Van Buren, May 1, 1823, Bernard C. Steiner, "Van Buren's Maryland Correspondents," *Maryland Historical Magazine*, VIII (1913), 141.
[56] M. Morton to J. Taylor, December 1, 1821, Taylor Mss, NYHS.
[57] Reprinted in the *Portsmouth* (N.H.) *Journal*, October 12, 1822.
[58] Plumer to W. Plumer, Jr., March 22, 1824, Plumer Mss, LC.

adumbrated by James Wilson of New Jersey. He assured a friend that his Republican successor in the Senate would give general satisfaction, "except to some Aristocrats, who think such an Honorable office ought to have been given to *a respectable man!*"[59]

Republicans, on the other hand, often held Federalists in a kind of awe or envy, and suspected them of seductive powers over unsophisticated Republican worthies. The Federalist *Philadelphia Union* was amused by reports that Boston Republicans had opposed Webster's election to Congress in 1822 on the grounds that Webster was a man "of powerful talents . . . extensive learning, and of great weight & influence."[60] One of Van Buren's lieutenants in New York state reported to him that many local Republicans were grumbling about Van Buren's conduct since he had been elected to the U.S. Senate. They charged that he had moved to Georgetown "in order . . . to get into the society of new fashioned aristocratic republicans," and further, that Van Buren was "wedded to Mr. King, & felt gratified in his society, &c." The correspondent warned that however "preposterous" the charges might appear, they were "industriously circulated."[61] One of the ways to prevent further seduction, most Republicans agreed, was to continue excluding Federalists from office. A typical reaction was that of George Dallas when he heard rumors that Monroe intended to appoint a prominent Philadelphia Federalist. "What earthly title to executive favor has Joseph Hopkinson?" he asked. "Not certainly as a politician, because he has ever been most bitter and hostile."[62]

During his first term, President Monroe had not tried to "heal the wounds of party" by picking his appointees from

[59] Wilson to W. Darlington, February 5, 1821, Darlington Mss, LC.
[60] November 5, 1822.
[61] M. Ulshaeffer to Van Buren, February 17, 1822, Van Buren Mss, LC.
[62] Dallas to T. Rogers, February 24, 1821, Dallas Mss, PHS. A similar reaction to another rumor was expressed in W. Lewis to J. Bailey, January 3, 1825, Bailey Mss, NYHS.

both sides of the fence. He made a feeble overture or two in this direction later, but at the end of his second term Federalists were still deeply disappointed. Monroe confessed to Adams in 1825 that he had not been able to do as he wished. Adams paraphrased Monroe's words: "He wished on his retirement to give some token of his disposition to conciliate that class of our citizens. He regretted that it had not been in his power to show the same disposition more frequently in his appointments. He had gone as far as was possible without forfeiting the confidence of his own supporters and thereby defeating the very object that he had at heart."[63] A few Federalists were appointed during this period, but most of them were assigned to minor diplomatic posts. However eager the president may have been to conciliate the Federalists, it is clear that he was effectively thwarted by the opposition of Republican party leaders.

Many historians have assumed that Monroe, especially during his second term, appointed many Federalists and generally relaxed the proscription policy. In large part, this estimate has stemmed from the appointment in January 1822 of Solomon Van Rensselaer to the postmastership at Albany. This incident aroused a storm of controversy at the time and superficially appeared to represent a new policy. A careful study does not bear out this conclusion.

Van Rensselaer, a firm Federalist, though one who had taken an active part in the War of 1812 and had received serious wounds, was removed from a state office by a Bucktail Council of Appointment in 1821. He was promptly elected to Congress from his Federalist district near Albany. When he heard that the administration contemplated removing the Albany postmaster, Van Rensselaer scurried about among New York's Congressional delegation to get recommendations

[63] Adams, *Memoirs*, VI, 494.

for the post if it became vacant. All but four of the delegation obliged. They did so, apparently, without much thought, at least on the part of the eleven Bucktails, except to reward Van Rensselaer for his military services and wounds. The postmaster-general, Return Meigs, settled upon Van Rensselaer, but first asked Monroe if he should proceed. Monroe advised him to ask Secretary of the Navy Smith Thompson. The latter at once objected. Thompson then notified Vice President Tompkins and Senator Van Buren. They also vigorously opposed the appointment. Monroe did not initiate the action, nor was the appointment part of any general plan, notwithstanding the fact that, when it was made public, partisans on both sides professed to believe the contrary.

Martin Van Buren led the fight to prevent the appointment. He induced his colleague, Rufus King, to join in asking Monroe to delay until New York Republicans could have time to consider the matter and possibly recommend another person. At the same time, he wrote home immediately to ask his followers to set in motion a vigorous protest campaign. He suggested that they circulate petitions in the legislature, agree upon a party regular as the approved Bucktail candidate for the post, and then write the Bucktail Congressmen who had signed Van Rensselaer's recommendation. Van Buren believed those men had signed "without appreciating at the moment the importance of the place in a political point of view." Because of the hubbub, Monroe called a special cabinet meeting, at which considerable disagreement was expressed. Monroe believed the matter to be "a very unpleasant affair" and announced gravely to his ministers that he would neither take any part in it, nor would he interfere with Meigs' action.[64] The appointment was made official two days later.

Van Buren was angry. To a friend in Albany he insisted: "This point must be settled one time or other, and no time

64 *Ibid.*, v, 479-81.

more appropriate than the present. . . . I am for taking the bull by the horns at once, and if our friends at home will sustain us we will effect it."[65] That Van Buren considered this appointment important is further revealed in this excerpt: "The disjointed state of parties here, the distractions which are produced by the approaching contest for president, and the general conviction in the minds of honest but prudent men, that a radical reform in the political feelings of this place has become necessary, render this the proper moment to commence the work of a general resuscitation of the old democratic party; and circumstances imperiously point to New York as the source from which the good work ought to emanate. . . . All good democrats here who understand the matter sympathized with us, and are happy to learn that the vice-president and myself have held a language on the subject which, though obsolete here, must again come in fashion. . . . If you submit tamely to this decision you must expect hereafter to employ soft, soothing milk and water petitions to get a republican preferred to a federalist by the government instead of that manly simplicity and characteristic boldness which distinguished the conduct of our public men in the early years of Mr. Jefferson's administration."[66] Not only was the issue of Federalist appointments involved, but also Van Buren's influence within the Bucktail Party. Van Rensselaer's victory convinced many that Van Buren would "not controll [sic] at Washington as he . . . [had] done at Albany."[67]

Van Buren's Albany friends duly held a protest meeting, which was pitched almost entirely upon the Federalist issue. This action stirred Federalists and Clintonians to stage a countermeeting. Their principal speaker hit hard at the fact

[65] Van Buren to B. Knower, January 6, 1822, Bonney, *Legacy*, I, 377.

[66] Van Buren to C. Dudley, January 10, 1822, *ibid.*, I, 382-83.

[67] S. Shaw to J. Taylor, January 5, 1822, Taylor Mss, NYHS.

that Rufus King had joined in the move to delay the appointment, although admittedly he had not participated in recommending a substitute. This effort by a Federalist to block the advancement of a fellow Federalist was, in the speaker's words, "truly remarkable," and he tellingly recalled that Tompkins and Van Buren had vigorously supported King's bid for re-election in 1819.[68] Months later, Van Buren expressed to King his satisfaction with the efforts they had made. "Our conduct last winter," he related, "meets with the approbation of all my old political friends; their feelings on the subject are very strong & universally the same as far as I can learn." Van Buren added that since he was not regarded as in opposition to the administration, his course was "clear & comparatively easy."[69]

The Federalist press was agog with joy when the appointment was first announced. A *New York Post* correspondent in Washington rejoiced: "Nothing that has transpired here for a long time, of a similar nature, has given such satisfaction as this appointment."[70] The *Baltimore Federal Republican* was sure that it heralded a new era. "Placed . . . upon an exalted ground of independence," the editor pronounced, ". . . [Monroe] will most probably endeavor to realize a wish he has . . . entertained during a long lapse of time, to see the people united as a nation, without which it cannot prosper, either at home or abroad."[71] Most of the Federalist prints, in spite of their general good humor, were disturbed by King's role in the affair, but they argued that it was probably due to some misunderstanding. It remained for the *Salem* (Mass.) *Gazette* to print the most lively comment about the appointment. " 'Burnam-wood moving to Dunsinane,' " it read, "We live in an age of wonders—federalists appointed to office—

[68] Bonney, *Legacy*, I, 395.
[69] Van Buren to King, May 31, 1822, King, *King*, VI, 472.
[70] Reprinted in the *Baltimore Federal Republican*, January 14, 1822.
[71] February 2, 1822.

the Catholics emancipated by George IV—and the inquisition overthrown at Lisbon without an earthquake!"[72]

But the victory, if it was one, was short-lived. Van Buren meant business. In January 1822 he led Senate Republicans in rejecting the nomination to a minor post in Pennsylvania of one William Irish. The charge was Federalism, though poor Irish's sin was not that he himself was a Federalist, but rather that he had supported Governor Heister. Soon Federalists were bemoaning their plight as they had in past years.

"And yet," the *Philadelphia Union* complained several months later, "all those men who were most active in promoting this great and glorious work [establishing the national government] must be condemned, and all who adhered to them proscribed. The very name of Federalist is considered by many, an indelible stigma."[73] A Connecticut Federalist fumed over the "millstone" about the necks of his friends and charged that to obtain appointments from Republicans it would be better for men to be "tories, refugees, foreigners, or traitors."[74] The distinctions remained even in South Carolina. The *Charleston Mercury* complained in 1824: "One of the rules it appears by which every true Republican should be guided, is not to vote for anyone who was a member of the federal party, otherwise he proves himself a heretic, and a fit subject for the political auto-de-fe."[75] When a Virginia Republican claimed in early 1823 that Republican presidents since Jefferson had made their appointments from both parties, Timothy Pickering was nettled. "Pray do you know of an instance?" he asked, "You will recollect the clamor and bustle in the ranks of democracy about a year ago, in consequence of the appointment of . . . Van Renselaer [*sic*]." "With all Monroe's marked civilities to federal gentlemen," Pickering

[72] Reprinted in the *Niles Weekly Register*, January 22, 1822.
[73] November 22, 1822.
[74] *Connecticut Mirror*, May 3, 1824.
[75] October 9, 1824.

added, "I do not recollect one that has rec^d from him an office; not even since his second & last term of sitting in the President's chair, when he had nothing to apprehend as to official consequences to himself."[76]

Monroe and his administration were thoroughly cowed by the threats of Van Buren and his friends. In the midst of the Van Rensselaer furor Monroe asked Adams to find out whether a North Carolinian being considered for a South American mission was a Republican. Adams duly learned that he was a firm Federalist, whereupon Monroe ruefully dropped the idea with his customary little speech that he could not lose the confidence of his own party.[77] Later, in 1823, the cabinet considered several possibilities for a minister to France. Again Adams noted: "Federalism was the principal objection to most of them."[78] Monroe's skittishness appeared once more in his correspondence relating to the appointment of a Supreme Court justice. Chancellor Kent, a firm New York Federalist, was strongly recommended, but Monroe was apprehensive. He delayed and delayed until Smith Thompson was finally prevailed upon to accept.[79] Federalists had buzzed with the rumors that Kent might get the appointment, although Richard Stockton, New Jersey's leading Federalist, observed archly: "A firm, unyielding Federalist stands no more chance *here* for a great office than a Roman Catholic in Ireland."[80]

The fact that Van Rensselaer's appointment was regarded by Federalists as a symbol far out of proportion to its ostensible importance revealed clearly the political position of Fed-

[76] Pickering to D. Foster, January 30, 1823, Pickering Mss, MHS.
[77] Adams, *Memoirs*, vi, 127-28.
[78] *Ibid.*, vi, 187.
[79] A number of letters in the Monroe correspondence refer to this matter. See especially, Monroe to S. Gouverneur, March 31, 1823, April 20, 1823, and May 5, 1823, Monroe Mss, NYPL.
[80] Stockton to J. Hopkinson, April 28, 1823, Konkle, *Hopkinson*, 250.

eralists. Whenever rumors were floated that a prominent Federalist might be in consideration for an important place, his friends were quick to congratulate the man as a deliverer. This fact colored a Bucktail Federalist's plea for an appointment. "But mine," he wrote Van Buren: "is a case in which necessarily the feelings of a particular *class* of republicans [former Federalists] are interested. For that class something should be done to show that they are received and cherished —so that those already pledged may have their ardor confirmed and increased, and that others, (and great Numbers there are of them) who are looking to see what Treatment the first Venturers will meet, may be encouraged to 'go and do likewise.' Appointments of this description are not of local concern. They are calculated to affect the Party throughout the State; and every general Politician is bound to see, that in respect to them, a Policy, at once just & discreet, be pursued."[81]

In the last months of his last term Monroe was still looking for an appropriate way to prove his goodwill. He included in the draft of his last annual message a paragraph pleading for reconciliation, but it included a reference to Federalists as a party which had once been hostile to republican institutions, though it had since come to understand their merits. Adams patiently explained that such words would not endear the Virginian to Federalists and advised him to omit the paragraph.[82] Monroe reluctantly did so, though later he eagerly reminded Adams that his draft paragraph had been similar to passages in Adams' inaugural address.

[81] B. Gardener to Van Buren, January 20, 1821, Van Buren Mss, LC.

[82] Adams, *Memoirs*, vi, 432.

CHAPTER VI

The Last Struggle of Federalism?

THE SIMMERING frustrations and suspicions that marked Monroe's second term were both determinants and reflections of local political currents. For Federalists on the hustings these years brought little but despair. On occasion they struck back with sullen wrath at their tormentors, but the smell of decay grew stronger.

"Notwithstanding the general concurrence of parties in the election of Mr. Monroe," a Baltimore editor observed in 1821, "a new flame appears to be bursting forth, in most of the states to the North." Massachusetts Republicans, he reported, were combining their attacks upon parts of the new state constitution with "the old obloquy against the federalists," and in Connecticut the editor had heard that the terms Federalist and Democrat were "almost as frequently used and contrasted as they were before the conversion and promotion of Mr. Oliver Wolcott." The Clintonian-Bucktail conflict in New York was confusing to those at a distance, but the editor believed he knew enough to recommend to Federalists that they have "nothing to do with them." Blackness covered Federalist prospects in his own state of Maryland, where Republicans had both the power and the will to mistreat Federalists grievously. Only in Pennsylvania was there even a flicker of hope. There the newly elected governor had at least promised to obscure party distinctions.[1]

Van Buren's Bucktails, in tough political infighting, were slowly overwhelming the Clintonian-Federalist alliance, but the most news-worthy group remained the Bucktail Federalists, more often denoted the "High-minders." Vociferous, talented, and ambitious, these gentlemen caused steady Bucktails to be

[1] *Baltimore Federal Republican*, April 3, 1821.

uneasy, affronted old-line Federalists, and provided potent ammunition for Clintonian counterattacks. "New converts must not have too much to say, or jealousies will be excited," was a typical warning passed on to Van Buren.[2] When the Bucktail leader eased one of his Federalist protégés into an important state office, loyal Republicans were jolted. While Clintonian presses cackled with charges of hypocrisy, the principal Bucktail editor, Mordecai Noah, lamely produced certificates showing that the appointee had fought in the late war.[3] A Clintonian Federalist observed in 1823 that these men were becoming more and more odious to old Republicans because they continued to be "very hungry and clamorous for office" and claimed for "their treachery to federalism, and brief service in the bucktail ranks, the same pay & emoluments as republicans of 98."[4]

The constitutional convention was the single most absorbing political issue in 1821. Van Buren's followers, by then dominant in the legislature, were determined to weaken their opponents by a series of fundamental constitutional changes, among them widening the suffrage, changing the system of making state appointments, and eliminating the so-called

[2] Smith Thompson to Van Buren, January 30, 1821, Van Buren Mss, LC. One disgruntled New York Republican poured out his unhappiness with Van Buren's policy in a long letter to John Quincy Adams. "This contemptible faction," he wrote: "have enlisted the Blue light federalists of the Southern District into their ranks, & even got their King Mr. Coleman by Invitation to attend the Vice president Palace (the Bucktail Paradise) at Staten Island. Blue Lights of every description attended that Splendid feast of Welcome into the Vice Presidents Ranks, they feasted & was drunken, Coleman also made fair promises but after consulting his pillow and returning to his sober senses, he Backed out & remonstrated at his & their Conduct of a Drunken Scrape."

"No Matter who" to Adams, January 30, 1821, Adams Mss, LC. There is evidence that Van Buren tried to get Coleman's support for Tompkins in 1820, but it is doubtful that this bacchanalian episode actually took place.

[3] Reprinted in the *New York Evening Post*, April 24, 1821.

[4] E. Baldwin to S. E. Baldwin, January 17, 1823, Baldwin Mss, YL. "Republicans of 98" refers to those who opposed the Alien and Sedition Acts in 1798.

Council of Revision. This latter body, in part composed of state judges, could delay legislation by challenging its constitutionality or legal form. This is just what the Federalist judges chose to do with the convention bill itself. Their action assured them of special attention when the convention finally met. William Coleman, like most Federalists, was uncommonly nervous about the impending convention. His first reaction was to print furious editorials denouncing the concept of equality among men. Then he switched to soothing assurances that Federalists did not intend to compete for delegates. On the eve of the convention's first meeting, however, he was back describing the demons that would leap full grown from a universal suffrage provision. Rufus King was not dismayed that the Bucktails intended to destroy Clinton and his Federalist friends, but he was apprehensive that the judiciary might be seriously injured and the suffrage widened too far.[5] King's Senate colleague, Van Buren, was busy assuring King's followers that the Bucktails would not put forward radical innovations.[6] The convention, nevertheless, promised gloomy results to Federalists, whether they were friends of Mr. Clinton or not.

Few Federalists had any hope of preventing a major revision of the suffrage requirements, but the occasion was irresistible for Federalist delegates to deliver themselves of deep-felt antipathies toward the whole course of democratization since 1800. By speaking out against the Bucktail proposals they risked exposing themselves to a hostile public, yet they were fully aware that many good Republicans were not yet ready to accept universal suffrage. That the Federalists emphasized the potential threat from the dependent urban worker was astutely calculated to frighten rural Republicans.[7]

[5] King to C. King, October 4, 1821, King, *King*, VI, 408-09.
[6] Van Buren to R. King, January 14, 1821, *ibid.*, VI, 375-77; King to Van Buren, February 18, 1821, Van Buren Mss, LC.
[7] See, for example, the speech of Abraham Van Vechten in *Proceedings and Debates: New York Constitutional Convention, 1821* (Albany,

While there is little question that the Federalist delegates were sincere in this argument, they were willing to try anything that might help to retain some restrictions. Their zeal was heightened by the reports of Federalists from other states who cited the miserable consequences of a wide suffrage in their local elections.[8] The convention stopped just short of universal suffrage, and rueful Federalists reflected that only two states, Virginia and Rhode Island, retained substantial curbs on the rabble. Although the great majority of Federalists, along with a striking number of Republicans, opposed the work of the convention, few believed that the consequences would be disastrous. Many even praised some of the proposed amendments.[9]

The Bucktails in succeeding years continued to bedaub Clinton with the taint of Federalism. Clinton himself acknowledged the effectiveness of this approach. "The odium attached to the name of Federalist," he confided to a friend, "has been a mill-stone round the neck of true policy." This reminded the literary politician of the tale of Tristram Shandy, wherein "the Hero got a deprecated name fixed on him, which, like a bird of evil omen, pursued him thro' life."[10] The most effective charge a Bucktail could level against a candidate for patronage was that he was a Federalist or at least that he was supported by the Federalists.[11] Some zealous Bucktails termed all sup-

---

1854), 226-31. Chancellor Kent's oft noted speech at this convention provides a convenient summary of the Federalist position. See *ibid.*, 220-24.

[8] For a particularly impassioned example, see S. E. Baldwin to E. Baldwin, November 10, 1821, Baldwin Mss, YL.

[9] R. King to C. Gore, November 9, 25, 1821, King, *King*, VI, 423-25; J. Adams to R. Peters, March 31, 1822, C. F. Adams, ed., *The Works of John Adams* (10 vols.; Boston, 1856), X, 403; P. A. Jay to J. Jay, November 15, 1821, H. P. Johnston, ed., *The Correspondence and Public Papers of John Jay* (4 vols.; New York, 1893), IV, 455.

[10] Clinton to H. Post, October 21, 1822, J. Bigelow, "DeWitt Clinton as a Politician," *Harper's New Monthly Magazine*, L (1874-75), 567.

[11] See, for example, the many letters sent to Perry G. Childs, a member of the Council of Appointment in the period 1819-22, Childs Mss, NYPL.

porters of Clinton Federalists, but most made a distinction between his Republican and Federalist friends. During these years individual Federalists in New York state often made solemn declarations that their party was dead, but a strong group consciousness clearly persisted among the followers of Hamilton, and Republican politicians still calculated upon a sizable "Federalist vote."

The Federalist party suffered serious losses in the neighboring state of Massachusetts. The constitutional convention in 1820 demonstrated that the Federalist maxim which held suffrage restrictions to be right and proper no longer commanded majority support in the Bay State. Federalist delegates, however, made only token resistance to a wider suffrage. Instead they concentrated upon protecting the judiciary and maintaining the existing over-representation of Boston in the state senate. Federalist speakers contended throughout that one house of the legislature must be based upon taxable property. Although this position infuriated most Republicans, Joseph Story led a small but decisive group of fellow-travelling Republicans in support of the Federalist position. Federalists from other parts of the country freely offered their condolences, yet most Massachusetts Federalists, especially those who participated in the convention, were pleased that the damage was not worse. What seemed most important to Daniel Webster, a commanding figure in the proceedings, was that he and his friends had "increased their reputation a good deal."[12] Jeremiah Mason bubbled with the news of their "increased stock of reputation," and Story wrote: "Our friend Webster has gained a noble reputation. . . . It was a glorious field for him, and he has had an ample harvest."[13]

Since the war Massachusetts Federalists had rallied behind a kindly but innocuous war hero, John Brooks. When Brooks

[12] Webster to J. Mason, January 12, 1821, Hilliard, *Mason*, 258.
[13] Mason to D. Webster, January 20, 1821, *ibid.*, 259; J. Story to J. Mason, January 21, 1821, Story, ed., *Story*, I, 394-96.

117

decided to retire in 1823, a more rigorous Federalist, Harrison Gray Otis, was selected to lead the faithful. The very personification of the Hartford Convention, Otis aroused the strongest party feelings on both sides. Because discipline among the Federalists had grown lax during the years, many leaders feared that a group of followers would balk at his candidacy. This possible rift was foreshadowed in Boston by the rise of what was known as the "Middling Interest." Disparaged by most orthodox Federalists, this "Middling Interest" was composed of men who were dissatisfied with the party leadership, although some claimed it was a collection of insolvent debtors.[14] What was feared came to pass. Otis was defeated. Stung by this blow, the Federalists girded themselves for another struggle in 1824. They nominated a less controversial candidate, but again the Republicans won by a small margin.

Two successive defeats in the stronghold of Federalism called for explanations. Christopher Gore had noticed in 1822 that only "the mediocrity & moderation" of Governor Brooks had prevented an earlier collapse, since in his opinion the Federalist party had already "died long since by Suicide." The obsessive desire of many, Otis foremost among them, to obtain payment of the militia claim by bowing low before Monroe and his administration, had prevented the Federalists from pursuing, in Gore's words, a "manly" course.[15] A Springfield youth of sixteen reported sadly that the Federalists simply did not make the effort to get voters to the polls that the Republicans did.[16] The future leader of Jacksonian Federalists in Massachusetts, Theodore Lyman, confessed that the second defeat in 1824 was crushing. "I am aware," he wrote Webster, "that this change of the government is attributed by many to

[14] For descriptions of this curious animal, the "Middling Interest," see the *Portsmouth* (N.H.) *Journal*, April 13, 1822, and the *Philadelphia National Gazette*, May 22, 1822.

[15] Gore to R. King, June 2, 1822, King, *King*, vi, 473-74.

[16] J. Lathrop to W. Lathrop, April 8, 1823, Lathrop Mss, SPL.

the unavoidable course of things in states where popular elections prevail to an excessive degree—the disposition under such circumstances being irresistibly to democracy—But it appears to me that the Federal party in Massachusetts and the great mass of the Federalists themselves is as democratic as the democrats—the only difference is that the last are known by that name—certainly a great advantage if it has secured them the voices of those who are carried along by the current of society. There is another notion somewhat prevalent. The Democrats must prevail—ergo, a great many will be democrats. Pompey or Caesar said more worship the rising sun. The increase of democratic talent, respectability and wealth in Boston the last two years, entirely owing to gradual secessions, is very great and having once begun, will constantly be greater. What can we do, therefore, having lost our own fortress, but take the enemy's camp."[17] Lyman's last suggestion fell on receptive ears. Webster soon organized a most successful incursion into the enemy camp. Federalists as a party never again contested the governorship of Massachusetts.

Events in New Hampshire took a much different course. There the Republicans had maintained their rule since 1816 while the Federalists had remained relatively quiet. In 1823, however, the Republican ranks were split and two candidates were offered for the governorship; one the choice of the legislative caucus and the other sponsored by a separate meeting of Portsmouth Republicans. Federalists at once saw an opportunity to reassert themselves. William Plumer reported with alarm: "The Federalists have it absolutely in their power to settle the question."[18] Webster was ecstatic when he learned that the non-caucus candidate had won. "You have accomplished a great affair in New Hampshire," he wrote his brother, "I have seen the returns, and it is clear enough which way

[17] Lyman to Webster, April 12, 1824, Webster Mss, LC.
[18] Plumer to W. Plumer, Jr., February 17, 1823, Plumer Mss, LC.

the Federal votes went."[19] The successful candidate in 1823, Levi Woodbury, was again elected the next year over a "regular" Republican. This result convinced Isaac Hill, the fiery Republican editor at Concord, that discipline had to be stiffened. Accordingly he stepped up his abuse of both Federalists and "wishy-washy" Republicans who had defied the caucus decisions. The manifest jubilance of most Federalists was his chief exhibit. Hill's tireless exertions bore fruit. Later in the decade the Federalists were again brought out into the open, and their Republican collaborators were mercilessly abused.

New England Federalists pursued differing policies in other states. After the failure of the "Union Ticket" in 1820, Connecticut stalwarts lay back and awaited the disruption of the Republican alliance. They remorselessly attacked the caucus and played upon the antagonism that existed between veteran Republicans and the new converts. Governor Wolcott, however, proved to be a powerful and resourceful leader. Maine Federalists were hopelessly outnumbered from the beginning, although a Federalist gubernatorial candidate ran in 1823, and Portland, the center of Federalist strength, returned a Federalist congressman in both 1821 and 1823. Old-line Federalists mused wistfully on the fact that Congressman Stephen Longfellow, elected in 1823, had been a member of the Hartford Convention.[20] The majority party was apparently unimpressed with the caliber of Republican lawyers in Maine, because in the first few years of statehood Federalists were appointed in numbers to important judicial posts. Rhode Island's political climate was more congenial to the dying party. In 1822 the legislature was evenly divided, but Federalists were not able to elect their men to statewide offices.

Governor Heister of Pennsylvania, elected by a Federalist-

[19] Webster to E. Webster, March 25, 1823, Webster, *Webster*, XVII, 322-23.

[20] S. A. Bradley to D. Webster, November 25, 1823, Webster Mss, LC.

Republican coalition in 1820, did not grant Federalists the preferment they had expected. He did, nevertheless, extend to them better treatment than they had earlier received. Accordingly, Federalists worked hard to maintain their alliance with the "Old School" Republicans. In many places they even dropped their name and campaigned under the designation "Independent Republican," the public designation of their allies. The *Philadelphia Franklin Gazette* explained succinctly that "Independent Republican" was the name assumed by Federalism wherever the latter term was "odious to the people."[21] It was an unhappy business. Federalist editors tried to establish that their readers were really good Republicans who concurred in most national policies. Yet most editors could not resist defending "principle" against Republican "demagogues," or crowing when a prominent Federalist was elected. The editor of the *Chester Village Record*, for example, exhorted the clan before an election: "The Federal Republicans must be true to themselves. Our only hope of liberty and political salvation is in firm union."[22] All the while insisting that Federalists were no different from other thinking Americans, another editor reported with pride in 1822 that eight of Pennsylvania's twenty-six man congressional delegation were Federalists, as were nearly a third of the state legislators.[23] This curious mode of thinking could have had no other effect upon Republicans than continued animosity and contempt.

The gubernatorial election of 1823 was waged almost entirely upon the issue of Federalism. The "New School" Republicans nominated one John Shulze, a mediocre, little-known gentleman, and their campaign address directed most of its attention to the charge that Federalists would support his opponent, thereby threatening all the benefits of democracy.

[21] August 17, 1824.
[22] Reprinted in the *Philadelphia Union*, September 17, 1822.
[23] *Philadelphia National Gazette*, October 26, 30, 1822.

George Dallas solemnly warned a friend that Federalism, "scotched, not killed," was counting on the expected rift upon the presidential question "to resume its most organized, efficient, and proscriptive operations."[24] Federalists were even more open in their support of Andrew Gregg, the "Old School" candidate, than they had been for Heister. Robert Walsh filled his columns with variations on the theme that Gregg had "manifested, on several occasions, a patriotic independence on party-views and distinctions."[25] Walsh, on the other hand, felt constrained to deny at great length that Gregg himself was a Federalist or that "an ascendancy of the Federalists" would follow upon his election.[26] When Shulze supporters accused Walsh of being "an open and avowed ultra-federalist," he replied firmly, but outrageously, that he had "always disclaimed any party connexion or appellation."[27]

"New School" stump-speakers and publicists, by their persistent and ruthless charges, gradually forced Gregg's Republican supporters into the uncomfortable position of appearing to be errand-boys for Federalists. Gregg's record was searchingly examined for deviations, and a few damaging items were uncovered, such as the fact that he had once supported severe naturalization laws and that he had voted for a restricted suffrage in the Mississippi Enabling Act. This broad attack provoked one group of Gregg Republicans to denounce publicly the efforts to cast them "without the pale of the democratic party," and "to publish as federalists . . . the advocates of Andrew Gregg generally, among whom are found soldiers of the Revolution, and distinguished and uniform members of the democratic party."[28] But such pathetic outpourings failed; Gregg lost. Professor Klein ascribes the defeat almost entirely to a "reaction against the old Federal party."[29] In their eager-

[24] Dallas to G. B. Porter, August 8, 1823, Dallas Mss, PHS.
[25] *Philadelphia National Gazette*, May 27, 1823.
[26] *Ibid.*, October 14, 1823.   [27] *Ibid.*, June 21, 1823.
[28] *Philadelphia U.S. Gazette*, June 24, 1823.
[29] Klein, *Pennsylvania Politics*, 147. One Federalist editor, however,

ness Pennsylvania Federalists had overplayed their hand. By seeking immediate gains they only succeeded in isolating themselves.

Elsewhere in the middle states Federalists continued to contend only as a party. They offered their own candidates and disdained combining with a dissident Republican faction. The results were mixed, although the Republican organizations were forced to stay together and Federalists could soothe themselves with the meagre consolation that they had retained their honor and their principles.

Maryland Federalists wearily resigned themselves to a steady decline in the strength of their party. One party leader described Maryland politics in 1821 as having "the very worst possible character."[30] The *Baltimore Federal Republican* editor roused the faithful to one more struggle the same year, but the results were disastrous. He announced after the election that he was, at least temporarily, resigning from the political wars. "While any encouragement existed," he sighed, "to contend on federal grounds for federal supremacy in the State, we trust we have not been found backward." What the party then wished was "repose."[31] Only fifteen Federalists were elected in 1822 to both houses of the legislature—a new low. Because the Republican majority had been lax in redistricting, however, four of the nine Congressmen elected that year were claimed by the Federalists. From along the shores of Delaware Bay came the news in 1823 that Federalists had elected a state governor and a majority in a state legislature. The last triumph of the wounded party came not in Massachusetts or in Connecticut, but in the three fertile counties of New Castle, Kent, and Sussex, which formed the state of Delaware. "Federalism,"

---

ascribed Gregg's loss to the fact he had once been "too prominent" an opponent to unite the votes of all Federalists. The editor claimed that most Federalists had declined to vote at all. *Philadelphia U.S. Gazette*, October 31, 1823.

[30] V. Maxcy to W. Sullivan, January 10, 1821, Maxcy Mss, NYPL.

[31] November 13, 1821.

the *Delaware Gazette* proudly announced, "has again reestablished itself in Delaware. It had suffered a partial eclipse, but its glories have only been concealed for a season, to display the greater radiance and beauty on its reappearance."[32] This resurgence was reflected to a lesser degree in New Jersey where Federalists reported a small gain in 1823. For every five legislators elected by Republicans three were returned by Federalists.

In spite of occasional victories, this period was a depressing one for Federalists, alleviated perhaps by the fact that Federalists were constitutionally pessimistic and by a few faint rays of hope some could see. Rufus King glimpsed no prospect for brighter days unless some scheme were invented to make man's individual desires subserve the rightful objects of government. "Montesquieu has somewhere a reflection to this purpose," he commented wryly, "but gives no hint in respect to the formation of so extraordinary a plan."[33] Even the beauties of spring could not cheer up the usually bumptious Webster in May 1823. "I never felt," he moaned, "more downright sick on all subjects connected with the public than at the present moment."[34] Illustrative of the Federalist penchant for pessimistic fatalism were the words of an editor criticizing the famous *Sturgis v. Crowninshield* decision. Witness a divided court, he exclaimed, "pronouncing, that all the state legislatures and courts of justice in the Union have been for 20 years in the habit of acting against the constitution. How the conferring of such an unlimited power upon a court, has a tendency to exalt their intellectual competency above that of the sum-total of all our statesmen, judges and lawyers we do not know. Yet, that they possess this power, is as certain as the existence of the constitution itself. They may be mistaken, but there exists no moral or political control over their error, if it be

[32] Reprinted in the *Philadelphia U.S. Gazette*, October 17, 1823.
[33] King to C. Gore, February 3, 1822, King, *King*, vi, 456.
[34] Webster to J. Story, May 12, 1823, Webster, *Webster*, xvii, 325.

one. We presume that the great men who framed the constitution, could not have anticipated this overpowering phenomenon, which, nevertheless, is produced in the just and fair exercise of an organ of government which they created."[35] Lo, the treasured Federalist doctrine of judicial supremacy itself harbored evils!

Federalists were continually angered by the unceasing democratization of the day. A friend of Rufus King went to Monroe's second inauguration and reported sourly: "Of all the mobocratic collections I have ever seen, it was a match for any."[36] It would appear that remnants of the "old order" did not have to await Jackson's famous White House "brawl" in 1829 to be shocked at the degradation of the presidency. Young Alexander Hamilton was equally appalled at the New York reception for Lafayette who was touring the country in 1824. "The stinking inhabitants of the Jersey meadows," he complained, "who partaking of the general enthusiasm have migrated to the Castle Garden and from their furious onsets seem to consider themselves rightful occupants."[37] The tormented Federalist soul was clearly revealed by a Baltimore editor as he attacked the same quality of self-sufficiency that Ralph Waldo Emerson would soon exalt: "This is one of the most detestable traits of character which can be enumerated— it induces the unfortunate victim to look down with contempt on his superiors, and causes him to hate those whose worth and qualities are far above his own. It induces the man who is governed by it, to assume the style of a dictator, when that of an humble and petty being would best befit him. . . . It induces beings whose minds are low and contemptible to attack and pass judgment on the sentiments and conduct of others who are as much above them as the heavens are distant

[35] *Baltimore Federal Republican*, November 1, 1821. This decision had struck down certain state insolvency laws.
[36] J. B. Eaton to King, March 5, 1821, King, *King*, VI, 389.
[37] Hamilton to N. Biddle, September 14, 1824, Biddle Mss, LC.

from the earth. It delights in the defamation of the wise and good, and glories in slander and detraction. It is shunned by the wise, and detested by the sincere."[38] The wise and sincere were sinfully set upon by the lowly in these dark years.

Nor was the Federalist morale bolstered by the continuing stream of apostates and deserters. Soon after the outburst just described, the same editor denounced "the little group of office-hungry men" who claimed to be Federalists but who were really their "rancorous enemies." He read them out of the party, though not before predicting that they would probably enjoy "all the self-importance and brilliant rewards" that had come to other deserters, particularly the "High-minders" in New York.[39] Old John Jay was less splenetic but no less critical of those once firm Federalists who had been "induced to think it expedient for them to join the opposing party," and thus mistook cunning for wisdom.[40] Federalists were particularly annoyed at those apostates who behaved in the time-worn manner by unceasingly berating their former colleagues. The *New York American* noted coldly that two of the editors of the *Albany Argus*, which reserved its choicest invective for Federalist idols, were recent converts.[41]

Those Federalists who remained true to the faith, however, were hard-pressed to set off a body of fixed views on major issues that were distinctively Federalist. The protection of domestic manufactures and national sponsorship of internal improvements were the two most discussed issues in the press and the Congress. On neither was there a clear-cut Federalist "position." The national bank was not a serious issue, at least in New England and the middle states, though the unwritten agreement that both parties would share equally in the director-ship of the bank (except for the government directors) and many of its branches was still meticulously honored.

[38] *Baltimore Federal Republican*, October 20, 1821.
[39] *Ibid.*, October 29, 1821.
[40] Jay to R. Peters, March 12, 1821, Peters Mss, PHS.
[41] June 7, 1824.

Federalists continued to hold sharply different opinions on the desirability of higher tariff rates. No constitutional issues were involved, only a policy decision. Yet, although many individual Federalists were engaged in manufacturing operations, the evidence indicates that the weight of Federalist opinion was opposed to the protectionist program. William Coleman became progressively more and more opposed to the tariff in his *New York Post*, and he found comfort in the columns of the Boston Federalist press. Both the *New York American* and Walsh's *Gazette* were opposed, but the Baltimore Federalist newspapers were uncommitted. The *Connecticut Mirror*, a staunch Federalist print, was a powerful advocate of higher duties. The direction of a particular Federalist newspaper seems to have been determined only by the editor's estimate of his readers' economic interests.

The tariff debates and votes in the Congress indicated no pattern of Federalist support. Among Federalists and Republicans alike, geography was generally the key to a member's position. The resistance of the Massachusetts Federalists, led by Webster, is well known. In New York the Federalist members of the House of Representatives all voted for higher protection, though they were joined by two-thirds of the Republican members. Nonetheless, the most prominent New York Federalist, Senator Rufus King, voted against the bill, thereby parting from his colleague Van Buren. To his son, King wrote in 1823: "I consider all violent, or exclusive efforts, to protect manufactures impolitic. Protection sh'd be afforded, under limits, to such manufactures as can be effected by machinery."[42] This moderate view differed from the flat disapproval expressed in a memorial written on behalf of the Philadelphia Chamber of Commerce by Horace Binney, a leading Federalist lawyer. "To the principle of the law," Binney wrote, "your memorialists are, however, more opposed

[42] King to J. A. King, February 15, 1823, King, *King*, vi, 502-03.

than to its details."[43] The only Pennsylvania vote against the bill was cast by Samuel Breck, a Federalist.

Similarly, Federalists disagreed over the question of internal improvements. In this case there was doubt both as to the policy and the constitutionality of federal aid. This lack of unanimity was evidenced by the votes on a bill in 1824 to authorize the undertaking of surveys for possible government projects. Massachusetts Federalists were split. Five of the eight representatives voted for the bill, but both Federalist senators opposed it. Daniel Webster had earlier stated to his friend Mason: "I believe you and I have the fortune, good or ill, to have committed ourselves in favor of the constitutional power of Congress to aid such projects."[44] This somewhat flip sentence demonstrated that by no means all Federalists were prone to adopt the more elastic version of the government's basic document. New York Federalists were also divided on the bill. Senator King was again listed among the nays. The constitutional issue was apparently uppermost in his mind, and he later told John Quincy Adams that the internal improvements section of the latter's inaugural address went "beyond" his reading of the Constitution.[45]

This lack of agreement and the apparently irresistible march of Republicanism led many Federalists to appraise the future of their party. A cryptic sentence in the *New York Post* attracted the attention of a Philadelphia editor in 1822. "Are we to infer from this," he asked critically, "that Mr. Coleman considers a formal dissolution of the party to have taken place?" Yet the same editor himself intimated that perhaps it would be a better policy for the harried Federalists to cease formal opposition. He recalled that a Republican had once told him:

[43] C. C. Binney, *The Life of Horace Binney* (Philadelphia, 1903), 89.
[44] Webster to J. Mason, November 20, 1823, Webster, *Webster*, XVI, 79.
[45] King to C. Gore, March 22, 1825, King, *King*, VI, 600. See also King to Gore, February 1, 1824, *ibid.*, VI, 549-60.

"You Federalists . . . do not act with true policy. If you would only give us rope enough, we'd soon hang ourselves."[46] Simeon Baldwin of Connecticut sadly noticed in the New York newspapers that Federalism appeared to be completely destroyed in that state, and he confessed to his son that he did not expect that it would ever revive in New York or in Connecticut. But like the Philadelphia editor, Baldwin professed to see a bubble of hope. He firmly believed that the watch-word of Republicanism, universal suffrage, was "an unwieldy instrument, a double edged sword," which might upset the dominant party and conceivably herald the return of "correct principles."[47] From New Hampshire Jeremiah Mason lamented that the 1823 defeat in Massachusetts was probably the last struggle of Federalism, an unhappy idea, but one which should convince Federalists to drop their name and compete in other ways. In Mason's seasoned judgment, maintenance of the Federalist standard in Massachusetts had "been injurious to neighboring States, by impeding . . . the amalgamation of parties."[48]

Webster too believed that "the best means of restoring the body politic to its natural and wholesome state" lay in breaking down the Republican system, a goal that would require a lessening of Federalist discipline and combat.[49] Well aware that to attack the caucus was to affect a democratic posture, Webster continually advised his friends to keep up their fire against it. To assure success, however, it was necessary that there be no glass shingles on the Federalist house. This inevitably meant further loosening the bonds of party.

Other Federalists sensed the clouded destiny of their still proud ranks, but if they had to go they wanted the world to know that the stain of defeat could not hide the worth of their

[46] *Philadelphia Union*, November 5, 1822.
[47] Baldwin to E. Baldwin, December 27, 1822, Baldwin Mss, YL.
[48] Mason to C. Gore, April 17, 1823, Hilliard, *Mason*, 271.
[49] Webster to E. Webster, December 4, 1823, Webster, *Webster*, XVII, 331.

views. One of Timothy Pickering's friends proposed to him that he undertake an ambitious literary project. "It is only before the tribunals of God and Posterity," the friend repined: "that Federalists can hope for justice, and duty to themselves demands more than has yet been done, to vindicate their names before the present and future generations.

It has long been my opinion that a volume with some popular title, containing a historical view of the whole controversy, making a kind of federal manifesto, written with candour and moderation, might be of great use in destroying the high pretension of the Democratic party, to exclusive loyalty and patriotism. . . . Such a book resting on facts and documents, and appealing to men of reason and candour and claiming only to vindicate the right of the federal party to be considered as *equally* wise, honest and patriotic, as their opponents, might be a kind of text book, furnishing an antidote . . . to the bold confident assertions and accusations of unprincipled editors. . . .

Ascendancy as a party, is perhaps scarcely to be looked for, but the obliteration of the party, and the 'Union of all honest men' may perhaps be promoted by proving that the federalists were the real authors and friends of almost every measure which has stood the test of experiment."[50] Although Pickering apparently never undertook the work, he must have mused by the fireside over what should properly appear in such a book.

As the presidential election of 1824 approached, perceptive Federalists saw that internal stresses within the Republican party might produce an instability that could yield savory fish. Though Republicans were uniformly disdainful of Federalism, the heat of a bitter presidential contest might convince some of them that it was sometimes desirable to "be on good terms with a respectable minority."[51] The *Philadelphia Union* ob-

[50] J. Spofford to Pickering, May 24, 1824, Pickering Mss, MHS.
[51] *Baltimore Federal Republican*, October 20, 1821.

served that the several candidates seemed able to agree on nothing but contempt for the Federalists. "The world must not be amazed," it continued, "if, before the day of election, the Federalists are as much courted on all hands as they are now abused." The editor then added: "Be civil, gentlemen— *if you can*: it will be for your interest."[52] The prophecy proved to be correct; the admonition wise.

[52] February 25, 1823.

CHAPTER VII

Federalists Bedevil the Front-Runners

NEAR THE END of a long, active political career, Martin Van Buren reminisced about the tangled presidential campaign of 1824, and about the able candidates who had entered that campaign. "A better field for the display of political ability and tact," he recalled, "than that presented to those distinguished gentlemen could not have been presented. The old Federal Party, yet strong in numbers, and rich in its traditions, had been reduced to a low condition by the course it had taken in regard to the War. Its former leaders, either from policy or conviction, acquiesced in the condemnation that had been pronounced upon it, and the future allegiance of its members seemed to be offered as spoils of conquest to democratic aspirants to the Presidency."[1] Van Buren named Clay and Calhoun as the two candidates who most demonstratively offered "relaxation of the rigors of party discipline and acts of amnesty" as bait to Federalists, but all the candidates indulged in this sport, not excepting Van Buren's favorite, William Crawford of Georgia, or his future chief, Andrew Jackson. They all courted Federalists in spite of the fact that most "good" Republicans, especially in New England and the middle states, would have agreed with one New York Bucktail who wrote: "One thing ought to be a sine qua non with the republicans . . . and that is that the man whom they support should be a decided republican who would not sacrifice his old friends and old principles upon the altars of 'good feelings.' "[2]

Federalists displayed the whole gamut of feelings toward the election, from cold indifference through lukewarm and

[1] Fitzpatrick, *Van Buren*, 116.
[2] R. N. Walworth to A. C. Flagg, January 27, 1822, Flagg Mss, NYPL.

wholehearted preference for one of the candidates. Early in the canvass some entertained the hope that a Federalist (Rufus King was usually mentioned) might become a serious contestant. A Federalist friend from Maryland, Henry Warfield, reported confidentially to Henry Clay in 1821 that a prominent Boston Federalist had proposed to him that "the Eastern States" could be induced to support King and Clay if it were understood that King would retire in four years and that Clay would be his successor.[3] Warfield was enthusiastic about this bit of fancy though apparently it did not appeal to Clay. Another group of Federalists was eager to support Clinton. The opinion of the largest body, however, was succinctly stated by the editor of the *Connecticut Mirror*. "When a Federalist," he wrote, "looks around for the men whom he could choose for the President . . . [he] does not find him among any that the prevailing politics propose for that office." If a Federalist did express a preference, he concluded, "it must be with some reluctance and much qualification."[4]

The overriding Federalist interest was with the proscription policy. It cut deeply. "In the hour of danger," a Philadelphian exclaimed, "our party may pour its wealth into the public treasury, and its blood upon the nation's bulwarks . . . but in tranquility and prosperity it must see honors and emoluments showered upon those who have at best but shared in the dangers and sacrifices which secured them."[5] A Bostonian warned that it would be absurd for Federalists to give power to any man who would use it to "degrade and reproach them."[6] When the election was over and it was clear that the choice would be made in the House of Representatives, Federalist editors stepped up their appeals for the end of proscription.

[3] Warfield to Clay, December 13, 1821, Clay Mss, LC.
[4] May 3, 1824.
[5] Reprinted from the *Philadelphia U.S. Gazette* in the *New York Post*, April 30, 1824.
[6] Reprinted from the *Boston Daily Advertiser* in *ibid.*, October 8, 1824.

The *Connecticut Mirror* prayed that "partialities for old names, and old nominations, hopeless and useless, and prejudices against honest men and sound principles" would be speedily erased.[7] William Coleman implored the new president to promote "the reconciliation of men of honest views, of integrity and of enlarged capacity."[8] Most of the editors noticed too that Georgia, Kentucky, and Virginia had all recently elected former Federalists to the United States Senate. Would this phenomenon spill over into the policies of the new president?

The same theme cropped up constantly in private correspondence. Timothy Pickering confided to a friend that prior to 1824 he had taken little interest in the election, convinced as he was that "whichever of the candidates succeeded—as all professed to be democrats—Federalists would remain under proscription;—the ruling principles of democracy being *to engross all the National as well as State offices*; admitting Federalists to the honour of paying taxes for their support."[9] Daniel Webster consistently plotted his course during the long campaign along the coordinates that offered the best hope of elevating deserving Federalists to office. In February 1824 he reported to Mason that all the candidates were "very civil towards *Federalists*."[10] Webster believed that Federalists should not at that time commit themselves to any one candidate, a policy that he scrupulously observed himself. If the Federalists continued to stand aloof, the various hopefuls would be tempted to offer explicit assurances that Federalists would be well treated under their administration. A shrewd young Federalist military officer, John A. Dix, later a Jackson stalwart, observed from Washington in the spring of 1824 that Adams would be the least likely to appoint Federalists. "But as Mr. Adams," he wrote, "has been a federalist the least inclination towards federal men or federal measures would

[7] December 6, 1824.   [8] *New York Post*, December 31, 1824.
[9] Pickering to R. Troup, September 30, 1824, Pickering Mss, MHS.
[10] Webster to J. Mason, February 15, 1824, Hilliard, *Mason*, 282.

excite alarm and disturb his popularity." Jackson, on the other hand, could freely appoint them because his Republicanism had never been doubted. Next to Calhoun, Dix concluded, the Hero was the only man who could "resuscitate" the party of Hamilton.[11]

To bolster their contention that the proscriptive policy was no longer based upon reality Federalists advanced many arguments. They insisted, for instance, that they agreed in the main with Monroe's policies, though they could not resist the temptation to mention occasionally that those policies often derived from Federalism. Rufus King observed that in regard to the tariff and internal improvements issues there were slight differences among the candidates, which might influence some Republican voters, but for Federalists there would be no compelling preferences based upon these issues.[12] The *New York Post* could find no candidate who would promise support for a low tariff policy. A pro-tariff Federalist paper in Rhode Island advised its readers that Clay or Crawford would be most friendly to their cause.[13]

Federalist writers also insisted that their party had long since ceased to exist. The editor of the *Philadelphia United States Gazette*, a steady defender of the faith, stated in 1824 that he was satisfied to see the enshrinement of Federalist principles under Republican auspices. He believed that "former" Federalists must vigorously dispute the Republican charge that they planned a revival of the party.[14] Because James Buchanan, a leading Pennsylvania Federalist, believed that the election would bring about a new division of parties, which in principle would "be nearly the same as the old Federal and anti-Federal parties," he took a conspicuous part

---

[11] Dix to G. C. Shattuck, February 22, 1824, *Massachusetts Historical Society Proceedings*, L (1917-18), 3rd Ser., 146-48.

[12] King to C. Gore, February 9, 1823, King, *King*, VI, 500.

[13] *Providence Gazette*, November 13, 1824.

[14] Reprinted in the *New York Post*, June 22, 1824.

in persuading fellow Federalists to dissolve their party.[15] The *New York American* insisted again and again that Federalism had "gone down to the tomb of the Capulets."[16] These efforts by men who either sincerely or tactically argued that the party had dissolved were constantly vitiated, however, by those Federalists who publicly exhorted their colleagues to act in the campaign as Federalists.

Galling to all was the frequency with which Republican candidates and their friends accused rivals of bearing a Federalist "taint." One editor noted glumly that in past days any critic of Republican policy was promptly labelled a Federalist, but more recently, leaders of the *"great republican family"* had used the term to mark their immediate opponents, hoping thereby "to establish . . . claims to exclusive republicanism."[17] Robert Walsh called this practice "one of the most despicable tricks of the Presidential Electioneers."[18] Federalists tried to put an end to it by pointing out that well-known Federalists had publicly ranged themselves in the corners of each major candidate. With undeniable truth Robert Walsh could write in 1824: "Federalists and Democrats are so intermingled as the advocates of each of the candidates, that neither of them can deem himself especially obliged to one denomination more than another."[19] This, of course, did not divert the steady stream of charges and countercharges that flowed from rival camps.

In the early part of the campaign there was substantial agreement among Republicans that, of the two strongest contenders, Adams would be more likely to attract Federalist votes. Crawford would make his prime appeal to the "Republicans of '98." From New York in January 1823 young Alex-

---

[15] Buchanan to H. Hamilton, March 22, 1822, quoted in Klein, *Pennsylvania Politics*, 214.
[16] January 21, 1825.
[17] *Philadelphia Union*, November 1, 1822.
[18] *Philadelphia National Gazette*, January 31, 1824.
[19] *Ibid.*, May 22, 1824.

ander Hamilton reported: "Republican feeling is in favour of Crawford. Adams is spoken of with regard, rather however as a man of talents, than as a *Republican* Presidential Candidate."[20] The same chariness tinged the thinking of Senator Edward Lloyd, a Maryland Republican. A friend summarized his views thus: "He is a strong advocate of the election of Crawford on the basis of the old democratic party which he says must rally & do it by a caucus here, or surrender its ascendancy & combination. He thinks that Mr. Monroe has done more harm to that party than was ever done by any man, by his era of good feelings; and I confess I seconded cordially his opinion that parties on principles are the only alternative for parties for men. . . . I asked him how Maryland stands, and if Mr. Adams has not the ascendent here. He said that his adherents had been taking great pains to forestall public suffrage . . . [but] when the people come to understand that the bulk of Adams's adherents are federalists he does not believe they will submit to such leaders. He acknowledged however that many of the most established democrats are adherents of Adams."[21]

Adams' former Federalism harassed him constantly after his apostasy in 1808. He learned later that when Monroe had first proposed him for a cabinet position, the disappointed Henry Clay had raised the issue of his political reliability. Monroe, ever cautious, wrote to Joseph Story. "So it would seem," Adams recorded laconically in his diary, "that Story undertook to answer for my Republicanism."[22] Smith Thompson of New York was inclined to favor Adams in early 1822 on sectional grounds, but he was worried. "The objection to him I apprehend," he fretted, "which will weigh most strongly with the great Republican interest of the northern and middle States is his former Federalism." Thompson asked a New

---

[20] Hamilton to J. W. Taylor, January 25, 1823, Taylor Mss, NYHS.
[21] William M. Meigs, *The Life of Charles Jared Ingersoll* (Philadelphia, 1900), 125.
[22] Adams, *Memoirs*, IV, 131.

York friend to nose about the state and report back whether the Republicans there would "support him warmly and pretty generally."[23] A Philadelphian, Charles Ingersoll, remonstrated with Thompson that if the Federalists all gathered to Adams, the latter would be forced to make a coalition with them. Ingersoll added: "I dare say he [Adams] might avoid it in *framing* his administration, but I don't believe it would be possible to do so *in the course* of his administration. A large, intelligent, respectable and bold party *would* be heard and felt, and he would have either to gratify them or to break with them. There are no other alternatives. . . . To be sure, as Mr. Thompson justly remarked, Adams can't prevent the Federalists voting for him, and electing him should it be so, but can he prevent their in part at least ruling him afterwards? if they should be able to say, we made you President."[24] The partisans of other candidates harped on these same apprehensions, which were fanned by countless tales, some true and others fabricated, about Adams' relations with prominent Federalists.

A Calhoun supporter observed in 1823 that the most difficult problem for the Adams men in New York State was "preserving . . . their democratic consistency & purity." He predicted that although the Crawford forces were "resting" upon the party issue they would not succeed. The delicate task for Calhounites was to dispose the people "to yield their northern preferences to the obvious democratic objections to Mr. Adams."[25] From Pennsylvania came a report that Adams seemed likely to attract most of the Federalists, thus making his Republican friends "doubtful or fearful, or even opposed." Because of this, it appeared unlikely that any prominent Republicans would dare go over to Adams after having previously announced for another candidate. To do so in Penn-

[23] Thompson to an unknown correspondent, February 3, 1822, Thompson Mss, LC.
[24] Meigs, *Ingersoll*, 120-21.
[25] C. Van de Venter to V. Maxcy, July 10, 1823, Maxcy Mss, LC.

sylvania's prevailing political climate would probably jeopardize their own party standing and injure Adams' prospects.[26]

Adams and his Republican friends were fully aware that if he became popularly grouped with the Federalists his chances for election would at once be reduced to nothing. When Joseph Hopkinson and Robert Walsh, both prominent Philadelphia Federalists, indicated early in the campaign that they were disposed to take an active part for Adams, the secretary was uniformly guarded. He would offer them no encouragement beyond normal courtesy.[27] Adams, at the same time, was not reluctant to discuss political strategy with his Republican intimates. William Plumer, Jr., who often urged Adams to take a more active role, wrote happily to his father in January 1822 that Adams had finally consented to a nomination from the Massachusetts legislature. If done, however, Adams insisted that only the Republican members should participate. The presence of any Federalists in the caucus would "do much more hurt than good."[28] This condition was scrupulously honored. Another trusted friend, John Bailey, was urged by a Baltimore editor to have nothing to do with a rumored project that would bring out for Adams the influential *Baltimore Federal Republican*. "It is the desire of the friends of Mr. Crawford," the editor cautioned, "that this course should be adopted, but I hope it will not be. . . . The real friends of Mr. Adams in this decidedly republican city do not want such an auxiliary."[29]

If it were true that many Federalists did favor Adams at this time, certainly few of them were enthusiastic. A considerable body was implacably opposed. His defection from

[26] T. Coxe to C. A. Rodney, September 28, 1823, Rodney Mss, NYPL. See also P. B. Porter to H. Clay, August 6, 1823, Clay Mss, LC.

[27] Adams, *Memoirs*, v, 297-99; vi, 130-37, 245.

[28] Plumer to Plumer, January 3, 1822, Everett S. Brown, ed., *The Missouri Compromises and Presidential Politics, 1820-1825* (St. Louis, 1926), 57.

[29] Isaac Monroe to Bailey, April 15, 1823, Bailey Mss, NYHS.

the Federalist ranks in 1808 was constantly urged as an insurmountable barrier to general Federalist support, and memories of his father's disruption of the party still haunted the minds of those who revered Hamilton. All of this was highlighted in 1823 by the publication of the famous Cunningham correspondence, wherein the elder Adams scored many Federalist worthies with vitriolic animosity. Should John Quincy Adams be elected, Timothy Pickering wrote, Federalists could look ahead to "the same exclusive executive appointments, which . . . characterized the Presidencies of Jefferson, Madison & Monroe."[30] New Jersey's most revered Federalist, Richard Stockton, shared Pickering's fear,[31] though when the Bay Stater raised aloft Crawford's banner, Joseph Hopkinson remarked with gentle sarcasm: "To be a democrat, faithful or unfaithful, has not heretofore been a recommendation with Mr. P--- for anything but a gibbet."[32] Webster found that Adams had few Federalist supporters in New York City, though some in the rest of the state had come forward.[33] The charge was made constantly that Federal newspapers generally supported Adams, but the facts did not bear out the contention. Deeply felt hostility in Federalist circles effectively obstructed the efforts of those Federalists who approved of Adams to stir up widespread support among their colleagues.

During 1824, Federalist rancor against Adams mounted. On the eve of the popular election in Pennsylvania, the Federalist editor of *Poulson's Philadelphia American Daily Advertiser*, a Jackson supporter, outlined the many reasons why Federalists should oppose the son of John Adams. First, he was a Republican like all the others. Then, Federalists had been rigidly excluded from the Massachusetts legislative caucus that had nominated Adams. He had treacherously

---

[30] Pickering to J. Lowell, October 20, 1823, Pickering Mss, MHS.
[31] Stockton to Pickering, February 21, 1822, *ibid.*
[32] Hopkinson to D. Webster, September 12, 1823, Webster Mss, LC.
[33] Webster to E. Webster, November 30, 1823, Webster, *Webster*, XVII, 329.

apostatized after the Federalists had granted him important offices. He had reviled such Federalist heroes as Fisher Ames and James Bayard. His supporters had consistently and vigorously denied that he was the Federalist candidate; and lastly, Adams had plainly intimated that, if elected, old distinctions would be observed in his appointments. "His own peculiar position," the editor continued, "would compel him to this course. The Democrats know him *as a deserter from the Federal ranks*. They believe he deserted that he might gain power and influence in the general government. . . . His own party therefore will watch him with a jealous eye, and he must go on proving the sincerity of his conversion by subserving to them, and continued neglect, and perhaps a persecution of their opponents. . . . If *Federalists* will humbly bend themselves to the promotion of this candidate, from whose success they can expect nothing but contempt, I am sure the day of their severe mortification and regret is at hand, and that it will not soon terminate."[34] "In politics," another die-hard cried, "the sin of apostasy can never be atoned for."[35]

After the Cunningham correspondence was printed in 1823, old Timothy Pickering, incensed and spiteful, set to work writing a long commentary. It was finished in the spring of 1824. In his pamphlet Pickering labored to cover the son with the same offal that he heaped upon the father. Coleman, with other Federalist editors, set aside long columns to reprint this commentary. They were careful to add their own savage remarks. "I am much gratified," Coleman wrote Pickering, "to inform you that your pamphlet has warmed once more into life numbers of staunch old federalists who have been torpid for many years, but have appeared at my office in person to express their revivified feelings of times that are past."[36] In August, a Bostonian reported that John Quincy Adams had

[34] Reprinted in the *Providence Gazette*, November 10, 1824.
[35] *Boston Courier*, June 10, 1824.
[36] Coleman to Pickering, August 1, 1824, Pickering Mss, MHS.

written the critical introduction to a new edition of the life and works of Fisher Ames, and at about the same time Adams was moved to make public some mild criticisms of Pickering's recent work.[37] This conjuncture was too much for Coleman. "The blood-thirsty vampire," he charged, "has already sought to glut his maw in the tombs of Hamilton and Ames, and he finishes his repast in the grave of Cabot."[38] The editor of the *Delaware Gazette* followed all these events with a malevolent eye. Thus, when a writer in a neighboring newspaper began a series of pieces praising Adams, the *Gazette* editor retorted that the Adams drum-beaters might as well attempt to write Benedict Arnold into favor with Delaware Federalists as John Quincy Adams.[39] Such were the passions aroused among Federalists as the election neared.

Those Federalists who became almost frenzied with rage at these events ran wildly off in many directions. The *Boston Courier* asserted that Federalists, most of them, would support any other major candidate, "even Jackson," and a correspondent in the *Haverhill* (Mass.) *Gazette* alleged that Clay, Crawford, and Jackson were all "infinitely superior" to the apostate.[40] William Coleman, always a strident opponent of the Bucktail forces and a warm supporter of the forces attempting to let the people of his state, rather than the legislature, choose the presidential electors, suddenly reversed himself in August 1824. He turned to support of the Bucktail candidate, William Crawford, and began writing pitiful editorials explaining why he was now against allowing a popular vote for electors. His previous position, Coleman claimed, had been taken "*as a probable means to attain a desirable end;* but not as being connected with any moral principle."[41] Such

[37] *New York Post*, August 21, 1824.
[38] *Ibid.*, August 21, 1824.
[39] Reprinted in *ibid.*, October 12, 1824.
[40] Reprinted in *ibid.*, October 26, 29, 1824.
[41] *Ibid.*, August 13, 1824.

feeble reasoning did little to increase the popularity of Mr. Crawford, nor decrease that of Mr. Adams.

New England Federalists railed at Adams unceasingly and they openly flirted with the Republican friends of Crawford, men theretofore considered the most demagogic and unlettered of the Republican fraternity. Although these Federalists could not agree upon a common candidate whom they could generally support against Adams, Crawford was certainly the most favored. John Holmes of Maine, himself an apostate, wrote ruefully to Van Buren that the Crawford cause among New England Republicans had been seriously compromised because "*some* of our politicians" had been "tampering with the Federalists."[42] Various slates were set up to oppose Adams but little organization was put behind them.

The actions of the anti-Adams Federalists during 1824 were repellent to those Federalists to whom Adams' virtues outweighed his shortcomings. Charles King, the principal editor of the *New York American,* and Robert Walsh both carried on an increasingly bitter verbal battle with the Coleman-Pickering wing of the party. Walsh characterized the Massachusetts dissidents as "by no means the most judicious or distinguished" of Federalists, and he stigmatized a writer in another Philadelphia press as representative of those "who remain in *soul* as loyal subjects of the British crown."[43] Coleman particularly irritated Walsh. In October he wrote: "We are fully of the opinion that the editor of the New York Evening Post has lost both his 'mental faculties' and 'moral instinct,' as regards the Presidential election."[44] Such battling among Federalists helped to draw away from Adams the imputation of Federalism that the advocates of other candidates were trying so hard to pin on him.

[42] Holmes to Van Buren, November 11, 1824, Van Buren Mss, LC.
[43] *Philadelphia National Gazette,* September 14, 1824, October 28, 1824.
[44] *Ibid.,* October 7, 1824.

143

From the beginning it was recognized that if no other candidate came forward from the free states, Adams would attract a wide following regardless of party or personal sympathies. True, it would probably be a passionless following, but votes knew no degrees of feeling. "After all," Rufus King mused, "as between Adams and any one of the Candidates from the slave States, the mo. powerful argument wh. could be used wd. be that which constitutes the Missouri Question," because only this would "overawe the old spirit of Party."[45] King's grudging support for Adams differed sharply from his view in 1816. "If J.Q.A. becomes Pr.," he had written, "all of N. England that is virtuous or enlightened, will be persecuted & degraded, manners, laws, principles will be changed and deteriorated."[46] Walsh's *Gazette* and the *New York American* hit hard at the sectional issue all during the campaign. In 1822 Walsh again vehemently denied that King and Adams had conspired to bring about the Missouri debates, but it was clear that the editor was not unhappy about the implication that Adams felt strongly about the matter.[47] If the South insisted upon asserting sectional claims in behalf of their candidates, Walsh argued: "We must appeal to northern feelings for a northern President."[48] By alternately denying and justifying Adams' special claims upon northern voters, the editors kept the slavery question shiny and potent.

The Federalist supporters of Adams, however, found themselves in exasperating circumstances. If they took an active role, they were held up as living exhibits to prove Adams' Federalist "taint." The editor of the *Connecticut Mirror* evinced his lukewarm support for Adams, but added mischievously; "We fear we can do Mr. A. no good. A federal paper to say, or even to hint, who shall be President of the Federal Union, under a federal Constitution! Preposterous!"[49] For recent con-

[45] King to C. Gore, February 9, 1823, King, *King*, VI, 501.
[46] King to C. Gore, November 22, 1816, *ibid.*, VI, 36.
[47] *Philadelphia National Gazette*, November 13, 1822.
[48] *Ibid.*, May 10, 1823.   [49] April 12, 1824.

verts to the Republican faith, men such as the "High-minders" and the editors of the *New York American*, Rufus King offered a few words of sound advice. These men, King wrote, should be very careful in supporting Adams in the face of Crawford's popularity among Bucktail leaders. "The claims," King continued, "which they will put forth to be credited on account of the antiquity of their faith, and the jealousy which they will endeavor to excite against the advice and arguments of the American, on account of the recent adoption of the Editor by the faithful are not mere shadows—or if they are, shadows are substances to defective vision."[50]

Robert Walsh was perhaps the most militant of Adams' Federalist supporters. Yet, in describing Adams meetings in other cities, Walsh always carefully stated that they were composed *both* of Federalists and Republicans. He took pride in describing a Philadelphia meeting as consisting "of our most substantial house-holders; professional men, merchants, and respectable mechanics, Democrats and Federalists, mixed." Yet, to quell Republican suspicions Walsh was compelled to deny that it was "a Federal assemblage," by calling attention to the fact that the chairman, two secretaries, and a majority of the corresponding committee "were well known to be of the Republican party."[51] As many times as Walsh tried to promote an Adams bandwagon among Federalists by stressing their participation in Adams' campaign, he had to deny vigorously that Federalists had taken a leading role in the movement. This was the kind of frustration that Federalists constantly met when they ventured into postwar politics. If they tried to rally behind Adams this frustration was at once heightened.

Adams himself fully recognized the anomalous position he held vis-à-vis the Federalists. Privately, he liked many individual Federalists and hated others of them. During 1824

[50] King to J. A. King, January 1823, King, *King*, vi, 495.
[51] *Philadelphia National Gazette*, October 21, 1824.

Adams was besieged by Federalists who were concerned lest he pursue a proscriptive course if elected, and by Republicans who begged him to wash his hands of any connection with Federalists. To a friendly Massachusetts Federalist, John Reed, Adams poured out his feelings on the whole vexing problem: "I asked him if he thought there was a doubt of my election by a large majority of the electoral votes but for an opposition from the Republican party on the very ground of my being suspected of too much federalism. He said there was not. I told him I had originally been a federalist, just such as President Washington had been. . . . Personally, the federalists had done me wrong, and I expected no favor from them. . . . [if elected] I should be the President not of a section, nor of a faction, but of the whole Union. If the federalists chose, as a body, to array themselves against me, I should not complain, and very probably they might prevent my election. Possibly their opposition, however, might strengthen me in the opposite party, and if, after a combined and continued movement against me, I should still be elected, they must be aware how much the difficulty would be increased of favoring them with appointments without disgusting those of the opposite party claiming the merit of friendly support against them."[52] Adams had suffered much from Federalists. The subtle but nonetheless potent threat in this passage proceeded from personal grief as well as sound political sense. If Webster and other skittish Federalists wanted to play in other fields, then let them do so at their peril. Adams was particularly incensed that Crawford, who had made "exclusive Republicanism" his principal campaign recommendation, was at this time feverishly cultivating Federalists.[53]

Because Crawford had set himself up as the most Republican of the Republican aspirants, the friends of other candidates took special delight in debunking this posture. In

[52] Adams, *Memoirs*, VI, 315-16.
[53] *Ibid.*, VI, 291, 391.

December 1822 a Calhounite queried: "Now I call upon Mr. Crawford to state, whether he did not say, some time since, to the Hon. Mr. Daggett, of Connecticut (who *then* was, and still *is*, a decided *Federalist*) that it was time the distinction between *federalist* and *democrat*, or federalist and republican, was done away."[54] Crawford's defenders heatedly denied the allegation, but, because Daggett had long been a fast friend of the Georgian, they never succeeded in laying it to rest. Then in 1823 some enterprising man uncovered evidence that Crawford had, in 1798, expressed approval of the Adams administration.[55] This too was widely publicized. A flurry of such stories went the rounds of hostile presses in succeeding months, most of them scurrilous fabrications.

In light of the fact that Crawford's purity was most often measured against Adams' mottled career, friends of the hard-working secretary of state took uncharitable delight in making Crawford's "record" a thoroughly public one. The citizenry was reminded interminably that the Delaware Federalists were among the earliest and most obstreperous advocates, and that Colonel Pickering was his noisiest if not most efficient champion in New England. Editorials in many Federalist presses which supported Crawford, from the *Salem* (Mass.) *Gazette* and the *Boston Courier* to the *Delaware Gazette*, were reprinted with relish by Adams editors. Time and again, the *New York American* joggled the gleaming pedestal upon which Crawford's minions had set up their image of "Mr. Republican." When William Coleman announced in August, 1824, that thenceforward he would zealously support Crawford, the *American* charged: "At last the mask is laid aside, and the holy alliance between the Evening Post and the Albany Argus [a Bucktail press] is openly avowed. . . . The leading ultra federalists, and the radical democrats . . . [will] easily

[54] *Philadelphia National Gazette*, December 30, 1822.
[55] *Ibid.*, February 27, 1823, April 17, 1823. For evidence that these charges unsettled firm Crawford Republicans, see C. Van de Venter to J. Calhoun, undated (probably 1823), Maxcy Mss, LC.

unite upon the common grounds, of dictating at Washington."[56] Day after day the *American* dilated upon the reports that crusty old Federalists, men like Pickering, Samuel Dana, and William Hunter, were openly singing the praises of the most exclusive Republican. This steady din had its effect. Soon after the general election in Connecticut, a firm Republican editor sullenly interpreted the returns as proof that Crawford had indeed *not* been the candidate of Connecticut Federalists.[57]

The most devastating evidence tending to tarnish Crawford's claims came from the mouths and pens of his Federalist friends. Timothy Pickering wrote all his friends in order to convey his reasons for advocating the Georgian, and some of these letters turned up in the newspapers. Pickering particularly liked Crawford's independence, his support of the first national bank in 1811, and his opposition to the embargo. The *Portsmouth* (N.H.) *Journal* detailed Crawford's role in requiring the Newport, R.I., customs collector to rehire a Federalist subordinate he had recently fired.[58] The *Delaware Gazette* acknowledged that Crawford was a Republican but did not believe that he harbored "enmity to the persons of federalists."[59] The *Providence Gazette* assured its readers that under Crawford's firm hand the "asperity of party feeling" would soon wash away when he formed a "broad-bottomed" administration.[60]

Such enthusiastic chatter from Federalists appalled many of Crawford's Republican supporters in New England and the middle states. They had based their whole campaign upon revivified memories of the great battles against Federalist oppressors in earlier years. It was Martin Van Buren who had principally engineered at Washington the caucus nomination

[56] August 12, 1824.
[57] *Hartford Times*, November 14, 1824.
[58] March 27, 1824.
[59] Reprinted in the *Providence Gazette*, October 9, 1824.
[60] October 2, 27, 1824.

148

for Crawford in February 1824. The group made public a long address which dwelt upon the divisions that had opened in the Republican ranks and the dangers that would arise from Federalists if the caucus candidate were not upheld. Friends of the other candidates had, of course, not attended the caucus, and they at once set out to discredit it. Federalists joined in with gusto. The *National Intelligencer*, a leading Crawford backer, tried to put the thin attendance at the caucus in a better light by stating that the forty to forty-five Federalists in both houses of Congress had not been invited. These figures seemed too high to the scoffers.[61] Charges were flung about that nine of the men who had voted for Crawford were or had been Federalists, and of the six New Englanders who attended, two were recent converts from Federalism, and three had voted for the Missouri Compromise.[62]

Observers quickly noticed, however, that there were "peculiar" facets to the caucus and the address. A letter appeared in the *Intelligencer*, purportedly from a Federalist legislator, which stated that there had been and remained many Federalists among Crawford's "most open and decided friends."[63] At the same time the *Intelligencer* editor, always a severe critic of Federalism, wrote: "For ourselves, of however little value may be our opinion, we should be wanting in candor, if we were not to say, that we believe there are to be found, among those who class themselves as Federalists, individuals illustrious for every civil and social virtue, and who would do honor to any station in which their country could place them. We should be glad to see such individuals placed in situations in government for which their natural and acquired talents qualify them."[64]

[61] See the *Philadelphia National Gazette*, February 24, 1824, and *Niles Weekly Register*, February 21, 1824.
[62] *New York American*, June 14, 1824. See also, D. Jennifer to V. Maxcy, February 15, 1824, Maxcy Mss, LC.
[63] *Philadelphia National Gazette*, February 24, 1824.
[64] *New York Post*, February 27, 1824.

Robert Walsh asked suspiciously: "What is there in the wind? Is the sting of the Address to be assuaged, in order that Mr. Crawford may not lose any of his Federal innamoratos?"[65] A week later, Rufus King's son fell in conversation with his uncle, William King of Maine. The latter, a Crawford man, confessed that the address was embarrassing, because in Maine he had assured his friends that Crawford would be "tolerant of all sects and parties." Uncle William further confided: "The principles contained in the Address could be explained it was true, but . . . the necessity of resorting to this humiliating office might well have been spared; seeing that New York and Pennsylvania alone could respond to the doctrine of party contained in it."[66]

To make this "humiliating office" easier Crawford carefully refrained from making any acknowledgment either of the nomination or the address. His Federalist friends in New England began to disclaim "the narrow party sentiments" in the address, and Crawford's intimate friends at Washington assured the "right" people that Crawford himself disapproved.[67] By election time the apparent dissimulation had been abundantly discussed. The lure of Federalist support had hurt Crawford seriously.

John Quincy Adams could have been easily isolated as the favorite of the Federalists and promptly buried under still smoldering Republican resentments. He was obligingly rescued by Mr. Crawford and the other candidates.

[65] *Philadelphia National Gazette*, February 24, 1824.
[66] J. A. King to R. King, March 5, 1824, King, *King*, vi, 553.
[67] *Philadelphia National Gazette*, June 19, 1824; S. Badger to D. Daggett, April 17, 1824, Daggett Mss, YL.

CHAPTER VIII

A Transporting Correspondence

ANOTHER Republican candidate, John C. Calhoun, found the lure of Federalist support too strong to resist. During his trips to New England in 1817 and 1820 Calhoun had impressed Federalist worthies with his attentive manner and vigorous mind.[1] Later he continued to charm, perhaps more deliberately as the remaining months of Monroe's tenure dwindled.

The theme which Calhoun wafted past Federalist nostrils was simple and appealing. "The present prospect," he wrote in a letter to Virgil Maxcy of Maryland, "is that the elements of party strife will assume quite new combinations, before the termination of the next presidential election, if the prominent men of the Federal party should cease opposition, as they ought to do, whether they regard their own interest, or that of the country."[2] That Federalists might, under Calhoun's banner, once again warm themselves in the political sun was more clearly outlined in another letter to Maxcy. "The line between the Republicans and Radicals," he predicted, "will finally be distinctly drawn, and they will become national parties, *where sides may be selected by all.*"[3]

Gossip had it by 1823 that Calhoun had already "fixed" a number of leading Maryland Federalists to his interest. He lavished attention upon Maxcy, Robert Goodloe Harper, and General Winder; he whetted their ambitions and imparted the subtle impression that he would rely upon them to manage his campaign in that state. Harper wrote with obvious enjoyment to Maxcy about his plans to build up Republican support

[1] Handwritten reminiscences of Samuel Lawrence, NYPL, 16.
[2] Calhoun to Maxcy, December 31, 1821, Maxcy Mss, LC.
[3] Calhoun to Maxcy, October 28, 1822, *ibid*. Italics mine.

for Calhoun. "As soon as the democratic papers are fairly enlisted," he suggested, "I will from time to time furnish them with short essays & paragraphs on the subject, and bring forcibly into view those peculiar merits of Mr. C. which may seem most likely to recommend him to the notice of persons belonging to that party."[4] After Hezekiah Niles had opened the columns of his *Register* to political communications in 1823, Calhoun asked Maxcy to organize a group of writers in Baltimore, headed by Harper, Winder, and, of course, Maxcy himself. That same year Maxcy complained that Calhoun's Washington newspaper had been overly critical of the Federalists. This evoked a quick response. The editor would be "more cautious."[5]

Together with his friends, Calhoun worked hard to cultivate Federalists in other states. Maxcy was asked to write William Gaston and other North Carolina Federalists, and Harper tried to stir the Patroon, Stephen Van Rensselaer, into activity. Lemuel Williams, a Massachusetts Federalist, reported gleefully in early 1823 that two Federalist presses in Boston would eventually come out for the ambitious South Carolinian.[6] Heady hopes swirled before the eyes of a leading Pennsylvania Federalist, James Buchanan, when Calhoun's protégé, George McDuffie, skillfully held out the promise of influence and office in an administration led by John C. Calhoun. James Hamilton, son of an immortal father, was wined and dined by the secretary of war when he visited Washington in 1824. He was told that his father's policy had been "the only true policy for the country," a view, Hamilton recorded laconically, which Calhoun had "doubtless supposed I would communicate to my Federal friends."[7] On another front, John Quincy Adams evinced little surprise that Calhoun's attitude toward the lingering Massachusetts militia claim

---

[4] Harper to Maxcy, April 6, 1822, *ibid.*
[5] Calhoun to Maxcy, June 1, 1823, *ibid.*
[6] Williams to Maxcy, September 15, 1823, *ibid.*
[7] James A. Hamilton, *Reminiscences* (New York, 1869), 62.

suddenly changed in early 1824. It seemed clear to the suspicious Adams that his rival was "tampering with the Massachusetts federalists for electioneering purposes."[8] No one suggested a more plausible interpretation of Calhoun's turn-about.

The influence of Daniel Webster was a highly prized goal in the Calhoun camp. Calhoun had stayed at Webster's home during a New England visit, and the next winter when Webster was in Washington on court business, Calhoun was "most particularly attentive to him." Such wooing had its effect, though Webster was loathe to commit himself publicly. Lemuel Williams explained this apparent anomaly to his friend Maxcy: "Tho' exceedingly friendly to Mr. Calhoun, he is so peculiarly situated that it will not answer to declare himself at present. He does much secretly, but nothing openly. Even in Boston he is thought of by Mr. Adams's friends to be favourable to their candidate. A few days since Mr. W made a journey this way on purpose, as he informed me, to converse with me on the Presidential question. He agrees with us entirely in our views on the subject, but it would not be prudent as it regards his interests or politick as it reflects ours that he should declare himself at present—tho his friends will understand his wishes."[9] Even after Calhoun's fortunes had suddenly collapsed in early 1824, Webster regarded him highly. He confided to his brother the hope that New England would support Calhoun for the vice presidency. "If so," he added, "he will probably be chosen, and that will be a great thing. He is a true man, and will do good to the country in that situation."[10] Not until the furious activity that preceded the House election in February 1825 did Webster's esteem wane.

Amid this flirtation with Federalists, Calhoun was well aware that he could not afford to become closely associated with Federalism. Outlining to a New York friend, General

---

[8] Adams, *Memoirs*, VI, 232-33.
[9] Williams to Maxcy, September 15, 1823, Maxcy Mss, LC.
[10] Webster to E. Webster, March 14, 1824, Webster, *Webster*, XVII, 347.

Swift, his ideas for forming a Calhoun party in that state,
Calhoun concluded: "Our standard then must be erected by
those, whose Union with the Republican party cannot be
questioned, and we must rally as far as practicable the supporters of the late war." Later, he asked: "How could we act
with acknowledged Federalists?"[11] But presidential politics in
the early 1820's were complicated. During a conversation
with Swift that same year, Calhoun blithely suggested that
the good general begin at once a correspondence with such
"acknowledged Federalists" as Roger Taney, General Winder,
and William Gaston![12] The nuances were well understood by
Robert Goodloe Harper. He asked Calhoun in 1823 for the
names of pure-bred New York Republicans who would form
the public leadership for a Calhoun movement in that state.[13]
It would not do for Harper's Federalist friends there to affront
the public eye.

The Calhoun forces were quick to publicize Crawford's
liaisons with prominent Federalists, partly in response to
persistent charges that Calhoun himself was at least a quasi-
Federalist. Reports had been spread by Crawford's admirers,
especially in the South, that Mr. Calhoun had succumbed at
last to the Federalist virus. Thus a New Jersey Calhounite
wrote plaintively to a Virginia friend: "Mr. C——N has been
much misrepresented in your State—He is not a Federalist."[14]

Henry Clay, another hopeful, relied principally upon the
allure of the American System and his urbanity to attract
Federalist support. He was not, of course, unwilling to make
politic "arrangements." An ardent partisan from western
Massachusetts reported hopefully in 1822: "With us, there

[11] Calhoun to J. C. Swift, April 29, 1823, October 14, 1823, T. R.
Hay, "John C. Calhoun and the Presidential Campaign of 1824. Some
Unpublished Calhoun Letters," *American Historical Review*, xl
(1934), 84, 94.

[12] Harrison Ellery, ed., *The Memoirs of Gen. Joseph Gardner Swift,
LL.D., U.S.A.* (Worcester, Mass., 1890), 192.

[13] Harper to Maxcy, May 7, 1823, Maxcy Mss, LC.

[14] S. Southard to Francis Brooke, November 15, 1824, Southard
Mss, LC.

is an interest advancing which will prevail—the manufacturing combined with the intelligent agriculturists—It has been proposed already to me, by men of both of the Old Parties, to sink old differences and unite in a new career."[15] Clay found some Federalist support in New England, the *Boston Courier* praised him occasionally for example, but the middle states seemed more promising.

Peter Porter, an ex-Federalist from Buffalo, was Clay's principal political agent in western New York. A former Congressman, Henry Storrs, and a distinguished lawyer, Elisha Williams, both leaders in the powerful Federalist stronghold on the Hudson, Columbia County, energetically paraded the Kentuckian's virtues before their friends in the eastern part of the state. Nor did they neglect to stir the imaginations of wealthy merchants in New York City with exciting visions of the commercial bonanza that would surely flow from Clay's stirring speeches in behalf of the South American independence movement.[16] Clay himself was enthusiastic about reports in 1823 that the *New York Post* might swing his way, though he was careful to add that such support would be "voluntary and unpurchased." He wished it known also that no one could properly daub him with a "Clintonian or Federal taint."[17] Coleman's *Post* finally embraced Crawford, an act that called forth words of disappointment from Mr. Clay. In Charles Miner, the colorful editor of the *Chester* (Pa.) *Village Record*, Clay had a zealous friend among Federalists in eastern Pennsylvania. A number of Philadelphia Federalists, men such as Thomas Wharton, William Rawle, and Benjamin Tilghman, joined heartily with Matthew Carey in publicizing the tangible benefits that would grace their city if Clay were elevated to the White House. The Kentuckian had counted upon substantial succor

[15] Henry Shaw to J. W. Taylor, February 25, 1822, Taylor Mss, NYHS.
[16] B. O. Tyler to H. Clay, June 24, 1822, Clay Mss, LC.
[17] Clay to J. S. Johnston, June 23, 1824, Johnston Mss, PHS.

in the bustling region around Pittsburgh, but by the autumn of 1823 the Jackson fever was sweeping all before it. The most prominent Pittsburgh Federalists, among them William Wilkins and James Ross, had scampered onto the Jackson bandwagon.

Even before publication of the celebrated Jackson-Monroe correspondence in May 1824, Federalists in many parts of the country had come to believe that support of Andrew Jackson promised much. A careful study of New Jersey politics during this period prompted Walter Fee to write: "In choosing Jackson the Federalist part of his adherents chose the candidate who was the less endowed with those mental and social qualities which leaders in their party had once so often emphasized. . . . On the other hand the military successes of General Jackson stimulated admiration. There was power in his name, and it may not be inaccurate to suggest that for some men allegiance to the General offered an opportunity to lose the burdensome implications of their political title and to become once more of political consequence."[18] An examination of political currents outside New Jersey would indicate that Professor Fee's suggestion was accurate. This motivation seems to have been consistently pre-eminent among Jackson's numerous Federalist partisans.

In part to dispel the widely held notion that he was an uncouth barbarian (or a brash despot, an illiterate farmer, or an unpolished upstart—descriptive phrases had rapidly multiplied in Federalist circles), Jackson went to Washington during the winter of 1823-24. He proceeded, of course, to charm even his bitterest critics. Webster wrote in February 1824: "General Jackson's manners are more presidential than those of any of the candidates. He is grave, mild, and reserved. My wife is for him decidedly."[19] A Massachusetts

[18] Walter R. Fee, *The Transition from Aristocracy to Democracy in New Jersey, 1789-1829* (Somerville, N.J., 1933), 258-259.

[19] Webster to E. Webster, February 22, 1824, Webster, *Webster*, XVII, 346.

156

Federalist senator, E. H. Mills, assured his wife from Washington that Jackson was "very mild and amiable in his disposition, of great benevolence, and his manners, though formed in the wilds of the West, exceedingly polished and polite." Mills concluded that the Hero would be "exactly the man with whom *you* would be delighted."[20] To meet the exacting standards of Federalist drawing rooms was no small matter. Rufus King might laud Jackson's "dignified course," but it was much more important that Jackson could delight Mrs. Daniel Webster of Boston.[21]

The Jackson fever had first struck the North in Pennsylvania. Observing that the "New School" Republicans had decided to support Calhoun, their Republican opponents, leagued with the major section of Federalists, began to put forth Jackson's name. One staunch and knowledgeable Republican, William Darlington of Chester, explained this phenomenon to a friend: "The artful Federalists & Greggmen, knowing the General's popularity, as a patriotic warrior, have started his name for the Presidency, as I believe, for the purpose of sowing dissentions in the Democratic party, & elevating themselves into some degree of consequence."[22] A group of Federalists outside Philadelphia was the first to set the Jackson fire. These men astutely judged that Jackson would have a broad appeal in their state, *without* standing for specific political principles in such areas as the tariff, internal improvements, or construction of the Constitution. Of supreme importance, Jackson had never indicated that he was a party man after the fashion of most Republican leaders in the middle and New England states. James Buchanan, a prominent Lancaster Federalist, had early calculated upon insinuating himself into the ranks of the dominant Republican faction by taking up Calhoun. He was therefore not privy

[20] Mills to his wife, January 22, 1824, Lodge, *Mills*, 41.
[21] King to J. A. King, April 19, 1824, King, *King*, vi, 566.
[22] Darlington to L. Coryell, February 18, 1824, Coryell Mss, PHS.

to the efforts of other Federalists to launch Jackson in Pennsylvania. A Federalist friend brought him up to date in October 1824: "If I have the pleasure of seeing you I will give a history of facts you never knew of—the *manner* Jackson was got into the minds of the people of Penn^a. *What is said here is confidential because it might do harm & can do no good*—I will now say that those who brought it about are the close friends of you & myself."[23]

The spectacular popularity of Jackson in Pennsylvania was clear to most politicians of all hues by the fall of 1823. Calhoun supporters first tried to abate the fever by attacking the Hero. When this appeared hopeless, they abided by the old adage and moved in on the Jackson boom. At the Harrisburg convention in March 1824, Jackson was proclaimed the candidate of Pennsylvania Republicanism. To preserve appearances, leaders of the convention ostentatiously excluded a few delegates on the grounds that they were Federalists or that they had been elected by Federalist caucuses in their local areas. The official address flayed Federalists in the customary manner, prompting Robert Walsh, who had carefully refrained from criticizing Jackson (probably because Adams had, during 1823 and early 1824, counted upon attaching Jackson's support to himself) to attack the convention proceedings. Walsh recalled that the Calhoun forces had once denounced the early Jackson meetings on the specific ground that they were Federalist inspired. Now it appeared that they intended to make Jackson their instrument in maintaining the vicious proscription system.[24]

Federalist Calhounites in Maryland and some Federalist Clintonians in New York suddenly perceived in early 1824 that they had seriously misunderstood Jackson's real character. Estimable virtues had escaped their notice. Crushed by Pennsylvania's disavowal in early 1824, Calhoun himself

---

[23] T. Elder to Buchanan, October 31, 1824, Buchanan Mss, PHS.
[24] *Philadelphia National Gazette*, March 11, 1824.

told faithful followers that the Hero was his personal choice. Robert G. Harper insisted to Maxcy that they must "openly and actively" support Jackson, and he sketched Jackson's peculiar merits. "The chief among them," he indicated, "are his sound practical judgment, his . . . firmness & good sense, his disinterestedness, and above all his perfect independence both in character & situation. If he should come in, it will be by a national feeling and movement in his favour; without any arrangement with any party, or any combination of any kind of politicians or intriguers. He is understood, & I assume correctly, to avoid and indeed to repel decidedly any such connection.

"Another & very strong reason with me in his favour is this. I have no doubt that should he be elected Mr. Calhoun will retain if he should think fit, as I hope he will, a high station in the cabinet, with great influence; that the present scheme of administration will be pursued & maintained; and that at the end of eight years Mr. C. will come in with great unanimity."[25]

Harper and Maxcy at once set to work convincing other Maryland Federalists that their interests would best be served by supporting Jackson. Benjamin Latrobe recalled in later life that he had given his first vote to Jackson "because of the convictions derived from my intercourse with General Harper."[26] Roger Taney became a Jacksonian at this time as did Francis Scott Key.

In Albany, DeWitt Clinton was, as usual, casting about for ways to elevate himself. Careful calculation led him to believe that support of Jackson offered the most fruitful prospects. Not surprisingly, therefore, the first Jackson meeting in New York City was principally attended by avowed Clintonians. Robert Bogardus, a prominent Federalist, was a leading speaker, as was Cadwallader Colden, a noisy Fed-

---

[25] Harper to Maxcy, March 1, 1824, Maxcy Mss, LC.
[26] John E. Semmes, *John H. B. Latrobe and His Times, 1803-1891* (Baltimore, 1917), 111.

eralist before the war.[27] Colden, however, was a member of that select group of pre-war Federalists, which also included Nicholas Biddle and Peter Porter, that had vigorously supported the war and had afterward ceased to act with the Federalists. These men were generally accepted as bona fide Republicans, but at the same time they retained the respect of most Federalists. They were not castigated as apostates by Federalists, nor was their Republicanism openly challenged by Jeffersonians. Few converts escaped one of these abysses.

"A correspondence more interesting, we venture to say," the *Philadelphia Franklin Gazette* editor wrote excitedly on May 13, 1824, "has never been made public." He referred to the publication of an extraordinary set of letters exchanged between James Monroe and Andrew Jackson. For months before the newspapers had been filled with feverish speculation about these letters and after they were published debate raged for years over their meaning. Professor Klein has termed this correspondence "the issue having most significance in Pennsylvania" during the presidential campaign of 1824.[28] Others have argued that Jackson's letters were chiefly responsible for attracting the considerable Federalist support which Jackson carried into the general election.

The public controversy began on January 14, 1824, with publication of a statement in the *Philadelphia Democratic Press*, a Crawford paper edited by sprightly John Binns, alleging that at the beginning of Monroe's first term, Jackson had recommended to him the appointment of two Federalists and two Republicans to the cabinet. A Jackson supporter at once obtained from both Jackson and Monroe denials of the *Press* story, but Binns replied with further details. He stated

[27] *New York Post*, April 13, 1824. One of Henry Clay's New York correspondents reported: "The story has become quite current that Mr. Clinton is to be *Prime Minister to President Jackson*." W. B. Rochester to Clay, May 29, 1824, Clay Mss, LC.

[28] Klein, *Pennsylvania Politics*, 146.

160

that, amid the William Irish nomination fuss during the winter of 1821-22, Monroe had shown to the Pennsylvania senators, Findlay and Lowrie, a letter written by Jackson which recommended the appointment of Federalists to cabinet positions. Findlay, a Jackson man in 1824, publicly denied that he had seen such a letter. This left Lowrie, a Crawfordite, to carry on the dispute.

The next bit of "hard" news came in early April. Following weeks of newspaper controversy about his role, Lowrie published a letter he had written Monroe on March 15, 1824. The letter made reference to "incontrovertible evidence" in Lowrie's possession that Jackson had indeed suggested an amalgamation policy. Lowrie asked that the president make public Jackson's letter. George Hay, Monroe's son-in-law, thereupon challenged Lowrie to publish a letter which Lowrie had earlier written to Monroe, in which he disclosed that he had just received from an anonymous source a copy, partly in Monroe's own handwriting, of the president's answer to Jackson's suggestion. Hay stated that Lowrie had at that time indicated to Monroe that he would hold the letter, presumably stolen, and await Monroe's advices. A series of newspaper exchanges followed. Hay accused Lowrie of holding stolen property that properly belonged to Monroe, and Lowrie indicated that the president was seeking to cover up an embarrassing situation by refusing to answer Lowrie's letters. Jackson and Monroe finally agreed early in May that, in order to stifle further speculation, the correspondence should be made public. Accordingly, there appeared in the *National Intelligencer* and the *Philadelphia Columbian Observer* a set of five letters exchanged by Jackson and Monroe in 1816 and 1817. They were accompanied by the letters exchanged between the two men in 1824.[29] This sensational correspondence was

[29] These letters, first published on May 9, 1824, have been reprinted many times. They may be readily consulted in volume 3 of John Spencer Bassett, ed., *Correspondence of Andrew Jackson* (7 vols.; Washington, 1926-35).

at once republished in almost every newspaper throughout the country.

A welter of evidence exists which bears upon the events leading to this publication, some of it contradictory and some unclear. In October 1816 Jackson included in a general letter to Monroe the suggestion that a wealthy North Carolina Federalist, William Drayton, be appointed secretary of war. Jackson acknowledged that Drayton was a Federalist, but he praised his record as a commander during the late war. Without waiting for a reply, Jackson again wrote in November to recommend Drayton, this time dilating upon the desirability of ending party quarrels during Monroe's impending administration. Monroe answered both letters on December 14. He confirmed Drayton's worthy record but politely brought to Jackson's attention the obligations that he, Monroe, owed the Republican party. The Virginian reviewed the past record of Federalist perfidy and emphasized the presence of leading Federalists who still looked dimly upon republican institutions. The goal of healing political wounds was admirable. It would, however, be a long process. Qualified Federalists should not be summarily excluded from office, but at the same time legitimate claims by the Republican party must take preference. Jackson answered graciously the next month, taking the occasion to add that if he had been the military commander in New England at the time of the Hartford Convention, he would have hanged the three principal leaders under the articles of war.

The charge made by the *Democratic Press* in January 1824 prompted both Jackson and Monroe to assemble a file of their earlier letters. Jackson wrote home and Monroe searched his records. They commenced a polite though wary correspondence, in which Monroe advocated public silence and Jackson the opposite. The letters and copies, with one exception, were found. Monroe could not find his copy of the letter written to

Jackson in 1816. It was a copy of this letter that Lowrie had received from an "anonymous" source. Jackson guessed that Monroe had shown the correspondence to several people, and that Abner Lacock, a Pennsylvania Republican, had stolen Monroe's copy. The president stoutly maintained that he may have referred to the letters when explaining his appointment policy, but that he had never actually read them to others. The copy sent to Lowrie was written principally in the hand of John Purviance, a former private secretary to Monroe. The last few lines, enjoining confidence on Jackson's part and wishing him well, were in Monroe's hand. No salutation or signature appeared. When the copy was finally returned to him by Lowrie, Monroe expressed wonderment at it. He could neither recall having added the last few lines nor indeed that he had ever even seen it.[30]

The best inference is that Monroe's only copy of the letter had been stolen by a secretary, possibly Purviance, or by a visitor to Monroe's office. There seems little question that Monroe had read one or more of the letters to visitors, principally Republican leaders who had come to complain about prospective appointments. Lacock wrote that he had seen the letters at the beginning of Monroe's first term, at which time the president stated clearly that he would not ruin the party by appointing Federalists.[31] Several other men testified that they were told about the correspondence by Findlay and Lowrie in 1821. Jonathan Roberts recalled that Monroe had shown him the letters on several occasions.[32] Yet Monroe still insisted that he had never read to callers any of Jackson's

[30] This copy is now in the Monroe Mss, LC. See, Monroe to an unknown correspondent, May 19, 1824, *ibid.*, for Monroe's reaction when the copy was returned. Monroe often discussed the Lowrie matter with Adams. The latter believed that Monroe was mistaken when he denied that he had shown the letters to others. Adams, *Memoirs*, VI, 342.

[31] Lacock to J. Monroe, April 24, 1824, Monroe Mss, LC.

[32] *Philadelphia National Gazette*, May 8, 1824. See also Klein, "Memoirs of Jonathan Roberts," 407.

letters. He would agree only that he might have alluded to their contents in conversation.

When the letters were published, many believed that Jackson's cause would be severely compromised among sensitive Republicans, particularly in New England and the middle states. Yet Jackson vigorously defended his statements. "I have allways [*sic*] been a republican, and acted with them," he wrote his nephew, "but the constitution secures to every man equal rights and priviledges [*sic*]; and the very moment I proscribe an individual from office, on account of his political opinions; I become myself, a despot, call me by what name you please."[33] Future exigencies would cause the general to modify somewhat these words. Albert Gallatin believed such a conception "not only in direct opposition to the principles of the Republican party . . . but [also] tantamount to a declaration that political principles and opinions [were] of no importance in the administration of government."[34] Jefferson termed the correspondence a "threatening cloud" over Jackson's prospects, and Martin Van Buren was scandalized.[35] Later, when political logic necessitated taking up Jackson, Van Buren assured a friend that the Tennessean had *once* acted upon sound principles. "We must trust," he said "to good fortune and to the effects of favorable associations for the removal of the *rust* they had contracted, in his case, by a protracted non-user and the prejudicial effects in that regard of his military life."[36] During the summer of 1824, however, Van Buren and other Crawford supporters lost no time in pressing their advantage.

[33] Jackson to A. J. Donelson, April 11, 1824, Bassett, *Jackson Correspondence*, III, 246-47. Professor Bassett erroneously states that the Lowrie letter was written by Jackson and George Hay and that it was stolen from Jackson. *Ibid.*, III, 231.

[34] Gallatin to W. Lowrie, May 22, 1824, Adams, *Gallatin*, II, 289-90.

[35] Jefferson to R. Rush, June 5, 1824, Paul L. Ford, ed., *The Writings of Thomas Jefferson* (10 vols.; New York, 1904-05), x, 304-05; Fitzpatrick, *Van Buren*, 237.

[36] *Ibid.*, 198.

The Republican presses that supported Jackson were badly shaken by the "amalgamating" sentiments of their champion. An instinctive reaction was to print again, with heavy emphasis, the names of prominent Federalists who had announced support of other candidates, especially Crawford. Jackson's defenders then insisted that he had not asked Monroe to form a coalition government as Lowrie alleged. He wanted merely to dispel party strife by appointing individual Federalists who were worthy of the place. The *Philadelphia Franklin Gazette* explained the distinction in these words: "As a party, holding their old opinions, and pursuing their old policy, federalists cannot but be viewed with distrust; *proscribed*, if you will; but should any individual, *formerly ranked* with that party, exhibit, in the support of his country, of its institutions and its laws, its *actual* government, its democratic measures, the qualities of 'probity, virtue and capacity,' then the democracy of the union is too wise and enlightened not to see the advantage of such an accession to its strength, too powerful to apprehend danger to its integrity from their admission as members, and too magnanimous not to extend to such individuals the hand of fellowship."[37]

The important criterion was whether the prospect was a "good" federalist. This left the door open for Federalist votes at the same time it permitted denunciation of "bad" Federalists. The Jackson Republicans, calling upon Washington and Jefferson to back Jackson's policy, declared finally: "Take the whole of the correspondence of General Jackson, compare all of its parts with each other, and there is nothing in it which tends to disprove the pure democracy of the veteran patriot."[38]

"There are federalists still living," wrote Major Lewis when James Parton was gathering materials for his Jackson biography, "who will remember laying down the newspaper

[37] May 18, 1824.
[38] *Philadelphia Franklin Gazette*, August 1, 1824.

containing . . . [the correspondence] with the feeling that a second Washington had come to judgment." Lewis believed that one had only to glance at the Hero's words to realize "how transporting" it must have been to "the remnants of the old federal party, 'proscribed' for twenty years."[39] There is no question that Jackson's views were highly entertaining to Federalists. Both Coleman and Walsh greeted the publication with cries of unalloyed joy. Coleman believed that it reflected the "highest honor" upon Jackson, and Walsh was sure that the general would "rise in the esteem of all American citizens of pure patriotism and elevated character."[40] Jackson was the only candidate who, in writing, had announced that he was willing to appoint qualified Federalists to office. Because he had written privately in 1816, Jackson's words were obviously not electioneering devices, nor did he ever attempt to disavow his words. Being a sensitive and querulous lot, however, some Federalists preferred to choke upon certain phrases in the letters.

The two sections of the correspondence that most annoyed Federalists were Jackson's statement that he would have hung eminent New Englanders and a phrase in one of Monroe's letters which characterized the Federalist party as one "which, at one time, was, in certain members of it, a monarchical one."[41] The excitement aroused in Federalist breasts over these two references would be incomprehensible without knowing of their inordinate pride and their tender feelings, rubbed raw by years of biting Republican criticism. The most charitable things Coleman could say about Jackson's remark were that Jackson either did not mean it or that he was grossly misinformed about the Convention's purpose.[42] The *Boston*

[39] James Parton, *Life of Andrew Jackson* (3 vols.; New York, 1861), III, 39.
[40] *New York Post*, May 11, 1824; *Philadelphia National Gazette*, May 13, 1824.
[41] Monroe to Jackson, December 14, 1816, Bassett, *Jackson Correspondence*, III, 227.
[42] *New York Post*, May 18, 1824.

Courier boasted that if Jackson had tried to hang any of the Convention leaders, they would have found "100,000 friends at their side."[43] Walsh led the pack in excoriating Monroe. Monarchism was a familiar charge coming from second-rate Republicans, but because Monroe gave it credence, mild and conciliatory Monroe, Federalists were incredibly angry. Harper wrote a long series of letters refuting the charge, and Rufus King would not speak to Monroe in spite of the efforts of mutual friends as late as January 1825 to heal the breach.[44] Webster nursed wounded feelings for years afterwards and took pains to insure unfavorable congressional action on certain claims that Monroe presented against the government after his retirement.[45] These protests perhaps soothed some Federalists, but they confirmed in Republican eyes the belief that the Federalists remained a discrete and unwholesome group. Federalist haughtiness once again vitiated the campaign to melt into the contemporary political scene.

The net effect of the correspondence upon Federalists is unknown. Clear it is, however, that Jackson had many Federalist friends during the last months of the campaign. The Jackson boom among Pennsylvania and Maryland Federalists took on new vigor, as did the movement among Clintonian Federalists in New York. By December and January, most of the anti-Adams Federalists in New York and New England were delighted at the prospect of Jackson's election in the House of Representatives. Coleman confided to Pickering his opinion that Jackson would, "with all the exceptions form the most independent, impartial & competent cabinet of any candidate that has been brought forward."[46] The *Philadelphia*

---

[43] Reprinted in *ibid.*, June 4, 1824.

[44] Harper's letters appeared in the *Philadelphia National Gazette* during December 1824. For King's anger toward Monroe, see Adams, *Memoirs*, VI, 472, 481; King to C. Gore, May 24, 1824, King, *King*, VI, 574; Monroe to C. F. Mercer, December 23, 1824, Mercer Mss, NYHS.

[45] C. F. Mercer to Monroe, March 6, 1826, Mercer Mss, NYHS.

[46] Coleman to Pickering, December 12, 1824, Pickering Mss, MHS.

United States Gazette, a violent Federalist print, announced that Jackson would "care as little about old party prejudices; as about the prejudices of those who lived before the flood."[47] A few weeks before the election, important Federalist leaders from Lancaster and Pittsburgh met with Philadelphia colleagues to urge support for Jackson. They represented, according to one account, "how long and how generally their party had been excluded from office under the United States Government; and that now according to General Jackson's letter to President Monroe, they, the Federalists, if he were elected, would have a chance of being appointed. The effect of these representations was evident in this Federal city, where General Jackson had a large majority."[48] This key idea cropped up again and again among Jackson's Federalist supporters.

Historians have tried manfully to unravel the chaotic pattern of the election. Convincing evidence remains that at least in some areas the picture was as confusing to the electorate as to future chroniclers. In New England, for example, the Adams men were well organized whereas the friends of other candidates turned first one way then the other. Voters in Massachusetts were confronted by a slate of Adams Republicans, a mixed unpledged slate, and a wholly Federalist ticket, also unpledged. The last two were put forward late in the canvass, mainly through the efforts of those Federalists who disliked Adams. The trouble was that they could not agree upon a single opponent. The result, in a light vote, was a convincing Adams victory. In Rhode Island the Republicans were content with Adams, in spite of an amusing "war" between the so-called "exclusive Republican" supporters of

See also E. Baldwin to S. E. Baldwin, November 12, 1824, Baldwin Mss, YL.

[47] Reprinted in the *New York Post*, November 2, 1824. See also, the *Boston Courier*, January 3, 1825.

[48] John Binns, *Recollections* (Philadelphia, 1854), 248-49.

Adams and the "exclusive" supporters of Adams.[49] The Crawford Federalists did not get around to forming an electoral slate until a week before the election, and they then promptly gave up the project. "Mature deliberation" convinced them that no effective opposition to Adams could be launched in so short a time.[50] The opposition to Adams in Connecticut formed an unpledged slate, variously thought of as favoring Crawford and/or Clay. The voters appear to have been disinterested in either ticket, especially Federalists (all the electors on both slates were Republicans), and the outcome was a pitifully small total vote.

The picture was more varied in the middle states. Confusion and angry feelings prevailed in the two states wherein electors were selected by the legislature. The titanic struggle in New York state has been exhaustively detailed elsewhere; suffice it to say that no one has ever quite understood all the shenanigans.[51] Of significance, however, is the fact that the defeated Regency forces did not afterwards maintain, as might be expected, that the selection of twenty-five Adams electors was the result of Federalist cabals. Because Delaware's electoral votes were but three in number, few observers noticed that the legislative proceedings were shrouded in mystery and sharply marked by seemingly justified charges of unconstitutionality against the presiding officer of the state senate. Federalists there were split between Adams and Crawford, a majority favoring the latter. Voters in New Jersey had a

[49] *Providence Gazette*, October 27, 1824.
[50] *Ibid.*, November 10, 1824.
[51] Three principal factions fought for electors in the legislature. The Van Buren Bucktails, the largest body, tenaciously supported Crawford; the Clintonians generally favored Adams (though several leaned to Jackson); and a third group, which was opposed both to Van Buren and Clinton, was split between Adams and Clay. The result of the incredibly complicated maneuvering was 25 electors pledged to Adams, 7 to Clay, and 4 to Crawford. A colorful, though not entirely correct, account appears in Harriet A. Weed, ed., *Autobiography of Thurlow Weed* (Boston, 1883). Three of the electors pledged to Clay actually cast their votes for other men in December.

169

choice among three tickets, all composed of Republicans. One was framed for Adams, another for Jackson, and a third mixed between Jackson and Crawford. The vote was close, although only a third of the usual number of voters went to the polls. The *Trenton Federalist*, a lukewarm Jackson press, commented: "In this election there was a general breaking up of the old parties of Federalists and Democrats."[52] The vote was also low in Pennsylvania, probably due to the general feeling that Jackson was an easy winner. Walsh tried to whip up Adams support, but the slate was made up so late and with so little organization that many counties were not even supplied with printed Adams tickets. Walsh expressed particular disappointment that so few Federalists had supported Adams. Instead, he moaned, they "distributed themselves among the candidates according to individual predilection."[53] Lancaster County, however, a leading Federalist stronghold, voted overwhelmingly for Jackson.

In contrast to most other states, the voters in Maryland took a strong interest in the election. Adams received the highest number of popular votes, though in some election districts the Crawford men combined with the Jackson forces to defeat Adams.[54] The "Federalist vote" was much disputed, but the best estimates were that Jackson and Adams had received about an equal number. Four of the Jackson electors were Federalists, two of them former speakers of the House of Delegates. The Crawford slate included five Federalists, while only two were on the Adams ticket. The Republican partisans of each candidate tried hard to pin a Federalist label on their opponents, and all were armed with convincing bits of evidence.

[52] Reprinted in the *New York Post*, November 12, 1824. See also the *Philadelphia National Gazette*, October 26, 1824.

[53] *Ibid.*, November 2, 6, 1824.

[54] Maryland selected presidential electors by districts, rather than the usual general ticket or legislative appointment.

The disintegration of Republican discipline and the lack of a concerted Federalist policy threw the election into the hands of Congressional delegations. This fact turned memories back to the dangerous confusion that had marked the election in 1801.

CHAPTER IX

Mr. Webster's Coup

A BEAUTIFULLY WROUGHT MANEUVER put John Quincy Adams into the White House. Weeks of planning ended in decision, almost anticlimactically, on the first ballot. Men from the broken ranks of Federalism, pressed by chance into the role of king-makers, had searched their hearts and then had acted. The ill-fated link, forged in ambition's fire, brought a glowing victory. Soon it would torment.

Bargain and sale! These words rang about the ears of Henry Clay the rest of his life after he had thrown his influence to Adams early in January 1825. Yet, even this powerful support, later to be amply rewarded, was not enough. Eleven days before the balloting was to begin, Rufus King accurately summed up Adams' tenuous chances: "If Kentucky, Ohio, Illinois, Missouri, & Louisiana unite with Clay to elect Adams these with six eastern States would make but eleven votes, and two more wd. be wanting to elect Adams: for these two votes the friends of Adams rely upon N. Yk. & Maryland. These States are each divided; the vote of N. Yk. may be more sure than that of Maryland, where Crawford, Adams, Jackson & Clay each have friends; and there may be difficulty in obtaining a majority for Adams."[1] Getting the necessary votes from New York and Maryland called for the full talents of Daniel Webster.

Webster's influence had been sought by most of the candidates. He was at times coy, at others cryptic, and the rest of the time apparently disinterested in the outcome. Calhoun was his favorite up to the early months of 1824, when the South Carolinian's cause collapsed. By summer, Webster had relapsed into outward aloofness. One theme did bring a

[1] Memorandum dated January 29, 1825, King, *King*, VI, 583-84.

sparkle to his eye. Which of the aspirants would be most likely to appoint Webster's Federalist friends to office? Who might be willing to send Boston's pride to the Court of St. James? Webster let it be known to Adams, among others, that his role in the election contest would depend upon answers to these questions. "His object," a friend concluded bluntly, "was the introduction of federalists into power."[2] Adams, in his turn, hinted that such terms, at least in part, were not impossible.[3] The news was pleasing, though Webster did not then agree that he would back the anxious secretary of state. Actually there was a powerful reason why Webster should stand behind Adams. He was, after all, the most prominent politician in the state that had reared and overwhelmingly supported Adams. The prospect of prominence in an Adams administration was good. For Webster to stand in opposition to the choice of New England would have been perilous.

By early December, Webster was confiding to Adams' friend, William Plumer, Jr.: "We must act with firmness, yet with moderation . . . supporting Mr. Adams, yet not quarreling with Gen. Jackson."[4] The possibility of Federalist appointments still transcended the value of success for his fellow Bay Stater. Even after Clay had come out publicly for Adams, Webster was still cautious. "This will not necessarily be decisive," he concluded, "but it will be very important. After all, I cannot predict results. I believe Mr. Adams *might be* chosen, if he or his friends would act somewhat differently. But if he has good counsellors, I know not who they are."[5] Not until the situation had simmered to the point where King could see Adams' chances as depending upon Maryland and New York did Webster drop his reserve. His moves were

---

[2] Adams, *Memoirs*, VI, 333.

[3] *Ibid.*, VI, 315-16.

[4] Plumer to W. Plumer, December 7, 1824, Brown, *Missouri Compromises*, 119.

[5] Webster to E. Webster, January 18, 1825, Van Tyne, *Webster*, 111.

complex but decisive, devious but perceptive. He ceased to be a passive advocate.

During December and January, Webster emphasized time and again to many friends of Adams that his chief concern was the treatment Federalists would receive. Regularly callers came into Adams' office to relay this story, and just as regularly Adams tried to quiet the fears. Webster himself came in a few times, never privately, and never did he discuss the appointment issue. He preferred to act through intermediaries. By late January, Adams was beside himself. He knew as well as anyone that Webster's active influence with other Federalists could be vital. What could he do? The election seemed to be slipping away from him, as the Crawford and Jackson partisans put increasingly heavy pressure upon undecided Congressmen. The moment came on the afternoon of February 3, six days before the balloting. Adams was told that Mr. Webster would call on him at his home that evening—alone! At last Webster's irritating circuitousness would be swept away. Two gentlemen would discuss their futures.

The amenities exchanged, Webster quickly showed Adams a letter he had received from Henry Warfield, a Federalist Congressman from Maryland, together with a draft reply Webster would send if Adams "should think proper." Warfield had, as expected, expressed apprehension about the treatment Federalists could expect from Adams. He was well disposed to the secretary of state, but he would appreciate Webster's assurances. Adams' caller added that he had been asked about the same point by John Lee, another Federalist Congressman from Maryland. Webster, in his draft reply, predicted that there would probably not be a pro rata distribution of offices among men "called by different denomination," but he did expect that "by some one clear and distinct case," Adams would indicate that he did not intend to bar Federalists from office. His own support for Adams, Webster emphasized in the draft, proceeded: "not from any understanding or communication with him, but from general considerations; from what I think I know of his liberal feelings, from his good sense and judgment, and from the force of circumstances . . . I assure you, very sincerely, that I have full confidence that Mr. Adams's administration will be just and liberal towards Federalists as towards others; and I need not say that there is no individual who would feel more pain than myself, if you and the rest of our friends should ever find reason to doubt the solidity of the foundation on which this confidence rests."[6]

As Mr. Adams sat reading this draft, Webster across from him, certain oddities floated before his eyes. The words: "not from any understanding or communication with him," were odd in themselves. Beyond that, Adams must have known that Warfield, a fast friend of Clay, had stated *unequivocally* a month before that he would go with Clay, either to Jackson or Adams.[7] Then too, it was strange that Warfield's letter was dated that day, February 3; that Clay had only a few days before expressed his anxious desire that Webster be conciliated; and that Webster, Clay, and Warfield must have been in frequent verbal consultation!

Adams in his diary gives no hint that he regarded Warfield's letter and Webster's draft as other than genuine. He apparently realized that he had been "had," and there was little use protesting the deviousness of Webster's conduct. The latter's influence was at this late stage priceless. Adams did insist, however, that his assent to Webster's reply should not be interpreted to mean that he would appoint a Federalist to the cabinet. Webster quickly suggested that perhaps a federal judge would be suitable. Adams recorded: "I said I approved

---

[6] Webster to Warfield, February 5, 1825, Webster, *Webster*, XVII, 379-80. See also, Warfield to Webster, February 3, 1825, *ibid.*, XVII, 377-78; and Adams, *Memoirs*, VI, 492-93.

[7] W. Plumer, Jr., to W. Plumer, January 4, 1825, Brown, *Missouri Compromises*, 126.

altogether the general spirit of his answer, and should consider it as one of the objects nearest to my heart." To soothe his conscience further, Adams added his belief, irrelevant if not pompous, that either of the other two candidates, if elected, would "necessarily act liberally in this respect."[8] As a postscript to his draft reply, Webster then added that Adams had both read and approved the letter. The daring and finesse of Webster's course were breathtaking; its scope even wider than Adams suspected.

Webster had planned this meeting with several objectives in view. The most immediate was to secure the vote of Maryland. A second was to influence the vote of Stephen Van Rensselaer. Another was to obtain leverage in bringing over Louis McLane, sole holder of Delaware's vote, to the Adams standard. Lastly, Webster was quite naturally thinking about his own position. He would be able to justify to Federalist colleagues his vigorous intervention on Adams' behalf only by offering tangible evidence that by doing so he had opened the way for the return of Federalists to positions of distinction and influence. Perhaps Mr. Adams would see fit to make Webster himself the symbol of Federalist regeneration. By striking at the moment when Adams was overcome with eagerness, Webster acted powerfully to further many ends.

The Maryland Congressional delegation was badly split. Three Republican members were firmly committed to Adams, and another was just as firmly a friend of Crawford. Henry Warfield would vote with Clay for Adams. Four remained. McKim, a Baltimore Republican, was wholeheartedly for Jackson; Little, also a Republican, was a friend of Clay but was known to be for Jackson (his district had voted heavily for the Hero); Mitchell, a Republican, leaned to Jackson though his district had voted by a small majority for Adams; and Lee, a Federalist from Frederick, was known to favor

[8] Adams, *Memoirs*, VI, 492-93.

Jackson, but he was peculiarly sensitive to the treatment Federalists would receive from the next administration. Webster hoped by a series of moves to get Lee's vote. First, he would seek explicit assurances from Adams. Second, he would ask Warfield to "talk" with Lee. Last, he would enlist the aid of Van Rensselaer, a move which also involved ensnaring his decisive vote in the New York delegation. The Patroon, notorious for appearing to agree with everyone, required constant nursing if he were to be carried safely into the Adams column.

Webster accomplished the first of these moves handsomely, and the approved reply to Warfield was undoubtedly brought to Lee's notice. Further to arm Warfield, Webster asked him to talk with Adams. Accordingly, on February 5, two days after Adams had approved Webster's reply to his letter, Warfield asked Adams for an interview. Adams sought out Webster to say that he would be happy to see the Marylander at once. Warfield called on schedule. He told Adams that he had not publicly said for whom he would vote, and that Roger Taney and Charles Carroll, prominent Maryland Federalists, had both told him that Jackson would not proscribe Federalists. Could Mr. Adams give him assurances? He could. Once again, Adams gives no hint in his diary that this was other than a straightforward interview.[9] Before he visited Adams on the third, Webster had sought out Van Rensselaer. He told him that Lee was wavering in his vote, being particularly concerned that Adams would not treat Federalists fairly. Webster asked that the Patroon see Adams and ask directly about his intentions. If Adams replied satisfactorily, Van Rensselaer should so advise Lee. To all of this Van Rensselaer agreed, and before Webster left Adams he told the secretary that the New Yorker would call the next day. After the by then familiar pattern, Adams banished Van Rensselaer's fears

[9] *Ibid.*, VI, 497-500.

with soothing words. True to his word, the Patroon relayed the news to Lee.[10]

Stephen Van Rensselaer was one of the more astonishing good-natured weaklings who have helped to make important decisions in American history. He advised his brother in December 1823 that although in the confidence of all the candidates, he would passively support Henry Clay. "I am too old," he sighed, "to engage in any active Electioneering business. I have worked against the Stream till I am exhausted and am now disposed to glide with the stream."[11] And glide he did! Van Rensselaer had blandly told Harper that he, like most New York Federalists, favored Calhoun.[12] To Van Buren, who had always carefully cultivated his company and good opinion, Van Rensselaer was always ready to imply strongly that he would support Crawford. An idol of the wealthy landlord, DeWitt Clinton also entertained a reasonable belief that the Patroon would do whatever he thought would advance Clinton's fortunes. The pleasant gliding continued into January 1825. Van Rensselaer wrote his brother that with Clay's support Adams' election seemed certain, though perhaps two or three ballots would be necessary. "We may be divided in our delegation at first," he concluded, "but Taylor, Storrs and Tracy think not. I feel inclined for 'Old Hickory' myself."[13] This last thought was probably the result of recent talks with a friend of Clinton who had gone to Washington specifically to tell Van Rensselaer that Jackson was Clinton's choice. At the same time, Clay still believed the Patroon committed to his corner, and two firm Crawfordites, Van Buren and Louis McLane, were both assured (or so they thought) that he

[10] *Ibid.*, VI, 492-93; Memorandum dated February 10, 1825, King, *King*, VI, 586-87.

[11] Van Rensselaer to S. Van Rensselaer, December 27, 1823, Bonney, *Legacy*, I, 409.

[12] Van Rensselaer to Harper, June 6, 1823, Maxcy Mss, LC.

[13] Van Rensselaer to S. Van Rensselaer, January 22, 1825, Bonney, *Legacy*, I, 415.

would not vote for Adams.[14] The Patroon always hated to hurt his good friend Van Buren.

Webster next turned to the vote of Delaware, held in the hand of Louis McLane. For a long time McLane had been a firm friend of William Crawford, as was the majority of Delaware Federalists. He confirmed this preference in many talks with Adams men, but on each occasion McLane stated clearly that he would never vote for Andrew Jackson. Knowing that Crawford had no chance, Webster went to McLane before the balloting. He felt sure that the Delaware Federalist would be attentive when he told him: "If the first attempt is not decisive, I then have in my possession a letter which I wish to show you, written to a member of the House in which Mr. Adams has expressly committed himself and designedly as to the course he will pursue towards the federalists."[15] Had not McLane the month before ringingly defended Federalism in the House of Representatives? Had he not proved, with heavy sarcasm, that the policies pursued by Federalist administrations had finally become those of a Republican regime? Had not this speech been prominently reprinted in Federalist newspapers everywhere?[16] "The first attempt," however, *was* decisive. McLane voted for Crawford, and Webster never actually showed him the Warfield letter. His constancy in not leaving Crawford, in spite of Webster's broad hint, was fully rewarded when Adams had fallen.

No one knew exactly what would happen on the morning of February 9, when the House would begin to ballot for president. John Lee of Maryland had let it be known to friends of Adams that although his vote would be for Jackson on the first ballot, he would then call upon Adams to seek an "explanation" for an obscure reference, which Lee said was offensive to Catholics, in a Fourth of July speech Adams had

[14] Memorandum dated February 10, 1825, King, *King*, VI, 586.
[15] William Coleman to T. Pickering, March 18, 1825, Pickering Mss, MHS.
[16] *Philadelphia National Gazette*, February 8, 1825.

made in 1821.[17] Mr. Adams would hardly choose the occasion
of chatting with Mr. Lee to abuse Catholics. The Marylander
had obviously listened well to the many assurances about
Adams' promised treatment of Federalists. A majority vote
in the Maryland delegation thus all but sure for Adams, at
least on the second ballot, Congressman Mitchell, whose
district had favored Adams, decided that it would not be
politic to hold out for Jackson. Mitchell's decision shifted all
eyes to New York. Seventeen representatives were known to
be for Adams; sixteen against him.[18] The remaining vote was
held by Stephen Van Rensselaer. The pressure he endured
was terrific. The anti-Adams men badgered him unmercifully.
Van Buren and McLane both stated later that Van Rensselaer
promised not to vote for Adams, and Mercer of Virginia
claimed that the Patroon had insisted Adams would not be
elected on the first ballot, a position Van Rensselaer had
taken many times before. Webster and Clay, knowing his
unbelievable suggestibility, drew Van Rensselaer aside on the
morning of the balloting. They sternly reminded the poor
man of certain statements he had made and actions he had
taken. On the first ballot, Van Rensselaer voted for John
Quincy Adams.

Devotees of historical speculation have long mused over
this crucial vote. Van Buren has reported that a few days after
the balloting, Van Rensselaer told him that just before the
vote he had prayed fervently and had looked up to see an
Adams ballot at his feet. A charming story![19] The most
credible account would seem to be that which Van Rensselaer
related to his friend Rufus King the day after Adams was
elected. Because he had heard of Van Rensselaer's promises

[17] Adams, *Memoirs*, VI, 502-03.
[18] There was considerable jockeying within the New York delegation during the few days before the balloting. Morgan, for example,
shifted from Adams to Jackson suddenly and mysteriously. Two other
Adams men, Tracy and Storrs, teetered until the last moment.
[19] Fitzpatrick, *Van Buren*, 150-52.

to Van Buren and McLane, King was particularly attentive when the Patroon came to his room and "entered into a free conversation respecting the election." Immediately afterwards, King recorded Van Rensselaer's words. "His purpose could not have been unknown to the opponents of Adams; that I might remember his expressing opinions favorable to Clay last winter; that Mr. Clay knew them, and early in the Session, he reminded Clay of this circumstance, and asked him what course he should pursue. . . . Soon afterwards Clay asked him how the State of New York would vote, and afterwards told him that the vote of N. York would have an influence upon the vote he might give, and urged him to give him an assurance that N.Y. would vote for Adams. Upon his, the Genl's, expressing his belief that N. Yk. wd. vote for Adams, Clay came out explicitly, and said that he should vote for Adams. . . ." At that time, said Van Rensselaer, Clay outlined to him the states that would go for Adams. The last was Maryland. Van Rensselaer then told King the story of Webster's request that he see Adams to ask, for the benefit of Congressman Lee, about the treatment Federalists could expect. "By asking this question," King wrote, "and its being answered in this manner, Genl. V.R. must be understood to have led Mr. A. to expect his Gen. V.R.'s support." Van Rensselaer argued that these facts pledged him to Adams.[20]

Van Rensselaer manifestly had no desire whatever to find himself holding the decisive vote on the morning of the election. Realization of this fact, which caused him to be assailed from many directions, reduced the Patroon to a state of shock and near collapse. He had consistently stated his opinion that Adams would be elected, though probably not on the first ballot. Wanting desperately to be liked, Van Rensselaer hoped to retain the affection of his friends by retreating into a pleasant dream world. In this world, Adams would eventually win, but he would do so with or without Van Rensselaer's vote.

[20] Memorandum dated February 10, 1825, King, *King*, VI, 586-87.

Thus he could tell Van Buren, McLane, and Mercer that Adams would not win on the first ballot, and even hint strongly that he, Van Rensselaer, would not vote for him. This would please them. When Clay and Webster reminded him that fateful morning that as an honorable man he must now vote for Adams, the Patroon's dream world must have been shattered pitifully. That he could tell Van Buren such a fanciful story after the election would indicate that he still could not face reality. Hoping to escape responsibility, he managed to project himself into the role of casting his vote in the full view of those to whom he had made so many contradictory promises. They had all, in turn, made calculations of the highest importance. Most men on the scene, whether they had been pleased or not by his vote, pitied Van Rensselaer. Few accused him of dishonesty or duplicity, for the Patroon was clearly an honorable man.

In spite of his failure to win over McLane, Daniel Webster had just cause to congratulate himself. He had helped to bring about Lee's equivocation, and to make it impossible for Van Rensselaer to turn back from support of Adams. Webster had acted as a Federalist with an acute sense of the Federalist mind. And he had his precious letter! Better days loomed ahead.

The later history of this letter, soon known as the "Webster Pledge," was long and stormy. Webster asked Warfield not to show the letter to anyone, a request Warfield apparently honored. Warfield did, of course, refer to such a letter in talks with Louis McLane and John Lee. Webster never actually showed his draft to others, either before or after the election. He did talk and write about it—often. Soon after the election, Webster confided to D. B. Ogden, a New York Federalist, a story which Ogden relayed to William Coleman, still a bitter opponent of Adams. Webster said that he had first liked Crawford, and only after much thought had he jumped to Adams. "But before he did so," Coleman reported, "he went to him personally to obtain an explicit declaration from him as to what would be his course with regard to the federalists & found it to be all he could wish, & either told Mr. O. or intimated to him, that Mr. A. has gone so far as to give him a pledge in writing, which he had in his possession."[21] Coleman had already heard from other sources that McLane was telling friends about Webster's cajolery. Webster also referred to the letter when explaining his course to friends. "I took care," he wrote Jeremiah Mason, "to state my own views and feelings to Mr. Adams, before the election, in such a manner as will enable me to satisfy my friends, I trust, that I did my duty. I was very distinct, and as distinctly answered; and have the means of showing *precisely* what was said."[22] Mason, Webster's brother Ezekial, Isaac Parker, Chief Justice of the Massachusetts Supreme Court, and Joseph Hopkinson of Philadelphia all heard of the letter and all approved Webster's action.[23] In 1827 the "Webster Pledge" would become an important campaign document for the onrushing Jacksonians.

Federalist reactions to the election were sharply varied. Thomas Robbins, the Connecticut preacher-diarist, was happy that New England again had a president, and that a duellist had not ascended to the White House.[24] To Harmanus Bleecker, a stiff-necked Albany Federalist, the best aspect of the election was that Henry Clay "resisted the wishes and views of a great portion of the western people." Bleecker piously argued that the House vote proved "the wisdom of referring the ultimate decision to some body of men more

[21] Coleman to T. Pickering, March 18, 1825, Pickering Mss, MHS.
[22] Webster to Mason, February 14, 1825, Hilliard, *Mason*, 297.
[23] Mason to Webster, February 20, 1825, Parker to Webster, February 21, 1825, Hopkinson to Webster, April 19, 1828, in the Webster Mss, LC. See also, Webster to E. Webster, February 16, 1825, Webster, *Webster*, xvii, 381.
[24] Increase N. Tarbox, ed., *Diary of Thomas Robbins, D.D. 1796-1854* (2 vols.; Boston, 1851), i, 995.

competent to judge than the people."[25] Isaac Parker reported
cheerfully to Webster that a mutual friend was planning a
public dinner in Boston on March 4. "There will be federalists
enough," Parker added, "to fill the table who sincerely rejoice,
so that there will be no need of the aid of those who are
merely acquiescent."[26] Among the latter group was Senator
E. H. Mills, who wrote his wife that, although on good terms
with Adams, he had "nothing to expect," nor would he "ask
anything at his hands." Mills indicated that he "might have
stood on different grounds" had Jackson been elected.[27] The
maneuvers and intrigues that attended the vote further convinced Ebenezer Baldwin in Albany that Jackson "would have
made a safer and more honest President."[28] Coleman, Pickering, and the many other Federalists who hated Adams were
naturally appalled by the news.

Most Federalists could agree on one point—the hope that
Adams would appoint at least a few Federalists to high offices.
"We should all feel anxious," stressed Robert Walsh, "that
the new President may select for secretaries, and ministers,
without distinction of party, men upon whom he can rely. . . ."[29]
Even crotchety old Timothy Pickering was sanguine that
Adams would select, in his words, "some who heretofore have
been federalists, & who have not yet renounced that character,
altho' they zealously promoted his election."[30] Coleman announced that he would judge Adams solely by whether he
distributed "posts and emoluments according to merit."[31]
Federalist editors everywhere voiced their fervent desire that
Adams would be "liberal" in his nominations. Most of Adams'

[25] Bleecker to S. Van Rensselaer, February 17, 1825, Gratz Coll.,
PHS.
[26] Parker to Webster, February 21, 1825, Webster Mss, LC.
[27] Mills to his wife, February 16, 1825, Lodge, *Mills*, 46.
[28] Baldwin to R. S. Baldwin, February 27, 1825, Baldwin Mss, YL.
[29] *Philadelphia National Gazette*, February 17, 1825.
[30] Pickering to W. Coleman, February 23, 1825, Pickering Mss,
MHS.
[31] *New York Post*, March 1, 1825.

Republican friends, however, wanted little to do with Federalists. A Poughkeepsie friend of Smith Thompson averred that Adams was the majority choice of New York Republicans, whereas most of the ardent Federalists, happily, wanted to follow Clinton in support of Jackson. The friend hoped Adams would do nothing to dissuade them.[32] The secretary of the navy, Samuel Southard, assured a Virginia Republican that certain fears about Adams were groundless. "I have consented to remain in his Adm^n," Southard revealed, "under the assurance & conviction, that he will consider the line marked out by Mr Monroe as the one in which it is his duty to walk. The policy of the Gov^t will be unchanged. His adm^n will be entirely republican—I say to you in confidence, that no man will be in it, whose republicanism is questionable, or ever has been so."[33]

Federalists were of course aware that there would be intense pressure put upon Adams to avoid the charge of an alliance. Webster did not sit back after his successful sortie on February 3 and expect that Adams would automatically take the lead in choosing Federalists for high posts. He must remind Adams that he had, after all, been quite explicit when votes were at stake. Reflecting upon a recent letter from Jeremiah Mason, Webster decided that Adams might find it "instructive" reading. Accordingly, under a disingenuous covering letter asking for no reply, Webster forwarded Mason's letter, which read in part: "I think you did perfectly right in explaining yourself to Mr. Adams. If he expects the support of the Federalists, he must remove the bar that excludes them from office. Confidence must of necessity be mutual. One of the Departments ought to be offered to a Federalist. Considering their number & talents this would naturally be the case, unless they are excluded by design. They ought not, & I trust will not be satisfied with mere

[32] T. Rudd to Thompson, February 19, 1825, Thompson Mss, NYHS.
[33] Southard to F. Brooke, February 27, 1825, Southard Mss, LC.

empty declarations of liberality in his inaugural speech."[34] Did Mason have in mind Webster himself? Certainly others were acutely sensible of his talents and recent favors. Robert Walsh, for example, put forward Webster's claims in the strongest language, and a Crawford Republican reported: "Mr. Webster must be in some way provided for; but how, is the difficulty. The holy political alliance are afraid of bringing so decided a Federalist into office."[35] Although Adams was not committed to providing for Webster, he was painfully conscious that he would have to make some arrangements.

Adams decided, in spite of Mason's sour comment, to make in his inaugural address a broad statement about party divisions. Adams, no doubt, sincerely believed that keeping up strict party lines in 1825 was archaic, but he was also prompted by his conscience to honor the professions of liberality he had made before the election. As a result, one quarter of his address was an eloquent plea for uprooting "the baneful weed of party strife." He called upon Republicans to make "one final effort of magnanimity, one sacrifice of prejudice & passion" to lay aside past standards.[36] The language was strikingly similar to Monroe's eight years before; in fact Monroe told his successor that the views were exactly as he would write.[37] Federalist editors, friendly to Adams or not, greeted the words with warm praise. Rufus King told Adams that this section deserved his "unqualified approbation," and Adams in turn told the venerable New Yorker that he intended to act upon his beliefs.[38] The joy was not shared by veteran

[34] Mason to Webster, February 20, 1825, Webster Mss, LC. See also, Webster to J. Q. Adams, February 26, 1825, Van Tyne, *Webster*, 112-13; and Webster to E. Webster, February 26, 1825, Webster, *Webster*, xvi, 101.

[35] R. H. Wilde to D. Blackshear, February 20, 1825, J. E. D. Shipp, *Giant Days or the Life of William H. Crawford* (Americus, Georgia, 1909), 193.

[36] *Philadelphia National Gazette*, March 8, 1825.

[37] Adams, *Memoirs*, vi, 512.

[38] King to C. Gore, March 22, 1825, King, *King*, vi, 600-01.

Republicans weaned on bitter party strife. Monroe's policies, at least his announced intentions, had already discouraged many, a feeling only heightened by the fratricidal battle that had split open the party during the presidential canvass. Martin Van Buren and others professed to see Adams' former Federalism glittering through the paragraphs which "embraced with avidity and supported with zeal the project of Mr. Monroe to obliterate . . . party distinctions of the past and to bury the recollection of their causes and effects in a sepulchre proposed by himself."[39]

Two days after his inauguration, Adams offered Rufus King the post of minister to England. He had first made the offer to DeWitt Clinton, knowing full well that Clinton would undoubtedly refuse. When King expressed doubt about accepting, Adams pressed him to reconsider, largely because of "the satisfaction which the appointment . . . would give to the federal party throughout the Union." Adams quite frankly told King that he was anxious to prove the sincerity of his inaugural address.[40] King's appointment was to be the great catharsis by which Adams could discharge his pre-election obligations. Moreover, King had supported the late war, and he had been re-elected in 1820 to the United States Senate by a Republican legislature in New York. Martin Van Buren, the personification of party regularity, had led the fight to re-elect King, and later had established close personal relations with King when Van Buren himself went to the Senate. If King were acceptable to Van Buren he must be acceptable to the most finicky Republican. Surely this was a master stroke.

A fearful row burst forth when King's appointment was made public in April. The *Intelligencer* estimated that it attracted more attention than any other in the past ten years, with the possible exception of Solomon Van Rensselaer's in

[39] Fitzpatrick, *Van Buren*, 193.
[40] Adams, *Memoirs*, VI, 523.

1822.[41] Outraged Republicans, unaffected by Adams' line of reasoning, sputtered and spluttered. The Southerners were almost uniformly disgusted, not only because King was a leading Federalist, but also because he had been stingingly effective during the Missouri debates and had lately proposed using the public land proceeds for manumission. Those already disposed to dislike Adams in the North fastened on the appointment to prove that Adams had opened the doors to Federalists. The protests by Adams supporters that King was a "good" Federalist were drowned in appeals to Republican purity.[42] Most Federalists were happy, though some were inclined to believe the appointment only a start, a sign that "talent" would count in filling future stations.[43] This note chilled the new president, who believed that he had "made good" on his obligations. To such as William Coleman and Timothy Pickering, however, the appointment was only a payoff for King's support during the campaign. Coleman, long devoted to King, took the lead in terming him overly ambitious and unfaithful. He even accused King in private letters of deliberately advising Hamilton to accept Burr's challenge though King knew that Hamilton would probably be killed. This vicious charge, seconded by Pickering, typified the inner hatreds that seized old Federalists as they watched their power dribble away after 1800.[44]

Federalists pressed their claims to executive favor upon Adams from the beginning to the end of his administration. They did this in spite of the fact Adams had selected only

[41] April 22, 1825.

[42] See, for example, the *Philadelphia National Gazette*, May 7, 24, June 7, 1825; and P. S. Markley to H. Clay, June 10, 1825, Clay Mss, LC.

[43] *Philadelphia National Gazette*, April 16, 1825.

[44] The two men had been abusing King since late in 1824 when King and his sons had been trying to get Adams electors chosen by the New York State Legislature. See Coleman to Pickering, November 21, 1824, February 13, 1825, and Pickering to Coleman, December 2, 1824, February 23, 1825, July 1, 1825, all in the Pickering Mss, MHS.

Republicans for his cabinet and had afterwards made very few Federalist appointments. Recommendations and appeals on behalf of prominent Federalists showered upon the new president in a swelling stream. The talent and respectability ascribed to the candidates approached awe-inspiring proportions; their zeal to serve the public interest proceeded from astonishing patriotism. Letters poured in from all directions. Jonas Platt, a high-toned New Yorker, had his eye fixed upon a district judgeship, and in August 1825 he asked Chancellor Kent to write Adams.[45] At the very same time, Kent's friends were mounting a formidable campaign to obtain for him the postmastership at New York City. Clinton wrote the postmaster general a long, flowery letter, which limned the Chancellor's many merits. "But the question," Clinton admitted, "is whether his former federalism, in case of his appointment, would injure the appointing power."[46] That was always the question! A prospective shake-up in the Philadelphia customs house brought forth a deluge of letters favoring a prominent Federalist, General Cadwallader, for the office of collector. Adams told his cabinet officers, Rush and Barbour, that "if Cadwallader's politics were to form no objection," Joseph Hopkinson was better qualified. Barbour quickly ended the discussion by stating that Hopkinson's political faith was an "insuperable objection."[47] As his father had long maintained, Adams soon agreed that making appointments was a president's most exasperating duty.

In the glow of Adams' announced intentions to disregard party distinctions, many Federalists, especially in New England, saw a chance to benefit from the widespread Republican support for Adams by promoting the cause of amalgamation. These men realized that Federalism, although still strong,

[45] Platt to Kent, August 29, 1825, Kent Mss, LC.
[46] Clinton to J. McLean, October 11, 1825, McLean Mss, LC. See also, J. C. Calhoun to S. Gouverneur, March 28, 1825, Gouverneur Mss, NYPL.
[47] Adams, *Memoirs*, VII, 93.

189

could never regain power as long as Republicans were able to unite against a formal opposition. If the body of Federalists would announce their support of Adams and give evidence of good faith to the Republican leadership, there was a chance that Federalists could once again share in the direction of public affairs. Planning to erase party strife, the amalgamators instead aroused in many states an intensity of party feelings during Adams' administration that was unmatched in the ten years previous. Seeing Federalists regain lost power by zealously advancing Adams' cause inflamed many a Republican stalwart who had little personal quarrel with Adams or his policies.

The first dramatic move came in Massachusetts a week after the House election. A caucus of Federalist state legislators met at Boston to endorse the Republican nominee for governor. Isaac Parker, "among the highest toned of the federalists," observed to Webster that Republicans in the state legislature had done nothing in recent years that Federalists would not have, and they had the added advantage of appearing to be "nearer allied to the people." In addition, the Republican nominee, Levi Lincoln, had, in Parker's opinion, gained in stature and steadiness from his year's tenure on the bench under Parker's watchful eye. Sure that Lincoln was then ready to maintain sound principles, Parker quipped: "Indeed there is no better remedy for democratic itching than a high judicial steam pressure."[48] Soon the amalgamators were making arrangements with friendly Republicans to run a "union" ticket of state senators from normally Federalist Suffolk County. The ticket would have three Republicans and three Federalists; surely an attractive offer by selfless Federalists.

Daniel Webster plunged wholeheartedly into the movement. On April 3rd he took the platform of Faneuil Hall before five thousand citizens to deliver a moving oration on

[48] Parker to Webster, February 19, 21, 1825, Webster Mss, LC.

the beauties of amalgamation. He began by saying that until then he had never given a political speech on that platform, because he had long held the view "that to preserve the distinction, and the hostility, of political parties, was not consistent with the highest degree of public good." He had come now to preach union and conciliation. After praising Adams and Clay, Webster began his peroration: "We tread on a broader theater, and if instead of acting our parts, according to the novelty and importance of the scene, we waste our strength in mutual crimination and recrimination about the past, we shall resemble those navigators, who having escaped from some narrow and crooked river to the sea, now occupy themselves with the differences which happened as they passed along among the rocks and the shallows, instead of opening their eyes to the wide horizon around them, spreading their sails to the propitious gale that woos it, raising their quadrant to the sun, and grasping the helm, with the conscious hand of a master."[49] Here was Webster at his soaring best, and the "shouting and cheering" lasted a quarter of an hour. This speech soon became gospel for amalgamators.

Other Massachusetts Federalists possessed less imagination than Daniel Webster. To them the amalgamation movement was simply a fraud, another outcropping of the accursed "middling interest," which had provided a haven for the "moderate, indolent, candid, canting, dunning, insidious & interested men" of the Federalist party. Why were there to be three Federalists and three Republicans on the senatorial ticket if the purpose of the movement was to destroy party distinctions? Why should the Federalists give up half their representation to the enemy when there was no evidence that the Republicans would reciprocate in their strongholds? What right had a few Federalist leaders to consign the party to ruin? The answer was plain. Ambitious men hoped to

[49] *Philadelphia National Gazette*, April 12, 1825.

191

flatter the president and amalgamate themselves into office.[50] The deftness and daring of the union men, led by Webster, carried the day, but setbacks lay ahead. Closing ranks a month later when Boston's representatives to the lower house were to be chosen, the regular Federalists trounced the union slate. Webster's magic was not equal for the moment to the ire of hard-bitten Boston Federalists. Those Republicans who had joined with Federalists became restive, angry, and suspicious.[51] Yet the political logic behind Webster's course was irresistible. Amalgamation went forward.

The movement in New Hampshire got off to a bad start and was destined to end in disaster. Jeremiah Mason had decided in 1824 to run for the United States Senate. A vigorous and acrimonious fight ended in a stalemate, but Mason resolved to try again at the legislative session that began in June 1825. Webster advised Mason to use the amalgamation theme among the Adams Republicans, and Webster even tried to get the personal influence of President Adams to further Mason's ambitions. Perhaps remembering Mason's impudent letter, Adams scornfully rejected the appeal.[52] The highhandedness of Federalist members in the New Hampshire legislature, however, thoroughly alarmed Republicans. "The conduct of the federalists," William Plumer grumbled, "has on this occasion, done more to perpetuate *party spirit* than every event that has occurred for this eight years. . . . Mason & his partizans *overacted* their part, & injured themselves."[53] The able and vitriolic editor, Isaac Hill, ran up the flag of Republican orthodoxy high on the standard. The Federalists

[50] The *Boston Courier* led the Federalist fight against the amalgamators. Its columns were filled with sarcasm and bitterness during the four months beginning in February 1825.

[51] See the *Boston Patriot* through this period, especially August 10, 1825. Just beginning his distinguished editorial career, Samuel Bowles, in the *Springfield Republican*, also lambasted the amalgamation movement. See especially, May 11, 1825.

[52] Adams, *Memoirs*, VII, 14.

[53] Plumer to W. Plumer, Jr., February 7, 1825, Plumer Mss, LC.

were coming and the troops were there for all to see. "The spirit of Jacobinism," Mason ruefully reported to Webster, "which you know exists in this State in abundance, is pretty thoroughly roused."[54] It would be months before the amalgamators could push forward in other states.

In addition to sponsoring the amalgamation venture, Webster and his friends sought other ways to organize Federalists into an integral auxiliary of the Adams party. They got the idea of soliciting from interested Federalists the sum of two thousand dollars to enable Robert Walsh to write a history of the period, 1797-1817. The *Gazette* editor was enthusiastic, but the solicitors made a bad error.[55] They went to William Coleman with the subscription paper. Coleman at once sounded the alarm in a flurry of letters to friends. He cried that Walsh would certainly praise scoundrels such as Adams, Jefferson, and Madison in an effort to show that John Quincy Adams was following in their steps.[56] Pickering echoed this interpretation. "The object of those federalists who originated the *plot*," he wrote, "is amalgamation; to gratify their ambitions and cupidity. John Adams, Jefferson, and Madison are all to be *written up*, to *purity* of *intention* and wisdom of administration, as equal to Washington's. . . ."[57] Federalist objections and the burst of hostile speculation that appeared in the press persuaded Walsh and his coadjutors that it was not wise to go on. The "history" died aborning.

Adams' inaugural address, his appointment of King, and the amalgamation activities of his Federalist friends all helped to fuel Jackson's war machine. The opposition forces formed rapidly, united in large part by a common fear of Federalism. Martin Van Buren, a forceful supporter of Crawford, recognized early, if privately, that if he were to save the Republican

---

[54] Mason to Webster, February 20, 1825, Webster Mss, LC.

[55] Walsh to D. Webster, August 22, 1825, *ibid.*

[56] Coleman to T. Pickering, June 17, 1825, Pickering Mss, MHS; Coleman to H. G. Otis, June 17, 1825, Otis Mss, MHS.

[57] Pickering to W. Coleman, July 1, 1825, Pickering Mss, MHS.

party from further ravages of the "gross delusion," amalgamation, he would have to attach the "old" Republicans to Jackson's cause. Deeply shaken by Jackson's advice to Monroe, Van Buren was willing to take the chance that he could be brought back to good principles through the agency of "favorable associations."[58] Everywhere possible, the opposition underscored the valuable services performed for Adams by his Federalist friends and hinted that these men would soon receive their reward. That stormy petrel, William Giles of Virginia, led the way. "Wonderful to behold," he raged, "the Federalists are smuggled in again. Nay, worse, infinitely worse than that—a new improved sect of Federalists. The ultra Federalists are upon us! ! !"[59]

Adams' opponents found in his first annual message a phrase, soon widely publicized, that seemed to lend further credence to the charge that Federalism was seeping back into the White House. In a passage asking for a program of internal improvements, Adams urged the Congress not to be "palsied, by the will of our constituents." The president was probably asking only for bold leadership, but he chose unfortunate words. Since the internal improvements issue was controversial itself, the outcry was deafening. Consolidation and Federalism!! Walsh tried to soften the impact of Adams' words by stressing that he was merely attacking the oft-stated view that the government should not vote an improvement program because the people *allegedly* did not want it.[60] The defense was lame and the damage to Adams was consequently severe.

The contest for Speaker of the House in December 1825 was bitterly fought. John Taylor of New York was Adams' choice, but the Crawford and Jackson forces could not agree on one man to oppose him.[61] In October, Louis McLane, still

[58] Fitzpatrick, *Van Buren*, 194, 198, 233-37.
[59] *Philadelphia National Gazette*, December 13, 1825.
[60] *Ibid.*, December 8, 31, 1825.
[61] Webster toyed with the idea of the speakership, but Clay and

a firm Crawfordite, had written a revealing letter to the Patroon. The latter's tragic conduct during the House election had been largely forgiven by that time, and Van Rensselaer had shown that he still valued the friendship of those he had disappointed. McLane, an active candidate for the speakership, believed he could be elected if the Adams and Jackson forces failed to put over their own man. McLane asked for Van Rensselaer's help in securing the support of northern Federalists. "I suppose," he guessed, "there are more than twenty federalists in the next Congress, and their votes would probably decide the contest." Because the most pungent memories of the Missouri question had passed away, McLane reasoned: "the federalists of the Eastern & Northern portion of the Union can have no predilection for Taylor and I should suppose might be induced to aid us in the coming contest—If those in *your* state & Massachusetts could be brought right, I have no doubt the rest would follow. Bailies [Baylies], avowed to *me his* determination to support me—Dwight was always my personal friend, and Allen, Lathrop, Reed & Nelson well disposed. You however could have more effect with them, than anyone else; and your interference would be necessary to counteract Webster. . . ." Although McLane cautioned Van Rensselaer to avoid rousing "the temper of fears of the opposite side," he did emphasize to the Patroon the pride he felt in being a Federalist.[62] Taylor was able, however, to combine a slim majority in his favor on the second ballot, thus thwarting McLane. In spite of this result, McLane's belief that Federalists could act decisively when the Republicans were evenly split was by no means fatuous. From a different perspective, Webster noted slyly after the decision: "It

---

Adams would have none of it. Webster's biographer, Claude Feuss, argues that he could have had the job, "if he had but said the word." This is not true. Taylor barely squeaked through as it was. Many Adams Republicans simply would not have swallowed Webster. See Feuss, *Daniel Webster*, I, 327.

[62] McLane to Van Rensselaer, October 15, 1825, Gratz Coll., PHS.

was not a bad thing that the friends of Mr. *Crawford*, generally, supported a *Federalist* for the chair."[63]

For administration supporters, nevertheless, it was an unhappy fact that although the opposition was effectively linking the new government with Federalism, great numbers of Federalists were either neutral or actively cheering Jackson. Southern Federalists, for example, ably led by Berrien, Rowan, and Tazewell, went over to the Jackson camp almost *en masse*. Buchanan, Taney, and Oakley in New York directed a strong corps of Jacksonian Federalists in the middle states, and a noisy group of Adams-haters remained to plague the administration in New England. Particularly galling was the readiness of most Republicans to believe that only unrepentant Federalists were leagued with Adams, whereas those who took Jackson's side had mysteriously cleansed themselves. If these phenomena were easily seen during the infancy of Adams' tenure, they were crushingly apparent in succeeding years.

[63] Webster to J. Mason, December 11, 1825, Webster, *Webster*, xvi, 117.

CHAPTER X

Impaled on the Pike of Federalism

⸻

JUST AS THE CAMPAIGN of 1824 was waged for years before the election, so too was the next one. From the day of Adams' inauguration, Administration leaders and supporters began to worry about the next election. One formidable obstacle was the aloof and colorless public image of Adams himself, who was exasperated by suggestions that he make even small efforts to adorn his Administration with trappings of a popular flavor.[1] Another was a political technique, which, with few exceptions, was consistently atrocious. Willing Republicans were turned away, Federalists often left disappointed, and major sources of potential strength such as Clinton and Calhoun needlessly antagonized.[2] Of immense importance was the thicket of troubles that sprang up from Federalism and Federalists. Contrastingly, Jackson was advanced as a vigorous and dynamic patriot, wreathed in military glory and Republican virtues. Adams men watched in frustrated rage as an army of shrewd and resourceful politicians used large sums of money and effective opinion-molding techniques to portray Jackson as a simple but willful servant of the people. Jacksonians smothered Adams in a Federalist blanket at the same time they adeptly gathered their own legion of Federalist auxiliaries.

The correspondence files of Henry Clay, secretary of state and the chief political officer of the Administration, were

[1] A supporter once suggested to Adams that if he would say a few words in German, a language Adams knew well, at a suitable occasion in Pennsylvania, he would make thousands of new friends on the spot. Adams scorned the idea as a cheap political trick. Adams, *Memoirs*, VII, 297.

[2] For an astute critique of the Administration's technique, by Adams' postmaster general, see J. McLean to E. Everett, draft dated 1827, McLean Mss, LC.

jammed with letters from the field pleading that Adams sack the many appointees who publicly opposed the government. "I am persuaded," Ninian Edwards of Illinois wrote, "that the time is at hand, when the wisdom of Mr. Jefferson's course in regard to the patronage of the administration must become too obvious to be any longer neglected."[3] This course was described tersely by another: "Take care of your friends and let your enemies take care of themselves."[4] The complaints poured in on Clay from all sections of the country, and nowhere more frequently than from the middle states. Porter, Rochester, and Tallmadge from New York; Wharton, Ingersoll, De Grand, and Sergeant from Pennsylvania; and Warfield, Kent, and Learned from Maryland all repeated the same story. "The administration must *demonstrate*," De Grand implored, "*that they look to their openly avowed friends to fill the places.*"[5]

Being a flexible politician, Clay was sympathetic to these appeals, but his chief was not. Thus Clay was forced to explain the President's position as gently as he could, and in the meantime do everything he could to persuade Adams to make certain appointments and not make others. "The President," Clay explained in October 1826: "has been heretofore very unwilling to exercize his dismissing power merely from the fact of the indulgence of individual opinion without some malfeasance—Moderation and forebearance I think was the true policy of his administration, as it would be throughout, if violence and intemperance should not render a departure, in some instances, necessary."[6] The departures were rare. Major appointees and minor ones alike began to sense that if Adams would rarely dismiss government officers, it would be well to look beyond the next election and put on the record at least cautiously pro-Jackson words or acts. Hints

[3] Edwards to Clay, September 21, 1826, Clay Mss, LC.
[4] J. Smith to Clay, October 7, 1827, *ibid.*
[5] P. De Grand to Clay, February 8, 1827, *ibid.*
[6] Clay to R. Peters, Jr., October 16, 1826, Peters Mss, PHS.

already abounded that General Jackson intended to look after his friends.

Whether to appoint only firm friends of the Administration and bar all enemies was a comparatively simple matter of judgment. The problem of the Federalists, however, was blurred by crosscurrents. The Jackson forces had set out from the start to label Adams' Administration a Federalist one, and every move in the direction of Federalism was seized upon as further proof. Republican supporters of Adams were acutely aware that an association with Federalists would be disastrous, especially in New England and the middle states where Federalists were most numerous. Yet Adams himself personally liked and respected many individual Federalists. His sense of fairness and his recognition that Federalists could never again wrest power from the Republican party ran counter to maintaining a strict proscriptive policy. Moreover, his "arrangement" with Webster just before the election might possibly demand more attention than the appointment of King. In a more narrowly political view, the legislative and rhetorical talent of a Webster or a John Sergeant offered a definite attraction, as did the possibility that vital campaign funds might be forthcoming from friendly Federalists. Clay often presented to Webster the sorrowful plight of deserving Administration editors, and he stressed that new sets of type, increased subscription lists, or outright grants from "your quarter" would do wonders.[7] As Jackson's strength grew, Administration forces became more convinced that to sustain the government they must marshal every bit of strength they could. They made a bad job of it. Adams and his advisors compromised and hesitated, never succeeding in attracting the bulk of the old Federalist party, and often swelling the widely held feeling that somehow they had com-

[7] See, for example, Clay to Webster, August 19, 1827, and October 25, 1827, Webster Mss, LC. For Webster's replies, see Webster to Clay, September 28, 1827 and November 5, 1827, Clay Mss, LC.

promised basic Republican principles by opening doors to the ancient enemy.

"In due time," an Adams man warned from New York in 1826, "the administration *is to be* charged as advancing federalists &c &c—& the Democratic party is to be aroused— &c &c."[8] This campaign had already begun the year before and it mounted in ferocity month by month. By 1828 a Boston Jacksonian was recommending even more publicity to stress "the excessively meagre support" Adams would get *"without the aid of the Federalists."*[9] Another critic voiced fears that "the Aristocracy of the country" would make the most strenuous efforts, thus demanding that the voters "be kept in a state of excitement till the close of the campaign."[10] A pamphleteer swore solemnly, though unjustly: "With scarce an exception, the ancient ringleaders of high Federalism, yet surviving, are devoted to Mr. Adams." Having given up hopes of winning by themselves, the Federalists, hyprocrisy in their hearts, had held forth the hand of reconciliation. "The Republicans had the simplicity," the writer continued, "to believe their professions and greeted them as friends." This touching picture of unsophisticated Republicanism was followed by vividly drawn scenes of Federalists creeping back into office and finally "restoring the once discarded house of Braintree."[11] The Young Jackson Men of New York exhorted the Republican faithful not to be lulled by "adversaries and false friends" who preached dissolution of the great Republican party.[12]

[8] J. Tallmadge to J. Taylor, February 2, 1826, Taylor Mss, NYHS.
[9] D. Henshaw to R. Jarvis, February 2, 1828, Jarvis Mss, LC.
[10] J. H. Prince to S. Dexter, May 14, 1828, *ibid.*
[11] "A Republican of the Jefferson School," *Who Shall be President? The Hero of New Orleans, or John the Second, of the House of Braintree?* (Boston, 1828), 4-5.
[12] *Address of the Republican General Committee of Young Men of the City and County of New York, Friendly to the Election of Gen. Andrew Jackson to the Presidency, to the Republican Electors of the State of New York* (New York, 1828), 46.

The principal attack was made on Adams himself, with Clay close behind. Adams was an easy target. His early career as a Federalist was raked over unmercifully; his apostasy painted as a mere trick to gratify a voracious ambition. "The high-toned federal spirit," a typical Jackson address charged, "which was lighted at the parental fire in the essays of Publicola, although for many years it was carefully smothered, was never extinguished in his bosom; and had blazed forth with all its 'original brightness.'" Adams was now, the address went on, "surrounded and influenced by Federalists; and the very men whom, upon his pretended conversion in 1807, he denounced as traitors to their country."[13] Jacksonians also attacked Henry Clay's new friends. "I confess," a Marylander grieved, "I never expected to live to see the day when Henry Clay would be *politically* associated with Daniel Webster of Massachusetts, and it is with real pain that I leave such a man as Henry Clay."[14] In Kentucky, where the citizens enjoyed pungent oratory, a Jacksonian Congressman detailed Clay's gradual alliance with Adams. "Had you seen what I have," he said, "you would feel as I do. Had you seen the brave West, still bleeding from the wounds of the late war, made to shake the traitorous hand of the Hartford Convention merely to satisfy the ambition of one man, you would have felt as I do. It is enough to call forth the indignation of the relatives of those who fell at Raisin, Miami, and Mississippi, and who were virtually murdered by those politicians with whom their fathers, brothers and sons are now called on to coalesce."[15] The words were bitter; the allusions pitiless.

Jacksonian charges ringing about the ears of Administration leaders were joined by desperate appeals from Republi-

[13] *Ibid.*, 44.

[14] *Speech of Thomas Kennedy, Esq. at the Jackson Meeting, Held at the Court-House in Hagers-Town (Md.), August 4, 1827* (Hagerstown, 1827), 6.

[15] *Speech of Thomas P. Moore, Esq. Delivered in the Court House in Harrodsburg (Ky.), June 3, 1827* (Harrodsburg, 1827), 34.

can supporters to ignore the ambitious Federalists. An Indiana friend begged Clay to leave "that Eastern faction" and return to his "old democratic station," and a Kentuckian admonished: "Alas! Alas! You have made sad work for the poor Republicans. . . . We now find you have made Webster & Sergeant 'the lords of the Ascendant.' "[16] A faithful friend from western Massachusetts set forth the feeling in his area. "I want you to bear in mind one thing," he wrote, "which will perhaps explain to you some others as they pass . . . that the old lines of party are not wholly extinct among us, and it is proper that the Republicans should at times protect themselves by acting in concert—old feelings are to be respected. . . ."[17] Administration Republicans were particularly alarmed by rumors that Webster would succeed King in England. "Not that there is anything in fact, in the name," one warned, "but public opinion is ag^t it, & you will know Sir how much this influences."[18] A sarcastic Long Islander was amazed at the "wonderful conversion" Webster must have experienced since 1814 "when he made speeches, & voted against raising money, taxes, or troops."[19] Adams, besieged by frenzied appeals from Republican leaders, recorded in his diary: "All the friends of the Administration are agreed that the political effect of the appointment of Mr. Webster would be very unfavorable."[20] Webster was not appointed.

State leaders in Pennsylvania and New York were the most insistent that Adams shun the Federalists. A knowing Pennsylvanian argued that all political moves in that state must be identified with "the Democracy of the State"—anything else would be "fatal."[21] Another was even more em-

[16] J. Garrigus to Clay, January 8, 1828, F. P. Blair to Clay, November 14, 1827, Clay Mss, LC.

[17] H. Shaw to Clay, August 22, 1827, *ibid.*

[18] J. Mower to J. Taylor, May 6, 1826, Taylor Mss, NYHS.

[19] E. Sage to J. Taylor, February 27, 1826, *ibid.*

[20] Adams, *Memoirs*, VII, 525.

[21] P. Markley to H. Clay, May 19, 1827, Clay Mss, LC.

phatic. "The old Federal prejudice," he counselled: "is yet warm & inveterate, and every effort is making by the friends of Gen¹ Jackson, to identify the Administration with the most odious relics of that Party. The effort has been, thus far, successful, and will continue to be so. . . ."[22] New York Republicans told the same story. James Tallmadge, who with John Taylor had set off the Missouri debates with their resolution, thought it imperative that Adams boldly pull together a solid Republican bloc behind him in that state.[23] An equally loyal supporter cautioned in 1826: "If Mr. A. wishes to *save* this State, he must do something *signijicant* if his disposition is to serve his *Republican* friends, & that *promptly*."[24] Adams Republicans did not content themselves with merely registering their protests to Administration leaders. In election addresses, campaign literature, and newspaper editorials, they tried manfully to dispute the Jacksonian claim to "exclusive Republicanism." They argued that the old parties had split up, thus making it as impossible for Jackson to be elected without his Federalist supporters as Adams without his Republican friends. A familiar theme in this effort was cataloguing the names of prominent Federalists enlisted behind Jackson. No one could question that such as Timothy Pickering, James Ross, James Hamilton, and Roger Taney were outspoken Jacksonians, nor that the *New York Post* and the *Delaware Gazette* were the Hero's journalistic friends.

Another line of attack was directed at Jackson himself. Was his Republicanism as pure as Jacksonians claimed? The record, minutely searched by Adams supporters, was somewhat murky. The leading exhibit was, of course, the Jackson-Monroe letters. Administration Republicans flung these letters in the face of their enemy with tiresome regularity. An enterprising Pennsylvanian discovered that a prominent Jacksonian

22 J. Learned to H. Clay, September 27, 1827, *ibid.*
23 Tallmadge to J. Taylor, May 13, 1826, Taylor Mss, NYHS.
24 H. Wheaton to H. Clay, March 29, 1826, *ibid.*

in Tennessee had declared in Jackson's presence and without his disapproval: "The high minded federalists, *of the Hamilton School*, will not be against us."[25] This foray was accompanied by evidence from the dim past that Jackson had voted for suffrage restrictions in the Tennessee Constitutional Convention. Though diligent workers, the Adams men were never quite as resourceful in this business as the Jacksonians. An Administration address in New York offered unwilling evidence of this fact when it damned those who drove voters into support for Jackson "by promising the appellation and favor of 'a Republican' to him who [voted] for the General, and by denouncing the stigma and woes of 'federalism' against the man who ventured independence enough to oppose him."[26] That Adams appointed few Federalists and that he relied principally upon Republican advisers and state leaders was often lost in the din of Jacksonian charges.

Even Federalist editors who supported Adams, though their efforts often bore the marks of reluctance and anguish, tried to dispel the notion that Adams was the chosen instrument of Federalists. The *Boston Courier*, for example, was often appalled by attacks upon Federalists made by Adams Repub-

[25] *Address of the Democratic Convention Held at Harrisburg on January 4, 1828* (Harrisburg, 1828), 5-6.

[26] *Proceedings of the New York State Convention Held at Albany on June 10 & 11, 1828 by Friends of the Present Administration of Our National Government* (Albany, 1828), 31. For other efforts by Adams supporters to challenge Jackson's Republicanism, see the *Proceedings of the Maryland Administration Convention, Delegated by the People, and Held in Baltimore, on Monday and Tuesday, July 23 and 24, 1827* (Baltimore, 1827), 14-16; *Proceedings of a Convention of the People of Maine Friendly to the Present Administration Holden in Portland on the 23d of January, 1828* (Portland, 1828), 5-6; *Proceedings and Address of the Republican Young Men of the State of New York, Assembled at Utica, on the Twelfth Day of August, 1828* (New York, 1828), 10; *The Presidential Question. To the Friends of Equal Rights* (Philadelphia, 1828), 1-2, 6-8; and *Sketches of Character; or Facts and Arguments Relative to the Presidential Election, 1828* (Philadelphia, 1828), 12, 23-4. For typical press statements, see the *Baltimore Marylander*, May 14, 1828; and the *Springfield Republican*, August 13, 1828.

licans. Yet when a Jackson press, the *Boston Statesman*, made an unusually abusive assault upon the Hartford Convention, the *Courier* editor retorted: "The Statesman . . . has been very noisy, especially of late, in denouncing that assemblage, without making a reservation for such of its members and supporters—nearly the whole of the Connecticut deputation, for instance—as are embarked in the cause of Gen. Jackson."[27] One of the leading amalgamation presses, the *Portsmouth* (N.H.) *Journal*, tried always to break down the force of old party ties. "The folly of those," the editor wrote sharply, "who attempt to *support* Mr. Adams on old party grounds, is as great as theirs who appeal to those old prejudices with a view to render him unpopular."[28] When Isaac Hill charged that one of the Adams electors was a Federalist, the *Journal* promptly answered that one of the Jackson electors was too, as well as one of the Jacksonian candidates for Congress.[29] On another occasion the *Journal* wondered aloud how Hill could reconcile the Jacksonian nomination for Congress of Joseph Hemphill in Philadelphia and James Bayard in Delaware, both Federalists, "with the pure, unadulterated, unamalgamating, republicanism of the Jackson party."[30]

The Adams Federalists and many Administration Republicans tried to find a formula that would ward off the charge of Federalism and still make the Adams cause alluring to Federalists. The author of a Maryland address dwelt upon the Jackson-Monroe letters to discredit Jacksonian claims to exclusiveness, but at the same time he praised Adams for having "the magnanimity and firmness . . . to appoint those who were distinguished for their virtues . . . regardless of political names or party distinctions."[31] Clay avowed to Webster that

[27] June 12, 1828.
[28] September 16, 1826.
[29] October 18, 1828.
[30] October 6, 1827.
[31] *Proceedings of the Maryland Administration Convention . . . July 23 and 24, 1827*, 14-15.

there were but two parties in the country, "the friends and enemies of the administration," and that all reference to old party names was for "the purpose of fraud and deception."[32] To other correspondents Clay lamented "the divisions between our Federal & Republican friends" in Delaware and the lack of "vigor concert and union" in New York state.[33] Clay goaded a Philadelphian in 1826 to work for a merger between the discrete Federalist organization there and Republican allies. "It would be remarkable," the secretary concluded, "to see [the Federalists] lend themselves to the support of an opposition which mainly counts upon success, in N. York, in New England, in the South and in the West, by endeavoring to revive animosities, divisions and names what belong to past times."[34] Beyond general appeals, Administration leaders quietly wooed individual Federalists, such as David Daggett and even Coleman. The governor of Maryland, Joseph Kent, gently advised Clay in 1827 to grant a clerkship to the son of a leading Maryland Federalist, because the father, an Adams man, possessed "considerable influence."[35]

Federalist support was needed not only at election time but also in the Congress. The Administration was badly in need of wise leadership. His own undoubted talents and the absence of forceful Adams Republicans made Daniel Webster, almost from the first, the chief Administration spokesman and tactician in the House of Representatives. When Webster wished to move up to the Senate, concern arose that his place could not be properly filled in the House. Even Republicans were agreed that the men who could best do the job were

[32] Clay to Webster, November 10, 1826, Webster Mss, LC. See also, Clay to Webster, April 14, 1827, *ibid*.

[33] Clay to J. Taylor, September 7, 1827, Taylor Mss, NYHS; Clay to J. Hammond, November 6, 1827, Gratz Coll., PHS.

[34] Clay to R. Peters, Jr., October 16, 1826, Peters Mss, PHS.

[35] Kent to Clay, January 26, 1827, Clay Mss, LC. See also, Clay to D. Daggett, December 13, 1826, Daggett Mss, YL; and W. Coleman to T. Pickering, April 25, 1827, Pickering Mss, MHS.

John Sergeant and Thomas Oakley of New York.[36] Doubts about Oakley's political views were quickly resolved when he became in 1828 a vigorous Jacksonian. Webster did take the Senate seat and Sergeant became the *de facto* Administration House leader. To nobody's surprise, Webster became Adams' champion in the Senate, opposing what Clay termed "the enormous talent" of the Jacksonians.

Webster continued to press upon Republican and Federalist alike the need for combining behind Adams. He used a host of arguments, but to many Federalists the amalgamation movement was attractive because a leading Federalist, Daniel Webster, was high in the councils of the Administration. When Webster went to the Senate, a Pennsylvanian reflected Federalists' pride in their leader's prominence by pretending to grieve at his leaving the House. "Who," the writer asked, "when the storm is up and the bellows roll, can we see at the helm, and each feel that the vessel is safe."[37] Some of Webster's distinction and reputation rubbed off on frustrated party veterans who had for years dreamed of again savoring the glory that came with public office. Federalists characteristically identified themselves strongly with one of their number when he reached a goal all of them wanted.

To those Federalists who hated the Adams clan because it had helped to ruin their beloved party, Webster's plea for amalgamation was anathema. William Coleman was scandalized upon reading that leading Federalists, Webster, Sergeant, and William Duer of Albany among them, had in public eulogies warmly praised Jefferson and his measures. "Who would have believed," Coleman asked rhetorically, "that such men as Webster & Sergeant would have descended to

[36] H. Clay to D. Webster, May 14, 1827, Webster Mss, LC; D. Webster to J. Taylor, July 15, 1827, Taylor Mss, NYHS; J. Sergeant to H. Clay, September 18, 1827, Clay Mss, LC.

[37] C. Miner to D. Webster, June 13, 1827, Webster Mss, LC. See also, I. Parker to D. Webster, February 12, 1826, *ibid.*, and J. Mason to D. Webster, March 27, 1828, Hilliard, *Mason*, 320.

prostitute, yes, to prostitute their talents & sacrifice their regard for consistency, decency & veracity in pronouncing wholesale eulogies on Thomas Jefferson. . . ."[38] Coleman had earlier asked if Pickering could explain to him "the conduct of such men at Boston as T. H. Perkins, J. Lowell & others of that description."[39] Pickering answered by comparing them to John Adams, whose ambition had "ruined himself and prostrated federalism." Joseph Story's ambition, on the other hand, led him to become a virulent Republican, though when appointed to the bench, thus satisfying his ambition, Story "sought for better company; and never appeared more happy than when in the society of respectable federalists." Pickering went on to explain the success of amalgamation. "There are," he despaired, "a good number of unchanged federalists; but no efforts of theirs could change the popular current; & therefore they are inactive. Others, comprising great numbers of federalists of *federal times*, seeing no chance that federalism will ever regain an ascendancy—yet wishing to be of some political consequence,—they act with the ruling party. I presume this is not peculiar to Boston; but that the same remark is applicable to New York, and to all other cities and populous towns in the U. States."[40] Thus were Federalists only too willing to ascribe to their own breed motives quite as base as those of Republicans.

Within this jungle of conflicting values John Quincy Adams and other Administration leaders tried painfully to form an appointment policy that would gain the greatest political strength. "And it is upon the occasion of appointments to office," Adams lamented, "that all the wormwood and gall of

[38] Coleman to T. Pickering, September 24, 1826, Pickering Mss, MHS. For the relevant sections of the eulogies made by Webster and Duer, see *A Selection of Eulogies Pronounced in Honor of Those Illustrious Patriots and Statesmen: John Adams and Thomas Jefferson* (Hartford, 1826), 126, 229.

[39] Coleman to Pickering, April 25, 1827, Pickering Mss, MHS.

[40] Pickering to Coleman, April 30, 1827, *ibid.*

the old party hatred ooze out. Not a vacancy to any office occurs but there is a distinguished federalist started and pushed home as a candidate to fill it—always well qualified, sometimes in an eminent degree, and yet so obnoxious to the Republican party that he cannot be appointed without exciting a vehement clamor against him and against the Administration. It becomes thus impossible to fill any appointment without offending one-half the community—the federalists, if their associate is overlooked; the Republicans, if he is preferred. To this disposition justice must sometimes make resistance and policy must often yield."[41] For the most part, Administration leaders believed that "policy" demanded the appointment of Republicans.

The only important appointments of Federalists, past or present, made by Adams were those of King as minister to England, John Sergeant as a delegate to the ill-fated Panama Congress, J. J. Crittenden as a justice of the Supreme Court, Joseph Hopkinson as a district judge in Pennsylvania, John Duer as a United States attorney in New York, and Nathan Smith as a United States attorney in Connecticut. Adams submitted the names of three of these men in December 1828 a month after his defeat. In five of these cases, opposition was made on the ground the appointee was a Federalist, and at no other time was opposition made in the Senate on this ground. Always in that body was a vigorous and ably led opposition force, made up of men ever ready to accuse the president of favoring Federalists or of sponsoring Federalist legislation. Typical of this feeling was the reaction of George Dallas to the rumor in 1827 that Webster would be sent to England. "Mr. Webster," he avowed, "cannot be voted for by any democrat not disposed to commit political suicide."[42]

Five of these six nominations were confirmed by the Senate. Most observers expected a sustained effort would be made

[41] Adams, *Memoirs*, VII, 207-08.
[42] Dallas to R. W. Meade, December 20, 1827, Dallas Mss, PHS.

in December 1825 to deny King's confirmation. The debate was brief, however, and only fourteen votes were cast against him. Debate on Sergeant's nomination in 1826 was similarly brief and the vote for confirmation closely followed votes on the mission itself. Though some Federalist editors saw in the appointment another sign that party lines were becoming meaningless, the issues in the Panama debate itself largely transcended the Federalist question. William Findlay, for example, a Jacksonian senator from Pennsylvania, voted for Sergeant.[43] One of the "High-Minders" from New York, John Duer, was appointed in early 1828, and his confirmation came with no debate or dissenting vote. Van Buren had stated that he would oppose David B. Ogden for the same office, but not Duer.[44] In the case of Nathan Smith, Adams submitted his name during the lame-duck session of 1828-29. Senator Levi Woodbury, a New Hampshire Jacksonian, tried to have the nomination tabled. His motion was defeated by a vote that roughly followed the usual Administration-opposition lines.[45] Adams also sent the nomination of Crittenden, who had once been an active Kentucky Federalist, in December 1828. Two months later, by a vote of 23-17, the Senate decided to table it after a debate in which Crittenden's Federalism was a leading issue.[46]

The appointment of Joseph Hopkinson, which provoked a lengthy and angry controversy in the Senate, had a labyrin-

---

[43] *Philadelphia National Gazette*, March 18, 1826. See also, the *Portsmouth Journal*, March 25, 1826.

[44] Adams, *Memoirs*, VII, 396; W. Duer to S. Van Rensselaer, January 5, 1828, Gratz Coll., PHS; *Journal of the Executive Proceedings of the Senate of the United States of America* (Washington, 1829), III, 595.

[45] *Ibid.*, III, 646. Two ardent Jacksonian Federalists, Tazewell and McLane, voted to confirm Smith's nomination. For the effect of this appointment in Connecticut, see A. Child to G. Welles, February 26, 1829, and N. Phelps to G. Welles, February 27, 1829, Welles Mss, LC.

[46] See the speech of Senator John Holmes in the *Register of Debates in Congress*, 20th Congress, 1st Session (Washington, 1830), 90.

thine background. More entreaties were made to Adams in Hopkinson's behalf than was the case of any other Federalist. His merits had even been brought to Monroe's attention many times; the appeals only multiplied when Adams was elected. Early in 1826 a rumor was floated that the United States attorney in Philadelphia would not be reappointed. Joseph Story quickly wrote Hopkinson urging him to "apply" for the post, though he cautioned Hopkinson "to procure the recommendations of some *Republicans* of real substantial influence in Phila. to aid in accomplishing so just an object."[47] Nothing came of this. Soon afterwards, Richard Peters, a veteran Federalist and long-time district judge in the eastern district of Pennsylvania, became seriously ill. Story, John Marshall, and Bushrod Washington all offered to write separate letters to the president.[48] Judge Peters' constitution proved too stern this year, but early in 1827 the well-wishers were again anticipating his early demise. Hopkinson himself wrote Adams a long letter setting forth his claims to favor. A major section of this letter was a detailed explanation of Hopkinson's conduct during the War of 1812, in which he agreed that he had not, as was the custom, illuminated his house to celebrate victories. He had voted for supplies, however, and now counted many Republicans among his friends.[49] Hopkinson's Federalism was obviously the rub.

The pressure mounted in March 1827 when Webster wrote Adams from Philadelphia that Robert Walsh would soon go to Washington. He first noted that Walsh had lately become cool towards Adams, an unhappy fact in light of Walsh's influence among the "40 or 50 thousand Electors, in Penna., who formerly belonged to the Federal Party." Walsh had no quarrel with the government's policy, but, as an old and attached friend of Hopkinson, he felt the latter had been

[47] Story to Hopkinson, March 4, 1826, Konkle, *Hopkinson*, 252.
[48] J. Story to J. Hopkinson, March 8, 1826, *ibid.*, 252-53.
[49] Hopkinson to Adams, January 27, 1827, *ibid.*, 212-14.

neglected by Adams. Webster had no doubt "it would gratify Mr. Walsh more than anything else whatever," if Hopkinson were appointed, and Adams would be gratified by "the appearance of quite a different tone & manner in the National Gazette." The effect of this would be helpful not only in Pennsylvania, but also in New Jersey where Federalists were acutely unhappy because their leader, Richard Stockton, had not been given a post he had been led to expect. As a parting shot, Webster made it clear to Adams that Hopkinson was a "particular friend" of his.[50]

Preceded by this broadside, Walsh visited Adams and Clay. The results were disappointing. "Nothing was obtained," Hopkinson lamented to Webster, "but general impressions, without any . . . certainty or assurance." Walsh believed that Adams had been generally receptive but was prevented from acting by those around him. The leading villain was Henry Clay. "He is full of subtile explanations," Hopkinson reported, "and politic reasons, derived from persons here who certainly deceive him; and he the more readily falls into their errors as they favour his inveterate dislike to all federalists, & particularly to the one in question—There is no faith to be put in this man—he is evidently playing his own game, without the least regard to the interests or character of Mr. A.—except so far as he is connected with them.—He said with one of his significant leers, 'Nobody can say that I neglect my friends.' " Walsh had gathered that although Administration leaders considered Webster "indispensable," they implied that he was already "perfectly secured in the service." If Webster *demanded* a particular action, however, they would probably have to accede.[51] Clay wrote Webster soon afterwards, apparently without the knowledge that Webster had been the

[50] Webster to Adams, March 27, 1827, Webster, *Webster*, xvi, 150-51. For the Stockton matter, see the *Proceedings of the New Jersey Historical Society*, ix (1924), 133; and Adams, *Memoirs*, vii, 313-14.

[51] Hopkinson to Webster, April 13, 1827, Webster Mss, LC. Adams' account of his conversation with Walsh is in his *Memoirs*, vii, 252.

prime mover behind Walsh's trip. The editor had been favorably impressed by his journey, Clay believed, but his request was troublesome. "I really fear," he protested "that any other Federalist in Penns[a] (not excepting James Ross) may be appointed with less injury to the Admin[n] than Mr. H."[52] Here the matter rested, and Judge Peters lingered on.

Peters finally died eighteen months later. Again Hopkinson's friends besieged Adams with a flood of recommendations and appeals. In late October, Adams, in spite of continued dissent by Clay and other Republicans (Adams had no hopes at this late date that he could be re-elected), sent Hopkinson the coveted commission. Although valid only until March, unless the Senate confirmed the appointment, Hopkinson's friends were elated.[53] Adams forwarded the nomination to the Senate in December, but it was not reported out of the Judiciary Committee until February. A storm was brewing. After two motions to table had carried, the third was defeated. Webster, who had worked hard to help his friend, asked for a roll call. It revealed that two Jacksonians of Federalist antecedents, Rowan and Ridgely, had voted to table; and three, Berrien, McLane, and Tazewell, had voted against the motion.[54] Heated debate had prevailed both in committee and on the floor, some angry opponents going so far as to call Hopkinson a monarchist.[55] The Philadelphian's friends received the news with a new round of mutual congratulations. All were deeply impressed by a note Adams sent to Hopkinson in which he compared the appointment to that of Marshall in the last days of his father's Administration.[56] The decade-long struggle was

[52] Clay to Webster, April 14, 1827, Webster Mss, LC.
[53] B. Washington to R. Peters, Jr., September 7, 1828, Konkle, *Hopkinson*, 257; J. Q. Adams to J. Hopkinson, October 23, 1828, *ibid.*, 259-60; T. Wharton to H. Clay, October 4, 1828, Clay Mss, LC; J. Marshall to J. Story, October 29, 1828, *Proceedings of the Massachusetts Historical Society*, xiv (1900-01), 2nd Ser., 339.
[54] *Senate Executive Journal*, iii, 646, 650.
[55] B. O'Sullivan to H. Clay, February 13, 1829, Clay Mss, LC.
[56] Adams to Hopkinson, February 25, 1829, Konkle, *Hopkinson*, 265.

ended, and though the appointment did not occasion much newspaper comment, there were many who charged that it was the final issue of the "Webster Pledge."

From October 1827 until the day of election, newspapers were filled with conflicting reports that Webster had forced Adams to make a pledge that Federalists would be "fairly" treated. These stories were printed in many versions by Jacksonian newspapers, and Administration prints usually denied the stories out of hand. Many hostile editors, Coleman among them, had been aware in 1825 that some kind of negotiation had preceded the House vote, but no one knew the details nor was there available documentation. The first public charge, which appeared on October 6, 1827, in the *Philadelphia National Palladium*, stated that John Bailey, a close Republican friend of Adams, had written a letter to Webster, with interlineations in Adams' hand, which promised Federalist appointments if Adams were elected.[57] Bailey flatly denied the story. William Coleman then alleged in the *Post* that Webster had shown a pledge to Congressman Allen of Massachusetts, as well as to McLane and Warfield.[58] The latter, sensing that the controversy must have some relation to his letter from Webster, turned to his friend Clay for advice. "Publish nothing for the present," Clay advised, "until McLean [McLane], Who I take to be at the bottom of the business, chooses to come out."[59]

This flare-up had abated somewhat when early in 1828 trouble erupted again. This time a Jacksonian editor claimed he had new evidence in the form of a letter allegedly written by Richard Stockton of New Jersey, which stated that Stockton had seen the pledge letter during a meeting with Webster in 1825. The letter printed in the newspapers, actually a forgery, included the names of Walsh and Hopkinson as

[57] *Boston Courier*, October 12, 1827.
[58] *Ibid.*, October 19, 1827.
[59] H. Clay to D. Webster, November 8, 1827, Webster Mss, LC.

persons who had been present when Webster displayed the pledge.[60] Greatly disappointed in 1827 that Adams had not appointed him to a district judgeship, Stockton in his pique had told persons hostile to Adams that Webster had informed him about his meeting with Adams. Stockton never actually saw the Warfield letters. Pleas by both Hopkinson and Stockton's son (his father had recently died) that this story be denied and the facts made public were met by Webster with the advice that nothing be said.[61] The press, however, kept up the clamor. A confidant of Adams, Tobias Watkins, asked Adams in May if his facts were correct in a proposed article Watkins had written to silence the rumors of a pledge. Adams replied that the charges had "no other foundations than casual conversations" with Webster and others in which Adams disclaimed any intention to carry on proscription.[62] He apparently did not choose to recall the details of his meeting with Webster on February 3, 1825. New bits of evidence, mostly in the form of statements by persons who claimed they had been told about the pledge, kept the controversy boiling through the summer.

By fall the essential facts of the Warfield letters were being accurately detailed in Jacksonian newspapers.[63] Webster, accordingly, sent Adams copies of the letters and asked if they should be published as a counter to the many false tales still circulating.[64] Adams would not consent and the election came and passed without any of the principals, Adams, Webster, or Warfield, stating publicly exactly what had happened. Their silence, of course, did little to discredit the persistent

[60] *New York Post*, April 18, 1828. See also J. Westcott to T. Ritchie, January 18, 1828, Van Buren Mss, LC.

[61] Hopkinson to Webster, April 19, 1828, R. Stockton to Webster, May 14, 1828, Webster Mss, LC.

[62] Adams, *Memoirs*, VII, 539.

[63] See, for example, the *New York Post*, September 2, 1828; and the *Boston Jackson Republican*, September 17, 1828.

[64] Webster to Adams, September 13, 1828, Webster, *Webster*, XVI, 181-82.

charges, founded as they were on the testimony of many persons to whom Webster and Warfield had talked in 1825. If anything, the harm was probably greater because editors could print many versions and offer new evidence during the course of many months. Warfield, in a long letter to Webster in 1830, recalled his surprise when the first allusion to a pledge letter had been made in the newspapers. Warfield assured Webster that he had shown the letters to no one, although he admitted that he referred to them in conversation.[65] The letter would indicate that Warfield still did not know that it was Webster who, in his jubilation, had been much less discreet than Warfield.

Administration leaders often expressed their bitterness, mostly in private, that in spite of all the allegations that Adams was busily reintroducing Federalists and Federalism into the national government, the fact was that Federalists, as a body, had not rallied to a vigorous support of Adams.[66] Besides the number whose sympathies were evenly balanced by complaints, there was an even larger corps enthusiastically huzzaing for the Hero. William Plumer noted in 1827 that four of the five United States Senators who were or had been Federalists were "bitter & constant in their opposition to the president," and in the only remaining Federalist state, Delaware, the Federalists as a party opposed Adams.[67] The editor of an Adams newspaper in Cincinnati, himself an active Federalist in former years, deplored the fact that the Jacksonians were most effectively organized in the Senate. "Most of my old federal friends," he fumed, "are parties in it. When Mr. Ridgely of Delaware can assort himself with Duff Green, God help us—I begin to distrust even myself."[68]

[65] Warfield to Webster, March 22, 1830, Webster Mss, LC.

[66] D. Webster to W. Gaston, May 31, 1826, Webster, *Webster*, XVI, 135.

[67] Plumer to B. Pierce, May 19, 1827, Plumer Mss, LC.

[68] C. Hammond to H. Clay, March 28, 1827, Clay Mss, LC.

Federalists had many reasons for not joining in support of the Administration. Some could not be convinced that Jackson's election would be desolating. Webster had tried to stir up activity in Philadelphia by warning in 1827 that the government would be overthrown, the judiciary destroyed, and constitutional decisions reversed if Adams failed. At least one life-long Federalist was not moved. "When the Federalists lost their power in 1801," he mused, "it was then as loudly proclaimed, and our fears as greatly awakened with respect to the consequences, as they can be now; yet our successful rivals stepped into our shoes only to tread in the same paths that we had followed."[69] To other Federalists, the Administration's sponsorship of higher tariffs and internal improvements was repellent. Almost without exception, Federalist newspapers which backed Jackson were anti-tariff, and even such a strong Adams paper as the *New York American* was vigorously free-trade throughout the period. Internal improvements rarely found New England Federalists enthusiastic, indeed most saw them as benefiting only the West, whence little good flowed. A powerful cause of unhappiness, one that increased with time, was Adams' refusal to appoint more than a token number of Federalists. Through newspapers and in countless private letters, Federalists fussed and blustered that their talents had not been rewarded.[70] As early as 1826 a friend wrote Jackson: "The federal party who supported him [Adams] are dissatisfied with the policy he has pursued— they expected he would bring into the Administration some of the Leaders of that party; and being disappointed in that, they have become restive."[71]

[69] Henry E. Scudder, ed., *Recollections of Samuel Breck with Passages from His Note-Books* (Phila., 1877), 258-60.

[70] Many Federalists were more angry that Adams had not fully honored the alleged "Webster Pledge" than that he had made it in the first place.

[71] A. Hayne to Jackson, July 20, 1826, Bassett, *Jackson Correspondence*, III, 306.

The sensitive pride of Federalists often stood in the way of active support for Adams. The president's apostasy, for example, still burned in many Federalist breasts. "The old Federalists, few in number," wrote crusty old John Pintard of New York, "owe Mr Adams no good will for his apostasy, wh has been rewarded, & his enmity to Gen. Hamilton."[72] The zeal displayed by some Adams Republicans in caustically denouncing Federalists was still another source of heartburning. Colonel Binn's *Philadelphia Democratic Press*, an extraordinarily effective Adams press, was a leading offender and the object of constant and bitter Federalist complaints. Federalists often believed that pleas for amalgamation were the last crushing blows. Such an explicit acceptance of defeat was unbearable. In October 1826 Clay asked Judge Peters' son why the Philadelphia Federalists still clung to their "old name & discipline," thus precluding cooperation with Adams Republicans.[73] Young Peters replied that he had long held Clay's views on the matter, but they were not the views of many colleagues. "Private grief," he explained, "disappointed ambition, a conviction that the entire surrender of the *name* will deprive some of the consequence they still retain as leaders, even of a broken corps, continue to influence many, and prevent their openly maintaining a cause, which upon their own principle, they must respect.

"Heretofore, also, very considerable obstacles have interposed to prevent numbers of the federal party from appearing in the field on the side of the administration—These were found in the pride of party, and in the influence of those who claim to have been martyrs to their principles; and more than from all these, there being no standard around which they could assemble with confidence, and upon the principles of approved constitutional and general policy."

[72] J. Pintard to his daughter, December 1, 1827, Barck, *Pintard*, II, 379.
[73] Clay to R. Peters, Jr., October 16, 1826, Peters Mss, PHS.

Peters begged Clay to remember these things when making appointments.[74] Already a significant segment of the old party in Pennsylvania had firmly decided to remain aloof; or worse, to become supporters of Andrew Jackson.

Jacksonian Federalists were compelled to rationalize many instinctive antipathies. The Hero's boast that he would have hanged the principal leaders of the Hartford Convention remained a bitter pill on many tongues. The hope was indulged that Jackson would retract, but he would only agree that he should have cited a different section of the Articles of War. Coleman then charitably suggested that Jackson had not been correctly advised about the convention movement, and had undoubtedly believed that New England really had teemed with spies. Still hoping that Jackson would modify his charge, Coleman sent him a copy of Otis's famous vindication, "in the hope & belief of disabusing him of the many errors with which false & gross information" had filled his mind.[75] Another Jacksonian Federalist, Vergil Maxcy, wrote an address in 1827 that was designed specifically to dispel the charge that Jackson's supporters were "mere followers of a mere military chieftain."[76] Others even tried to palliate Jackson's lack of education and notoriously bad spelling by stressing his courtly manners and genteel demeanor.

This process of rationalization, although painful, was often followed by an apparently genuine conversion to new political principles. In his 1827 address, Maxcy had advanced the theory that United States House of Representatives, acting in its electoral capacity, had a constitutional obligation to represent the views of its constituents. Maxcy confessed privately that he had become a "complete convert" to this doctrine.[77]

[74] R. Peters, Jr., to Clay, October 24, 1826, Clay Mss, LC.

[75] *New York Post*, April 4, 25, 1828. See also, the *Boston Courier*, August 7, 1827; and A. Jackson to H. Lee, December 25, 1826, Bassett, *Jackson Correspondence*, III, 318.

[76] V. Maxcy to T. Pickering, August 7, 1827, Maxcy Mss, NYPL.

[77] *Ibid.*

Ebenezer Baldwin, an active Jacksonian Federalist in Albany, proposed a plan that would require all eligible voters to cast their ballots at each election. Baldwin was enthusiastic, though quick to admit that he considered the plan "vitally important in our future operations."[78] The political principles spread across the pages of the *Boston Jackson Republican*, edited by an ardent Federalist, Theodore Lyman, Jr., must have amazed some of his friends. "The leading trait in the opinions of Mr. Adams," Lyman charged, "is a distrust of the qualifications of the people, in matters of government. His opinions were formed in the school of Burke, who adopted it as a leading principle, that government is, in sound theory, if not in its actual origin, a *compact*, in which the people and the government are respectively the contracting parties. Our government, on the other hand, derives entirely from the people."[79] Mr. Adams' "sin" would ordinarily be to Federalists a recommendation. Jacksonian Federalists found it politic in another dimension to show their fidelity by attending such public functions as an Albany Jackson celebration, which Moss Kent described distastefully as a "great feast & Ball at the Theatre, of all descriptions & sorts of People from Gov. Clinton & his Lady down to the humblest Walks of Life."[80]

Jacksonian Republicans used great skill in properly integrating and indoctrinating their Federalist auxiliaries. Duff Green explained to Jackson in 1827 that although he fully agreed with the strategy in New England and New York of identifying Republicanism with support of Jackson, he was "delicately situated" as editor of the *United States Telegraph* in Washington because "a large portion" of Federalists, patriotic ones of course, supported Jackson. "As names have charms which it is difficult to break," Green testified, "you will

[78] Baldwin to R. Baldwin, November 17, 1826, Baldwin Mss, YL.
[79] August 20, 1828.
[80] Kent to W. Kent, January 9, 1828, Kent Mss, LC.

understand the guarded position I occupy."[81] To his friend Maxcy, Calhoun carefully explained in 1825 that he had not intended to castigate only Federalists for their attitude during the War of 1812. He argreed that many firm Republicans had openly and freely stated then that however justified the decision to go to war no good could come of it.[82]

The acknowledged master of handling friendly Federalists was Martin Van Buren. When one of his "High-Minder" cohorts showed signs in 1826 of leaving the Jackson cause, Van Buren observed: "Nothing but the fear of being regarded as a deserter will keep him on the right side." The proper course, therefore, was to bruit about that his desertion was "a probable event attributable to the insincerity of his conversion."[83] Van Buren's part in bringing William Coleman, a testy fellow at best, to a harmonious place in the Jacksonian hitch was a thing of beauty. Van Buren wanted the influence of Coleman's *Post* in the campaign, and he spent considerable time and thought "caring" for him. Through intermediaries and flattering though firm letters Van Buren gently persuaded Coleman to be a tractable member of the Jacksonian coalition. He even convinced the old Federalist that the states' rights philosophy was a proper antidote for the Administration's swollen power.[84] These efforts would seem to belie, in part, the statement in Van Buren's *Autobiography* that Jackson had lost all his Federalist friends by 1828.[85] An Adams Republican, Jonathan Roberts, was convinced that without Fed-

[81] Green to Jackson, June 9, 1827, Bassett, *Jackson Correspondence*, III, 361-62.

[82] Calhoun to Maxcy, September 9, 1825, Maxcy Mss, LC. See also, Adams, *Memoirs*, VII, 491-93, wherein Robert Walsh tells of the efforts made by Jacksonians to secure his support.

[83] Van Buren to J. Hamilton, December 20, 1826, Hamilton, *Reminiscences*, 63.

[84] Van Buren to Coleman, April 4, 1828, *ibid.*, 77; Coleman to Van Buren, April 17, 1828, Van Buren Mss, LC.

[85] Fitzpatrick, *Van Buren*, 220, 449.

eralist aid Jackson could not have succeeded. "Ultra Federalism," he stormed, "panting after a system of Castes & Classes, & a strong executive; joined in the huzza for the hero . . . & thus laid the foundation on which to aspire to prominence."[86]

In some states Van Buren was more correct; in others, Roberts. The two men would agree, however, that Federalism and Federalists played a major role in the campaign. As in past years, this role varied from state to state.

[86] Klein, "Memoirs of Jonathan Roberts," 503.

CHAPTER XI

Amalgamation for Defeat

FEDERALISTS FLOWED FREELY into both presidential camps after 1824. Although the process varied in the several states, one characteristic stood out: The Adams Republicans tended to treat the Federalists as a bloc, whereas the Jacksonians tended to recruit them on an individual basis. Amalgamation, therefore, was a phenomenon associated with the Administration. Instead of being a mixture of the parties, amalgamation was really an alliance system. Being such, the Adams cause was made peculiarly vulnerable to Jacksonian charges of bargain and corruption (ironically, the "arrangements" Adams made with Clay and Webster before the election helped on the one hand to create the psychological "fix" that helped to determine the bloc approach and, on the other, to lend credence to the later Jacksonian charges that Adams was bargaining with Federalists). Reaction to this Jacksonian attack led the Administration to "pull back" at crucial times when an appointment or other action might have cemented an effective and vigorous alliance. The debilitating effects of indecision and confusion were but compounded by the suspicion that naturally arose within the ranks of Adams Republicans and friendly Federalists. Jacksonian leaders, ever alert and intelligent, fed upon the spoilage.

The state of New Hampshire was rocked by collisions between Federalists and Republicans in the late 1820's. The first moves toward amalgamation had floundered because of the way Jeremiah Mason and his friends had tried to win a Senate seat in 1824 and 1825. Tensions within the Republican party, however, caused two candidates, David Morril and Benjamin Pierce, to run in the gubernatorial race of 1826. Federalists, thus put in a decisive role, generally supported

Morril on the ground that Pierce was backed by Isaac Hill, the *enfant terrible* of New Hampshire Republicanism.[1] Hill's constant concerns were the purity of his party and the fear of resurgent Federalism. A Crawford man in 1824 but soon for Jackson, he kept his *Patriot* bubbling with hatred of Federalists and emotional defenses of the caucus system, which he insisted was the only means of preserving Republican ideals. At the same time, Hill tried to control the formal party machinery in the state by encouraging his friends to dominate local caucus meetings.

Filial devotion intensified Daniel Webster's constant interest in New Hampshire politics. During long and earnest conversations with Senator Samuel Bell, a leading Adams Republican, Webster decried the caucus and held out the promise of a strong Adams party based solidly upon a majority of both Republican and Federalist voters. If Bell and his friends refused to break with Hill and the caucus, Webster argued, the New Hampshire Federalists would not sit by quietly. Instead, they would take the lead in calling meetings of "all persons" friendly to the Administration, thereby leaving Bell's friends the unhappy choice of following the Federalists or joining Hill in opposition.[2] Since one-third of the legislature was Federalist in 1827 and an undoubted majority of New Hampshire citizens preferred Adams, the force of Webster's logic was compelling. Still, Bell was reluctant. The threat of Hill's fury hung like a pall.

The stage was thus set for the extraordinary events during and preceding the legislative session that began in June of 1827. Troubled by Webster's appraisal, Bell had returned from Washington, only to be swept into a meeting called by the "Republican friends of the Administration." The purpose of

[1] W. Plumer to L. Woodbury, March 9, and April 5, 1826, Plumer Letterbook, LC. See also, D. Morril to H. Clay, September 18, 1826, Clay Mss, LC.

[2] D. Webster to J. Mason, May 31, 1826, Hilliard, *Mason*, 304-305; Webster to Mason, April 10, 1827, Webster, *Webster*, xvii, 419.

the meeting was to express approval of Adams' policies in the form of resolutions that would later be introduced in the legislature. One speaker in effect apologized for Rufus King's appointment, and another damned the Jacksonian tactics in other states of tantalizing undecided Federalists with Jackson's friendly advice to Monroe while assuring Republican friends that no danger would flow "from the fraternal embrace of the former rival political parties." The object of all the speakers, Webster's brother charged, "was to prove Mr. Adams to be a democrat, & his administration to be strictly democratic, & more purely & entirely so, than Mr. Munroe's or Mr. Madison's or even Mr. Jefferson's. They vindicated him from the charge of being a federalist, or inclining to favor the Federalists. *This was the substance of their story.*"[3]

New Hampshire's Federalists were furious. To a man, Federalists in the legislature voted for postponement of the resolutions, and they were, of course, joined by the Jackson Republicans. As his brother had instructed him, Ezekiel Webster rose to explain his action. "Let the cause of the Administration be supported," he bristled, "on just and liberal principles: not proscribing men by classes, not for past political opinions, honestly formed, independently expressed, and honorably throughout maintained—or let it not be supported at all."[4] News went out over the country that the New Hampshire legislature had snubbed the Administration by a resounding vote of 137-70. The effect, both public and private, of these proceedings was devastating. Senator Bell and Ezekiel Webster parted "under a good deal of excitement" after a heated meeting, and Levi Woodbury, a leading Jacksonian, observed happily that the stinging defeat had disclosed "a firmness & independence among us."[5] The ardently amalga-

[3] E. Webster to D. Webster, June 17, 1827, Clay Mss, LC.
[4] D. Webster to E. Webster, April 4, 1827, Webster, *Webster*, XVI, 152; *Portsmouth Journal*, June 30, 1827.
[5] E. Webster to D. Webster, June 17, 1827, Clay Mss, LC; L.

mationist *Portsmouth Journal* tried desperately but vainly to repair the grievous damage.[6] Though angered, Daniel Webster kept at his friend Bell. If the Adams Republicans would not call a meeting of all friends of the Administration, Webster assured Bell that the Federalists would oppose every one of their candidates at the spring election in 1828.[7] Webster's words, alternately threatening and soothing, had their effect. Caught in a withering cross fire between Federalists on one side and the rampant Hill on the other, a group of Portsmouth Republicans finally issued a call of "all friends" to meet in December of 1827.[8]

This meeting marked the beginning of a slow and halting course of cooperation, made more painful by Hill's scathing editorials and the implacable insistence of the Jacksonians that the Republican party must stay pure. The Portsmouth meeting was followed by a "mixed" state convention which nominated a slate of state senators and put Senator Bell's brother at the head of their ticket. The Federalists had agreed not to put forward any of their men for these nominations, but they did so with the understanding they would be rewarded in the near future. Although the state senatorial slate generally succeeded, Bell lost. The *Portsmouth Journal* explained that the incumbent had only been in office a year and had not openly declared for Jackson. Added to this, the *Journal* confessed, were "some little remains of the old political prejudice against Mr. Bell because he was once a federalist."[9] By the fall elections in 1828 the Adams forces were acting in comparative harmony, but they had lost ruinously in numbers. The Jackson legions, working confidently

---

Woodbury to R. Jarvis, August 27, 1827, Jarvis Mss, LC; D. Webster to J. Q. Adams, June 30, 1827, Webster, *Webster*, xvi, 154-56.

[6] See issues of June 30, July 7, 14, 1827.

[7] D. Webster to S. Bell, October 15, 1827, Webster Mss, LC.

[8] *Portsmouth Journal*, December 15, 1827.

[9] *Ibid.*, March 15, 1828. See also, E. Webster to D. Webster, March 17, 1828 and E. Evans to D. Webster, April 4, 1828, Webster Mss, LC.

and decisively since the debacle a year and a half earlier, succeeded in breaking off great chunks of the overwhelming New Hampshire support Adams had enjoyed when he was elected.

The amalgamation forces in Massachusetts enjoyed happier days. Governor Lincoln was re-elected in 1826 over a feeble opposition candidate put up by disgruntled Federalists, but the alliance was still shaky, and many waited eagerly for its proprietors to stumble. The rise in 1827 of small and ephemeral parties based on local issues had allowed bitter-end Federalists again to harass the amalgamationists. A confusing mélange of tickets kept Boston from sending its full allotment of representatives to the General Court. Webster promptly denounced the Federalist obstruction as "folly," and "insanity," and in two major speeches pounded away at his central theme that all men of good will must stand together against the unsavory, slave-ridden Jacksonians.[10] Because the Bay State still backed Adams solidly, the Republican-controlled legislature later that year elected Webster, its second choice, to the U.S. Senate. Governor Lincoln was obviously the favorite, but he had declined to be a candidate.[11] No one else approached Webster as a talented and effective champion of the Administration. Only Adams' intervening election could have prompted Republicans, fresh from hard-fought victories in 1823 and 1824, to send Daniel Webster to the Senate in 1827.

For the masses of Massachusetts Republicans who supported Adams, however, the course of events after 1825 was deeply disquieting. They knew that the Federalists were gradually slipping back into power, yet they could find no way to curb them. The files of staunch Republican presses like the *Boston Patriot* and the *Springfield Republican* abounded with

[10] *Portsmouth Journal*, April 7, 1827, May 5, 1827; D. Webster to H. Clay, May 18, 1827, Clay Mss, LC.
[11] L. Lincoln to D. Webster, May 24, 1827, Clay Mss, LC.

signs of this frustration. The *Republican* editor, Samuel Bowles, had dedicated himself in 1824 to maintaining pure Republicanism, which naturally included regular attacks on the Hartford Convention and the "aristocracy of wealth." A firm Adams supporter, he tried in succeeding years to fight both amalgamation and Federalism, in spite of his acknowledgment that most Massachusetts Federalists stood behind Adams. Gradually Bowles shifted his main battery fire away from Federalists in order to combat the onrushing Jacksonians.[12] He had been caught in the same dilemma as those Federalist editors who, while supporting Monroe, had tried to rouse Federalists to independent action on the state level. An influential Republican relayed to Henry Clay in 1827 the general anxiety of his colleagues. "I have felt," he fretted, "that a bad policy has been pursued in relation to our own State, most certainly one that has effectually displaced the old Republicans and given the power into hands, that may not abuse it, but not as reliable, as I could wish—I urged upon Mr. Webster's friends the impolicy of placing him in the Senate—I had various reasons for it, but the one most operative with me was, that he was too strong a man to be made too Independent. . . . It was moreover too soon to commit so great a violence upon the old Republican feelings of the State —I hope however that he may be faithful—I hope to acquire more confidence in him hereafter."[13] The God-like Daniel left in his powerful wake a sea filled with drifting men, depressed by suspicion and distrust.

The amalgamation movement in Massachusetts reached a zenith in 1828. Webster was advised by the *Boston Patriot* editor in March that a large meeting of local Republicans had unanimously agreed to act with Federalists in the presidential election. "*From your exertions last year,*" the editor cooed,

[12] See files of the *Republican* through the period 1824-28, especially December 29, 1824, May 24, 1826, May 31, 1827, and April 9, 1828.
[13] H. Shaw to Clay, August 23, 1827, Clay Mss, LC.

"we think we shall reap a full harvest this."[14] A month later, a prominent Boston Federalist assured Webster: "The Union Administration Cause here can boast of an organization equal in efficiency and unanimity to that of the good old days of 1814-16."[15] At an harmonious convention called in June to choose Adams electors, a central committee was formed, which included the names of Henry Shaw, Timothy Fuller, and Joseph Sprague, all prominent Republicans, and Leverett Saltonstall, Abbot Lawrence, and John Winthrop, each a notable Federalist.[16]

There remained a group of Federalists who could not tolerate Adams the apostate. They gathered at the Exchange Coffee House in Boston to appeal to those brethren who had supported Crawford in 1824 and who had not since succumbed to the blandishments of amalgamation. Theodore Lyman, Jr., in the chair, the assemblage listened to perfervid speeches by Francis Baylies and Lemuel Williams.[17] The latter confided to his friend Vergil Maxcy that afterwards most fellow lawyers would barely speak to him in court.[18] Undaunted by meager success in the spring elections, this coterie began publication, with Lyman as editor, of an attractive newspaper, blithely styled the *Boston Jackson Republican*. It competed with the *Boston Statesman*, chief organ of the little band of Boston Republicans who had steadily supported Jackson. David Henshaw, leader of the Jackson Republicans, took a dim view of his new Federalist allies, and suggested that they had not come out openly until certain that Jackson would win the national election. Henshaw hoped they would stir up resentment in Federalist circles, but he intended to

[14] G. Fairbanks to Webster, March 12, 1828, Webster Mss, LC.

[15] B. Russell to Webster, April 14, 1828, *ibid.*

[16] *Address of the Central Committee . . . Friendly to the Election of John Q. Adams . . . Held . . . in Boston, June 10, 1828* (Boston, 1828).

[17] *Boston Columbian Centinel*, March 8, 1828; *New York Post*, March 14, 1828.

[18] Williams to Maxcy, April 1, 1828, Maxcy Mss, LC.

have nothing to do with them.[19] The two groups squabbled constantly during the campaign, each suspecting, with some justification, that patronage was the chief incentive for the other's activities. Lyman and Henshaw both openly thirsted for the collectorship of customs at Boston.

Although amalgamation did not develop as early in Connecticut, the pattern was similar. An ardent Jackson Republican, Gideon Welles, reported in June 1827: "A dish of amalgamation is ere long to be served up here as in Massachusetts and New Hampshire."[20] Connecticut Federalists, not blessed with a dominant leader like Webster, had wallowed in hesitation and conflicting advice from old captains. Most came to favor Adams though few sincerely admired him. A substantial number, including the most prominent, continued to despise the president. These men made common cause with Andrew Jackson.[21]

Republicans in the state, still nursing bitter memories of the 1817 election, tried manfully to keep the party together. Animosities stemming from differing presidential choices, however, together with long-standing jealousies within the party, led to an open rift in 1828. The naming of two slates of presidential electors, both entirely Republican, opened the way for Federalists to press amalgamation. A disgusted Jacksonian charged: "The Federalists altho innately divided in sentiment on the Presidential question will yet act together with a view to overthrow our Republican ranks. Alone they expect nothing under the national government. To divide & overthrow the republicans in the State is their whole object with us."[22] Jackson Republicans were well aware that Connecticut would go to Adams by a wide margin. Their hope

[19] Henshaw to R. Jarvis, March 5, and July 11, 1828, J. Boyd to Jarvis, March 5, 1828, Jarvis Mss, LC.

[20] G. Welles to H. Mitchell, June 26, 1827, Welles Mss, LC.

[21] T. Smith to R. Baldwin, March 14, 1827, Baldwin Mss, YL; J. Andrews to G. Welles, June 30, 1828, Welles Mss, LC.

[22] A. Sterling to G. Welles, June 22, 1828, *ibid.*

lay in the prospect that Jackson would win nationally, in which case they would make it easy for the Hero "to distinguish between his friends & enemies in this State." Yet the desire to attract a respectable vote for Jackson led a surprising number of fervent Republican supporters to recommend in the last months of the campaign that their friends avoid unduly affronting Federalists in election addresses and newspaper broadsides.[23] The break-up of the Republican party in Connecticut had cast up rich provender for Federalists.

In other New England states too, amalgamation was among the chief topics of political controversy. Many of the Republican leaders in Maine who had supported Crawford in 1824 soon swung over to Jackson. In spite of taunts from Adams men that these former Crawfordites had once tried to get Federalist support, the Jackson campaign was skillfully managed. Amalgamation was cut apart by tireless appeals to old Republican sympathies.[24] During an Adams convention in February 1828, one participant observed with pride and evident relief that although several Federalists had attended, all the committees were wholly Republican. This fact, he suggested, "should effectively silence the clamor, that it was a federal convention."[25] Such language was a tribute to the effectiveness of Jacksonians in a state that had backed Adams generously in 1824. A limited suffrage and a deep interest in manufactures led to successful amalgamation in Rhode Island, though again there was a hard core of Federalists which stood behind Jackson. Because Vermont Federalists had ceased for many years to act as a body, amalgamation there was a relatively minor issue.

Federalists and the image of Federalism greatly complicated the efforts of New York state voters to adjust to emerging

[23] See the Welles Mss, LC for the period June-October, 1828, especially R. Fairchild to Welles, June 23; R. Heinman to Welles, July 5; and J. Crawford to Welles, July 5.

[24] *Portsmouth Journal*, June 16, 1827, September 29, 1827.

[25] J. Hill to J. Bailey, February 4, 1828, Bailey Mss, NYHS.

national alignments. The twisting course of state politics after 1824, when a substantial majority of the electorate favored Adams over Jackson, led New York to give a majority of its electoral vote to the Hero in 1828. A variety of favorable circumstances in 1824-25 had pointed to the building of a powerful Adams party, firmly grounded in New York Republicanism. Among these were the strong sectional preference for a Northern man, the interest of New York in a high tariff policy, and the triumph of Adams Republicans over the Van Buren-Crawford faction in the 1824 electoral battle. The force of these factors, nevertheless, was blunted by the maladroitness of the Adams Administration, the skillful maneuvering of the Red Fox, Van Buren, and—not least—the actions of New York Federalists.

Adams and his advisers could not make up their minds what group in New York state should receive the Administration's blessings. By first offering the English diplomatic mission to Clinton, it appeared that Adams intended to make the Clintonians his chief support. This view was quickly dispelled when, after Clinton's refusal, the mission was given to Rufus King, an anti-Clinton Federalist. The appointment of another "High-Minder," John Duer, to a high position seemed to confirm the feeling that the Administration specially favored this coterie, articulate but few in numbers, which revolved around Charles King and his *New York American*. Such a policy, though foolish, would have had at least the virtue of consistency, but other major appointments went in turn to Clinton Republicans and Van Buren Bucktails. The possible advantage from these moves was, of course, largely destroyed by the total effect of a frantic scramble for votes from any quarter. This bungling was bad enough, but the one group that believed itself most entitled to executive favor, those Republicans who opposed *both* Clinton and Van Buren and who had carried the day in November 1824, received little encouragement from Washington.

Frequent pleas for aid by this last group were shunted aside in favor of various schemes to placate other factions. "Those Republicans who seceded from the Party—& won the Electors in this State," James Tallmadge complained in 1826, "now find themselves opposed by Clintonians—unsupported by the Crawford men & unacknowledged by the Genl Administration."[26] Clintonians openly scoffed at Tallmadge and his friends for having been let down by Adams, and Bucktails condemned them as renegades from the Republican party. Other Adams men deeply resented the Administration's continued flirtations with Clintonians. One termed this policy "a most fatal error," and the discontent grew worse when in the spring of 1826 Van Buren and Clinton entered into an "intimate negotiation leading towards an anti-Adams coalition."[27] Clinton's increasingly open support for Jackson was painful to those of his followers who preferred Adams, but the Administration offered these men no clearly defined and rewarding alternative.

Martin Van Buren was firmly convinced by the spring of 1825 that he must lead his Bucktail forces from support of Crawford to Jackson. He was equally aware, however, that an abrupt shift to the Hero in the face of general satisfaction with Adams' election and Jackson's poor showing in New York during the 1824 campaign would be disastrous.[28] Accordingly, the Red Fox first set out to intimidate and harass the Adams Republicans. He sidled up to Clinton, his ancient enemy, with the purpose of confusing his Republican opponents and possibly laying the base for a strong Jackson coalition. Then, in a startling *volte-face*, Van Buren suddenly threw his full support behind an Adams Republican who opposed Clinton in the 1826 gubernatorial election. The object was

[26] Tallmadge to J. Taylor, February 22, 1826, Taylor Mss, NYHS.
[27] J. Cramer to J. Taylor, January 10, 1827, *ibid.* Rufus King's son regarded the temporary Clinton-Van Buren alliance as a "coquette," which had assumed "the appearance of open prostitution." C. King to H. Clay, March 21, 1826, Clay Mss, LC.
[28] Fitzpatrick, *Van Buren*, 159.

to split sharply those Republicans who approved of the Administration but who disagreed violently about Clinton's merits. Not until the summer of 1827 did Van Buren feel strong enough to come out for Jackson openly. By appealing directly to Republican voters on the ground that Adams was the Federalist candidate, he further demoralized and weakened the Adams Republicans.[29] Their hopes of attracting Republican votes thus dimmed, the Adams forces began to listen to those Federalists who had offered their services to the Administration cause. The curse of amalgamation settled more firmly upon the Empire State.

A numerous body of New York Federalists, however, either supported Jackson openly or took no part for either candidate. The merchant community of New York City was nearly united in clamoring against Adams' tariff policy, and William Coleman's *Post* burnished rusting memories of John Quincy Adams' apostasy and his father's perfidy toward New York's adopted son, Alexander Hamilton. Jackson's advice to Monroe was not forgotten, nor were the many Federalists who had already gained prestige by following the Hero.[30] Of particular importance to the many Federalists who had become deeply attached to him was DeWitt Clinton's belief that his own fortunes would best be served by a Jackson victory. When Clinton stood behind one Enos Throop, for a vacant U.S. Senate seat in 1827, an Adams Republican bridled: "We cannot support our Clintonian Jacksonian candidate for the Senate. *We* prefer even a bucktail Jacksonian to a federal. Throop, you are aware I presume, is an old federalist, and

[29] M. Van Buren to A. Jackson, September 14, 1827, Bassett, *Jackson Correspondence*, III, 381-82.

[30] H. Martindale to J. Taylor, November 13, 1827, T. Rudd to J. Taylor, February 27, 1828, Taylor Mss, NYHS; E. Baldwin to S. Baldwin, February 27, 1827, Baldwin Mss, YL; J. Morgan to A. Flagg, December 4, 1827, Flagg Mss, NYPL; J. Townsend to I. & J. Townsend, January 21, 1828, Townsend Mss, NYPL.

then Clintonian, and his transition to Jacksonianism is natural and *necessary*."[31]

Clinton died before the 1828 election, which left many of his followers floundering about, though the intense loyalty Clinton inspired apparently caused many to do as "the great man" would have wished. More Clinton Federalists would probably have formed behind Adams if some of the "High-Minders," especially Charles King and other writers for the *New York American*, had relented in their abuse of Clinton.[32] Even among the "High-Minders," however, there was a schism as James Hamilton and Josiah Hoffman led a strong minority in support for Jackson.[33] A New York Federalist had to weigh many competing hates and desires in making his presidential choice. Many could make no firm judgment and remained aloof.

If Administration leaders were muddle-headed in directing New York affairs they were downright stupid in Pennsylvania, where sectional and economic factors (especially the tariff and internal improvements issues) were as favorable as in New York. Instead of forthrightly making every effort to build a strong organization rooted in Republican soil, letting Federalists come along if they wished, the powers at Washington harbored the strange notion that to amalgamate Philadelphians should be their chief concern. Adams made his Pennsylvania appointments with very few exceptions from among Republicans, but many of them had little influence or were outright Jacksonians. Often the impression got abroad that the Administration would rather have appointed Federalists.

Knowing Republicans suggested time and again that Jackson's many Federalist friends in Pennsylvania could be turned

[31] H. Martindale to J. Taylor, October 16, 1827, Taylor Mss, NYHS.

[32] J. Thomas to H. Clay, May 13, 1827, Clay Mss, LC.

[33] J. Campbell to G. Verplanck, April 9, 1828, Verplanck Mss, NYHS.

to advantage. Identifying Jackson with Federalism would, in the words of one supporter, "completely revolunize [*sic*] Penn^a in favour of the administration."[34] Samuel Ingham, a leading Jacksonian who lived in New Hope on the Delaware, hinted privately to Van Buren that there was substance to this theory. He lamented after a visit to a New Jersey county just across the river: "[There was] a good deal of torpor, owing to the fact of several active Federalists there having declared for Jackson—the Democrats seem yet at a loss and many are undecided."[35] A typical example of the Administration's foolishness was its treatment of John Binns, the tough Philadelphia Republican editor who had turned from Crawford to Adams during the winter of 1824-25. Obviously influential among Republican voters, Binns loaded his editorial salvos with charges that Jackson was remarkably popular in Federalist circles throughout the state. His sulphuric attacks upon Federalism itself brought howls of protest from Adams Federalists, who complained regularly to Administration leaders in Washington. Smitten with the will-o'-the-wisp of a triumphant liaison between Republicans and Philadelphia Federalists, these leaders treated Binns with less than candor and rarely heeded his pleas for money and perquisites.[36]

Philadelphia Federalists were among the most sensitive and prideful of the breed. They had maintained with outstanding success a tightly organized city machine in the fervent hope that at least one outpost of honor and respectability would survive the onslaught of Jeffersonianism. By 1826 they still retained a slight margin over the despised Republicans, but their whole focus, even more so than in past years, had become centered upon city affairs. Accordingly, cries of anguish drifted skyward when John Sergeant, after refusing a Federalist nomination for Congress, changed

[34] P. Markley to H. Clay, April 28, 1827, Clay Mss, LC.
[35] Ingham to Van Buren, July 31, 1828, Van Buren Mss, LC.
[36] J. Binns to H. Clay, May 10, 1826, B. Crowninshield to H. Clay, March 14, 1827, Clay Mss, LC; Binns, *Recollections*, 250.

his mind upon meeting with a Republican delegation which was both friendly to the Adams Administration and amenable to working with Federalists in Sergeant's behalf. Always moderate and thus acceptable to many Republicans, Sergeant hoped to force a realignment of Philadelphia parties by pitching his campaign upon support for Adams. But the majority of Philadelphia Federalists were mortally offended by his action. Acting from injured pride they promptly put up another candidate who would properly represent their narrow interests.[37]

An exciting three-way contest followed when the Jacksonians happily entered their own man. Oddity and chance provided the dismal climax: Sergeant and the Federalist candidate got exactly the same number of votes—a flip of the coin went against Sergeant. "There is a positive loss in Pennsylvania," mourned Adams in his diary, "and those who call themselves friends of the Administration have neither concert nor courage."[38] A young Federalist friend in Philadelphia assured Henry Clay that the Republican and Federalist friends of the Administration would thereafter work in concert.[39] The assurance was premature, and Adams' friends could not shake the delusion that if Federalists and Republicans could at last get together in Philadelphia, victory in the state would be theirs.

The wounds had not yet healed by the fall of 1827 when another Congressional race impended. Sergeant once more announced that he would be a candidate on a platform of outright support for the Administration. Those who controlled the Federalist machinery again thought seriously of running their own votary, but they compromised by withholding their imprimatur from any candidate. The Jacksonians thereupon

[37] S. Breck to W. Meredith, September 21, 1826, Meredith Mss, PHS; E. Ingersoll to H. Clay, September 22, 1826, Clay Mss, LC; *Boston Courier*, October 5, 1827.

[38] Adams, *Memoirs*, VII, 154.

[39] R. Peters, Jr., to Clay, October 24, 1826, Clay Mss, LC.

nominated a Federalist of their own with the hope of quietly drawing off dissidents. In spite of Sergeant's open preference, the speakers at a Federalist rally held in his cause avoided any mention of the presidential question. Sergeant felt called upon to apologize to Clay for the "politic" course.[40] Sergeant won, but still the Administration forces would not combine firmly. In July 1828 the Adams supporters called for a great peace meeting in Philadelphia to adjust their differences. Joseph Hopkinson and Sergeant were the main speakers at this highly publicized gathering, and each devoted most of his attention to the exhilarating effects of hoped-for amalgamation. Impressive resolutions were passed and tearful promises exchanged.[41] Here was prime grist for the Jacksonian mill and Adams' chances for winning the state slumped still lower.

The Jackson Federalists in Pennsylvania were led by James Buchanan, the leader of an efficient machine in Lancaster which could turn out a majority of 2,500 in a major election.[42] The *Lancaster Journal* followed Buchanan in his support for the Hero, it being one of three such Federalist presses in the state to do so—only five favored Adams. Outside Philadelphia no major Federalist leaders in Pennsylvania supported Adams in 1828. James Ross, Henry Baldwin, and William Wilkins, the captains of Pittsburgh Federalism, were ardent Jacksonians. Even in Philadelphia, Jackson ran surprisingly well in traditionally Federalist wards, and Joseph Hemphill, a Jackson Federalist, overwhelmed Sergeant in the Congressional contest.[43] It has been variously estimated that there were fifty or sixty thousand "Federalist votes" in the state, a fact that led one investigator—apparently un-

[40] Sergeant to Clay, September 26, 1827, *ibid.* See also the several letters from Sergeant to Clay earlier in the month.

[41] *Report of the Proceedings of the Town Meeting in the City of Philadelphia, July 7th, 1828* (Philadelphia, 1828).

[42] Klein, *Pennsylvania Politics*, 214-15, 221, 225; S. Ingham to M. Van Buren, July 31, 1828, Van Buren Mss, LC.

[43] *New York Post*, October 7, 17, 1828.

aware of the wide Federalist support for Jackson—to write that since Adams got about that number of votes in 1828 they were probably all Federalist votes.[44] Much closer to the truth is an estimate that Federalists divided their votes about equally between Jackson and Adams, a depressing result for the eager amalgamationists.

Federalists were also about equally divided in the other middle states. After a careful study of New Jersey politics in this period, Walter Fee concluded that although Federalists had no firm choice in 1824 they afterwards turned increasingly to Jackson.[45] When Richard Stockton and his son both came out openly for Jackson in 1827 (the result of their disappointment in not getting a federal judgeship from Adams) it became eminently respectable for New Jersey Federalists to become Jacksonians. Fee found that the most common and telling political argument used by the Adams Republican newspapers in New Jersey was the fact that Federalists dominated the state leadership of the Jackson movement.[46] The majority of Delaware Federalists had by 1828 turned from Crawford to Jackson, a factor which encouraged Adams Republicans there. Old party discipline on both sides had remained firm until 1827, when, for the first time, a Congressional election turned on the question of supporting the Adams Administration. Both men who contested for the seat in 1827 were Federalists, the Jacksonian nominee being the son of James Bayard, Delaware's most distinguished contribution to the Federalist hagiology. The Adams candidate won in a close election, but a majority of Federalists probably aided young Bayard.[47]

Maryland Federalists not only split down the middle in their presidential preferences for 1828, but they also assumed

[44] Florence Weston, *The Presidential Election of 1828* (Washington, 1938), 167.
[45] Fee, *New Jersey*, 272.   [46] *Ibid.*, 262.
[47] J. Sergeant to H. Clay, September 18, 23, 1827, Clay Mss, LC; *Boston Courier*, October 8, 1827.

commanding positions of leadership in both camps. At an Adams convention in 1827, Robert H. Goldsborough, a prominent Federalist, brought all the resolutions before the meeting and read the official address.[48] Appropriately, the semi-official Jacksonian reply to this address was written by Vergil Maxcy, Calhoun's Federalist protégé.[49] Maxcy was helped in his campaign for Jackson by such Federalist champions as Charles Carroll of Carrollton, Roger Taney, Charles Goldsborough, Benjamin Howard, and Charles C. Harper.[50] On the other side, Clement Dorsey, Henry Warfield, Daniel Jennifer, and George Hanson led the list of well-known Federalists who took an active part for Adams. Since the Federalists had given up their state organization before the 1824 election, formal amalgamation as such was not a pressing issue. Relations between Federalists and Republicans in their respective camps, accordingly, were more harmonious than was the case in most of the other New England and middle states. Adams and Jackson partisans, however, still tried on the one hand to stigmatize the enemy with the taint of Federalism and on the other to defend their own cause from such attacks. Contrary to its short-sighted policy in New York and Pennsylvania, the Adams Administration paid special attention to Maryland Republicans, particularly Governor Joseph Kent. He was in turn able to conduct a vigorous and effective campaign among Republican voters.[51]

By the spring of 1828, it was obvious to most observers that Andrew Jackson would be the next president. In spite of the unceasing anti-Federalist assaults that flowed from Jacksonian orators and presses, a large body of Federalists in the

[48] R. Goldsborough to H. Clay, August 9, 1827, Clay Mss, LC; *Proceedings of the Maryland Administration Meeting . . . 1827.*

[49] W. Grason to V. Maxcy, September 25, 1827, Maxcy Mss, LC.

[50] H. Niles to J. Taylor, May 10, 1827, Taylor Mss, NYHS; S. Smith to M. Van Buren, May 26, 1827, Steiner, "Van Buren's Correspondents," 142.

[51] C. Goldsborough to V. Maxcy, January 2, 1828, Maxcy Mss, LC.

various states had enlisted with the Hero. Motivated by a number of factors, these Federalists found most compelling the hope that under Jackson old distinctions of party would be erased and Federalists could once more assume their "proper" place in the conduct of public affairs. This hope was based in part upon an estimate of Jackson's character, the tone of his letters to Monroe, and upon the willingness of Jackson Republicans to forgive any man's past sins if he would swear loyalty to their leader. After his election, Jackson proceeded to appoint more Federalists to important offices than had been appointed by all his Republican predecessors combined.

CHAPTER XII

The Emancipation of a Numerous Class

THE ADAMS ADMINISTRATION crashed down in ruins— broken as well by its own political incompetence as by the commanding image of Andrew Jackson. What a supercilious Virginian termed "the first grand triumph of the rowdy principle in the U. States" was ushered in at the 1828 election by an altogether convincing host of voters.[1] Clear it was that the "respectable era" of national politics had come to an end.

Thus irony marked the challenge which the dumpy but very respectable man in the White House, with galling defeat looming before him, flung at the heirs of the once powerful Federalist party, the most respectable political assemblage of them all. Adams stated, in an article that appeared in the *Washington National Intelligencer* on October 21, 1828, that certain leaders of Massachusetts Federalism had, for a period of several years during Jefferson's presidency, contemplated the dissolution of the union and the creation of a separate confederation. Adams added that he had told Jefferson of these plans in 1808.

Yowls of anguished protest sprang from Federalists in swelling unison. The anger of Jackson Federalists was tempered with a quiet but malicious glee as they watched a sharp rift open between Adams and his Federalist supporters. "It is upon patriotic principles only," wrote one Adams man, "that he can be supported by old Federalists."[2] The *Salem* (Mass.) *Gazette* switched to Jackson, and William Coleman was probably not far from the truth when he wrote that New England would give Adams "a sulky, cold, dissatisfied sup-

[1] J. Harrison to H. Clay, March 18, 1829, Clay Mss, LC.
[2] T. Williams to R. Baldwin, November 3, 1828, Baldwin Mss, YL.

port."[3] Even such a militant adherent as the *New York American* expressed its disgust.[4] Adams' loyal friend, John Sergeant, reluctantly told his chief that the incident had provoked "a very extensive and unpleasant effect."[5] The controversy became even sharper after a series of public exchanges between Adams and a group of Massachusetts Federalists. Daniel Webster, with a heavy heart made wearier by a libel suit that had grown out of Adams' first charge, wrote his brother that there had never been a publication he "so regretted" as the *Intelligencer* article.[6] "Mr. Adams," wrote a bitter New York Federalist in March 1828 "goes out with little sympathy, having forfeited the confidence of those who made him president."[7]

To find Federalists who were genuinely grieved by Adams' defeat was difficult; those who were unhappy with both candidates or pleased with Jackson seemed much more numerous. Charles King, the *American* editor, feared the worst from Jackson, and Reverend Robbins, the parochial Connecticut diarist, termed Adams' loss a "pity."[8] Moving across the spectrum, the respective brothers of Daniel Webster and Chancellor Kent believed themselves "quite resigned" to the new president. Both approved of Adams' measures, but they had nothing but contempt for his "character."[9] Those Fed-

---

[3] *New York Post*, November 4, 11, 1828.

[4] *Philadelphia National Gazette*, February 10, 1829.

[5] Adams, *Memoirs*, VIII, 82.

[6] Webster to E. Webster, January 31, 1829, Van Tyne, *Webster*, 141.

[7] J. Pintard to his daughter, March 4, 1829, Barck, *Pintard*, III, 65.

[8] King to H. Clay, November 13, 1828, Clay Mss, LC; Tarbox, *Robbins*, II, 117. King was so exercised that he suggested to Clay that Virginia be induced to vote for Chief Justice Marshall in hopes that the election would be thrown into the House and with the understanding that all the Adams electors would also support Marshall. Clay endorsed the letter from King with the words: "Answered, disapproving decidedly the project."

[9] E. Webster to D. Webster, February 13, 1829, Webster, *Webster*, XVII, 469; M. Kent to W. Kent, December 16, 1828, Kent Mss, LC.

eralists who had campaigned for Jackson were, of course, overjoyed. Theodore Lyman, Jr., editor of the *Boston Jackson Republican*, expected an increased flow of Federalists to the Jackson banners, under which Lyman was confident they would be accepted with as much trust and respect "as any of the disciples of Jefferson, themselves."[10] Administration men were crushed by the course Robert Walsh pursued. For two years before the election he had become increasingly cool to Adams until in December 1828 he appeared entirely satisfied with Jackson's election. Adams' measures, he explained, "did not correspond with our hopes and anticipations. He selected co-adjutors, patronized systems, and pursued in his appointments a policy, quite different from those we supposed he would espouse."[11] Walsh was impelled primarily by his burning desire to help Federalists derive the distinction and self-fulfillment that flowed from public office.

Concern over Jackson's plans regarding appointments was not confined to the columns of Walsh's *Gazette*. A leading Boston Federalist, William Sullivan, had seen earlier in the year the probability that Jackson would be chosen. Sullivan asked his friend Webster: "Then comes the question, will the new president, attempt to live down the bad fame that has been affirmed of him—and call the first talents in the land into his counsels; or will he be forced to submit himself to the dominion of partizans, and persevere in a course of party favoritism,—& exclusion?"[12] Federalist editors, whether for Adams or Jackson, were as one in recalling the Hero's advice to Monroe. The *Portsmouth Journal* was sure that Jackson would act upon his own wise and magnanimous words, which Monroe "had not the moral courage to follow."[13] Walsh led the pack in these mouthings. In January he wrote a soaring piece depicting Daniel Webster's many talents,

---

[10] *Boston Jackson Republican*, November 29, 1828.
[11] *Philadelphia National Gazette*, December 10, 1828.
[12] Sullivan to Webster, May 12, 1828, Webster Mss, LC.
[13] January 3, 1829.

chief among them the fact "he never prompted, uttered nor countenanced invectives against General Jackson."[14] Henry Clay spoke sourly to Adams "of Webster's adhesion to the new Administration, proclaimed somewhat ostentatiously by a puffing article in Walsh's *Gazette*."[15] Such words, of course, were tinged with the bitterness both Clay and Adams felt toward Walsh in these grim months. Jackson Federalists were equally anxious that Jackson heed his advice to Monroe, but suggested one condition. "We may say what we will," warned William Coleman, "but the commander who refuses to reward the troops who have achieved for him his victories, will soon find himself without followers."[16]

Expectant Federalists eagerly scanned Jackson's list of cabinet officers. The name of John Berrien, a former Georgia Federalist, was at once singled out. Coleman characterized the new attorney general as a man of brilliant and substantial talents, who belonged to "the old Hamilton school of federalists."[17] Other editors soon learned that both Samuel Ingham and John Branch had at one time in their careers acted with the Federalist party. Jackson's action, the *Portsmouth Journal* rejoiced, was conclusive proof that "the bugbear, federalism, shall not terrify *him* at least."[18] Dispatching Louis McLane of Delaware to the top diplomatic post at St. James, however, was even more convincing. He came from a state north of the Potomac and had always been elected on the Federalist ticket. "Every patriotic citizen," Walsh wrote: "owes thanks and honor to General Jackson. He has first disregarded the unjust and mischievous distinction of quondam Federalist and Democrat, in the choice of functionaries of the highest rank. The *emancipation* of a numerous class of Americans, long proscribed after the original and every sound motive to their

---

[14] *Philadelphia National Gazette*, January 10, 1829.
[15] Adams, *Memoirs*, VIII, 89.
[16] *New York Post*, February 24, 1829.
[17] *Ibid.*, March 3, 1829.
[18] March 21, 1829.

disfranchisement had vanished, seems to have been effected as to the executive department of the General Government. This constitutes an era in our political annals, to which historians will refer as much more important and remarkable than it may now appear at slight observation."[19]

Other lesser appointments fell happily into the hands of grateful Federalists. Calhoun, for instance, used his influence to help a number of his Federalist friends. The post of solicitor to the Treasury was created in 1830 after much maneuvering, and Vergil Maxcy was named to fill it.[20] Two of Calhoun's New England friends, Francis Baylies and Lemuel Williams, received collectorships—though Baylies thought he deserved better and declined.[21] Other New England appointments went to a Federalist editor, installed as collector at Providence, and a New Hampshire lawyer, appointed U.S. Attorney.[22] An awkward situation arose when Jackson nominated James Hamilton to replace John Duer as U.S. Attorney in New York. Hamilton had always been a special protégé of Van Buren's, but Jackson made the appointment without consulting the new secretary of state. Restless New York Jacksonians, especially those who did not appreciate seeing their Federalist auxiliaries put in desirable posts, wondered whether Van Buren was as potent at Washington as they had supposed. Hamilton, for his part, did not wish to displace his fellow "High-Minder," Duer. In spite of these awkward circumstances, Jackson persisted.[23] Supreme Court Justice Bushrod

[19] *Philadelphia National Gazette*, June 18, 1829.
[20] See J. Calhoun to V. Maxcy, January 13, 1829, Maxcy Mss. LC.
[21] *Portsmouth Journal*, March 21, 1829. Williams was at first turned down in the Senate, but later he was confirmed. See, J. Calhoun to J. Hamilton, March 20, 1830, Calhoun Mss. NYPL; and J. Bailey to J. Davis, February 19, 1830, *Proceedings of the Mass. Hist. Soc.*, XLIX (1915-16), 219. Calhoun was probably responsible too for the appointment of C. C. Harper, son of Maryland's Robert Goodloe Harper, to a diplomatic assignment in June 1829. See the *Philadelphia National Gazette*, June 4, 1829.
[22] *Portsmouth Journal*, March 21, May 2, 1829.
[23] See J. Hamilton to "a friend," April 25, 1829, and J. Hamilton

Washington's death in 1829 set off a frantic scramble among the Jacksonian factions in Pennsylvania. Ingham's men hoped to elevate the Chief Justice of Pennsylvania's highest court and replace him with Horace Binney, a leading Philadelphia Federalist who had supported Jackson. The other main faction pressed upon Jackson the name of Henry Baldwin, a Pittsburgh Federalist. Baldwin was chosen amid considerable fluttering.[24]

For every Federalist who found his place in the new sun there were many more who tried and failed. If Adams had grown weary at the sight of a never-ending stream of Federalist supplicants, Jackson and his aides must have been utterly exhausted. Driven on by the number of Federalist appointments made in the early days of the new Administration and by a belief that Jackson was pleasantly naïve about political realities north of the Potomac, few of the prideful sect—young or old—doubted that the harvest season had at last arrived. Yet joy turned to sadness for most, in large part due to the watchful restraint of such Jacksonian stalwarts as Samuel Ingham, Martin Van Buren, and Levi Woodbury. These men had no wish to see Federalists devour the prize that had been brought to earth by a struggle in which Republicans had played the chief role. The jubilation of successful Federalist job-seekers and their friends was an added stiffener.

No state was free from a horde of hopeful Federalists. The clash between David Henshaw's Republican friends in Massachusetts and the Baylies-Williams-Lyman Federalist coterie was brisk. Both groups had their powerful friends, but the combined influence of Van Buren, and especially Woodbury, tipped the major share of patronage into the Henshaw camp, though he too had some Federalist allies whom he carefully

---

to W. Coleman, May 6, 1829, Hamilton, *Reminiscences*, 124, 137; and Fitzpatrick, *Van Buren*, 264-66.

[24] See H. Baldwin to J. Hopkinson, January 21, 1830, Konkle, *Hopkinson*, 284-85; and Klein, *Pennsylvania Politics*, 298-300.

slipped into patronage jobs.[25] Woodbury, who came from a state where Jacksonianism seemed to grow in proportion to the abuse dumped upon Federalists, also helped young Gideon Welles and Judge Niles, the leaders of the Jackson Republicans in Connecticut. The list of prominent Connecticut Federalists who had supported Jackson was a long one and few of them abjured the happy thought of a suitable place. Each side scored wins but Welles and Niles, both future cabinet officers, scored more often.[26] Republican jealousies frustrated Federalist ambitions in other states as well. James Ross was denied a judgeship in Pennsylvania and Roger Taney did not succeed in placing many of his Federalist friends in Maryland.[27] Although Solomon Van Rensselaer succeeded, by strenuous efforts, in keeping his Albany postmastership, young Alexander Hamilton was writing friends as late as 1830 in the vain search for a comfortable berth.[28]

Perhaps the most important reason for the resistance by Jackson Republican leaders in New England and the middle states to the appointment of Federalists was that such appointments might deprive them of a principal source of strength, i.e., local identification of Jackson with the "old" Republican party. Jacksonian orators and editors continued to label their opponents with the words "Federalist" or "aristocratic," without being careful or indeed interested in distinguishing genuine Federalists from Republican "renegades." If confronted with evidence that many leaders of the National Republican

[25] In a long, impassioned letter, Francis Baylies detailed some of the intricate maneuvering that had gone on in Massachusetts. Baylies to E. Livingston, November 20, 1829, Miscellaneous Mss, MHS.

[26] See the voluminous correspondence during 1829 in the Baldwin Mss, YL, for the astonishingly persistent efforts of Connecticut Federalists to get appointments. The other side of this effort is recorded in the equally voluminous correspondence for the year 1829 in the Welles Mss, LC.

[27] Adams, *Memoirs*, VIII, 351; R. Taney to S. Ingham, August 14, 1829, Steiner, *Taney*, 84-5.

[28] Sol. Van Rensselaer to his wife, June 29, 1829, Bonney, *Legacy*, I, 487; A. Hamilton to V. Maxcy, August 8, 1830, Maxcy Mss, LC.

party were respected Republicans of long standing, these editors and orators were quick to say that what they really had in mind was the fact that Federalist principles or policies had become those of the opposition. Thus, the address of the convention which nominated Jackson and Van Buren in 1832 could insist that Jackson had brought the country back to the clear lines that had existed in 1800 and that the National Republicans occupied "precisely the ground of the federalists."[29] Such a position was enormously effective politically.

Two other obstacles stood in the path of the Jackson Federalists. Jackson's lieutenants, especially Republican leaders from northern states, insisted that if Federalists wished to follow the Hero they must be willing to become obedient soldiers in the ranks, neither asking nor expecting special attention. Further, they must show an inclination to see the merits in the doctrine of states' rights and the Jeffersonian concept that the "people" could govern themselves.[30] The

[29] *Summary of the Proceedings of a Convention . . . for the Purpose of Nominating a Candidate for the Office of Vice-President . . . Held at Baltimore . . . May, 1832* (Albany, 1832), 11-12.

[30] When Vergil Maxcy sent his friend Timothy Pickering a copy of Maxcy's Jackson address written in 1827, he foresaw that Pickering probably would not accept all of its reasoning. "I fear," Maxcy wrote, "you will not assent to all the views taken in the address—and particularly to the construction we give to the constitution with respect to the duty of Members of the H. of Representatives, when acting in an electoral capacity. I confess myself to be a complete convert to the Doctrine of the Address in this regard." Maxcy to Pickering, August 7, 1827, Maxcy Mss, NYPL. In 1828 when Van Buren was trying to enlist William Coleman in the Jackson cause, he did not rest on purely expedient reasons. Instead, Van Buren set forth an extended defense of the states' rights doctrine and detailed several instances in which the central government had, in Van Buren's view, interfered unduly in state matters. Van Buren to Coleman, April 4, 1828, and Coleman to Van Buren, April 17, 1828, Van Buren Mss, LC. Many of the editorials that appeared in the *Boston Jackson Republican* contain sentiments that strongly suggest at least a partial "conversion" of its Federalist editor, Theodore Lyman, Jr. If not, they were the product of extremely clever stage-acting. See, for example, the issue of August 20, 1828.

mystique of Jacksonianism demanded the catharsis of conversion, which, in the case of Federalists, manifested itself in the denunciation not only of the character of Federalists who stood with the National Republicans, but also of their principles. As the years passed, however, certain policy decisions of the Administration were exceedingly repugnant to many Federalists who had joined their fortunes to those of Jackson. The great "Bank War" was, of course, chief among the causes that led Federalists away from the Hero.

The reward of distinction and office remained for loyal Jackson Federalists, in spite of these crosscurrents. James Hamilton, Roger Taney, and Louis McLane stood as continuing symbols of Jackson's generosity and power. Loyal followers continued to abuse and ridicule their wayward colleagues who stayed in opposition. Webster reported sadly to his brother in New Hampshire that among Jackson Federalists in the Senate he found as much bitterness as ever appeared in Isaac Hill's *Concord Patriot*.[31] Jackson's policies were accepted also. Robert Walsh, once Adams' fondest admirer, termed Jackson's first annual message a first-class performance; marked by "comprehensive views, clear representations, instructive suggestions, adequate diction, patriotic spirit, and personal good faith."[32] Walsh was, to be sure, unhappy about the section devoted to bank matters, and he became more critical in 1830. Still, he did not officially break with the Administration until the bank crisis had deepened.[33] Jackson's cause remained attractive to Federalists during the early years of the new decade, much to the disgust of a hostile New Yorker who described a Regency meeting in 1832: "What made the scene truly laughable, was to see so many old Federalists acting a conspicuous part in the farce—out of the fine speech-makers [*sic*] three were of the

[31] Webster to E. Webster, February 5, 1829, Webster, *Webster*, XVI, 187.

[32] *Philadelphia National Gazette*, December 10, 1829.

[33] *Ibid.*, December 11, 1830.

real old-fashioned thorrough [*sic*] Federal stamp, who, a few years ago . . . would have sent Van Buren and all his party to the Divel [*sic*] but now for-sooth they are flaming Democrats—and stand forth before the people the bold champions, and brave defenders of the much Injured—and *persecuted* Martin Van Buren . . . & denouncing with bitter execration those . . . who dare oppose the omnipotence of Andrew Jackson."[34]

After their terrible defeat in 1828 it fell to the lot of Clay, Webster, and other prominent Adams leaders to build a co-ordinated opposition party strong enough to overthrow Jackson's formidable legions. They failed in this enterprise for a number of reasons. Not the least was the same kind of political ineptitude that had plagued them earlier. Just as Federalists and Federalism had offered hope and brought despair to Administration leaders before 1828, so did they continue to titillate and scourge the anti-Jackson forces. Daniel Webster dreamed of a clear realignment of parties based upon the tariff and internal improvements issues, and he even believed that under his own leadership a united New England would swing the balance in favor of a president committed to the overthrow of Jacksonianism. Yet he and his Federalist colleagues, perversely, did much to frustrate their own hopes. They did so in spite of Webster's signal contribution to the cause and the fact that "the upper stratum of society" became increasingly disturbed by the program and methods of governing that marked Jackson's Administration.

Partisans of Adams and Clay intensified their efforts to dispute the Jacksonian claim to purity and "exclusive Republicanism." Using ridicule and sarcasm, anti-Jackson editors pointed accusing fingers at the many Federalists active in Jackson's cause at the same time they reeled off the names of "true-blue" Republicans who stood out against the Hero. "How these men can claim to be the exclusive republican

[34] S. Campbell to J. Taylor, March 24, 1832, Taylor Mss, NYHS.

party," one editor despaired, "while their leader is making his appointments from the old Federal party, is more than we can conceive."[35] It would appear, he wrote later, that "the moment a federalist is appointed by the president, he stands 'emancipated and disenthralled' from the fetters of federalism in the opinion of the Jackson party, and becomes as completely identified with *what they call the republican party* as if he had never belonged to any other."[36] He wondered what these men had done to purify themselves. "Where is the pool," he asked in mocking tones, "in which they have washed off the political leprosy of former years?"[37] This line of attack was not confined to public prints. A friend assured James Barbour, the displaced minister at London, that his recall, "& being supplanted by a federalist," had not been relished in Virginia.[38] A volatile Ohioan was more incredulous. "I thought he *dare not* select his whole important appointments from that old party," he raged, "but he has done it, and the country must bear the consequences."[39] He must have been even more excited when both Roger Taney and Louis McLane had been elevated to the cabinet.

Many Adams Republicans were as uneasy about those Federalists in their own camp as they were exasperated that Jackson had made so many Federalist appointments. A prescient Massachusetts Republican, Henry Shaw, conveyed the misgivings of many in a long and thoughtful letter to Clay. He began by acknowledging his "profound admiration" for the many talents of Daniel Webster. "What then," Shaw asked: "are the objections to following his suggestions! Mainly his name & his former associations—the Old lines should be maintained if for no other purpose, for this, that the cry which has put you down & put Jackson up, may be neutralized—It

[35] *Connecticut Mirror*, July 11, 1829.
[36] *Ibid.*, November 14, 1829.
[37] *Ibid.*, April 4, 1829.
[38] J. Pleasants to Barbour, May 30, 1829, Barbour Mss, NYPL.
[39] J. Heaton to C. Heaton, April 30, 1829, Heaton Mss, LC.

answers no purpose for us to say that the old Parties are dead, while the other side say they yet live, and avail themselves of this declaration to fasten odium upon us, while they are the friends of the People—It was the howl of saving Democracy that fixed Pennsylvania, & New York, & Ohio—and this will be kept up hereafter to promote the ends of the Combination."

The events of the late war had left a deep imprint upon the Republicans of New England, Shaw continued, and the associations of names and things would only gradually be forgotten. Webster had labored to keep Levi Lincoln in the governor's chair with combined Republican and Federalist support because he knew that he could control Lincoln, and that the Federalists would maintain "a real ascendancy" under Webster's auspices. "Well this would be true for a while," Shaw agreed, "and possibly Massts might be thus held for any period—but what is the effect elsewhere—decidedly *fatal*—the names of Webster, King, Storrs, Sergeant, Hopkinson, Quincy &c &c—will make us the *Federal Party*—& that is all that is necessary to secure us a quiet repose—You must be made a Democratick Candidate or you must fail—the feeling of N England is decidedly with you, it can only be turned from you by the too close adhesion of old Federalists."[40]

New England Republicans struggled to avoid the too close embrace of the Federalists, but in most states they were unable to stop the steady march of amalgamation. The *Boston Patriot*, most influential of the Adams Republican presses in New England, supported in November 1828 a meeting called in Boston to "reorganize" the Republican party. Held on the same night as a "Jackson Republican" conclave, the meeting did not kindle the fire needed to fuse anti-Jackson Republicans into a tough and lasting unity.[41] Efforts to

[40] Shaw to Clay, January 9, 1829, Clay Mss, LC.
[41] See the *Boston Courier*, November 24, 1828. Robert Walsh ridiculed this effort of Boston Republicans. See the *Philadelphia National Gazette*, December 2, 1828.

popularize the new sobriquet "National Republican" met with restive murmurings among those Massachusetts Republicans who had been bred on the power of the simple word Republican.[42] An era was passing. Up the Connecticut River, New Hampshire Jacksonians swept into power at the spring elections in 1829 and even before the election, William Plumer had recommended with regret to Adams Republican leaders that they must offer Federalists a few places on the anti-Jackson slate.[43] Plumer's friends complied grudgingly, thereby in effect, surrendering the Republican label to their opponents. It was sad work.

Amalgamation was a juicy enough target for Jacksonians, but in at least one major city the Federalists insisted upon maintaining their own organization into the early 1830's. The years might dim memories of amalgamation; they could not blur the fact of an open Federalist machine in Philadelphia, which remained to many Republicans a proof that Jacksonians were not pummeling straw men when they insisted the Federalists were still dangerous. A deep reaction had followed the great peace meeting in 1828 at which Adams leaders had tried to combine Federalists and Republicans into a single phalanx. Resentful of these efforts to destroy their carefully wrought machinery, many Federalists threw up their hands in horror when the city government was captured by Republicans in 1829. Their efforts to regroup opened old wounds and led John Binns, the battle-hardened Republican editor, to search for new ways to combine the opposition to Jackson. "You know my Dr Sir," he wrote John Sergeant in 1834, "how zealously & earnestly I laboured to induce our Federal friends from the earliest stage of the Jackson contest to associate under the Democratic banner & name. They would not do it, nay even to this day they have resisted such an organization although they have seen, for years, that the

<hr/>

[42] W. Lovering to J. Bailey, March 17, 1829, Bailey Mss, NYHS.
[43] Plumer to S. Bell, December 9, 1828, Plumer Letterbook, LC.

heretofore most thorough-going partizans of the Federal party—for example James Ross and Timothy Pickering—*as Jackson men*, were content to attend Democratic meetings & associate and act under that name. Shall we continue to keep our eyes shut against light & knowledge & remain deaf to the voice of experience? I ask the question because I would use a name, as well as principles, which are dear to the people to induce them to associate and preserve the institutions & with them the happiness & prosperity of our country."[44] Sergeant had long believed that the Philadelphia Federalists had acted stupidly, but for that very reason he was suspect among his old colleagues. Pride and frustration mixed badly.

The peculiar sensibilities of Federalists plagued the efforts of anti-Jackson leaders in other ways. A friend of Henry Clay, one William Lawrence, reported from New York City in 1830 that he and his friends had carefully wooed the Workingmen's party there as an instrument to help overthrow the Regency, but their efforts were being thwarted by the inability of certain wealthy Federalists to distinguish between Lawrence's group and the party of Robert Owen and Fanny Wright, the radical reformers. Both parties had the same name, but Lawrence could not understand why "those timid friends" did not realize that any group which attracted Chief Justice Spencer and "other men of property and education" was unlikely to favor agrarianism.[45] When Massachusetts Republicans suggested to Adams that he run for governor in 1833, the ex-president scoffed: "I am as you know, of long Standing an outlaw to the federal party and especially to its leaders in this State." Adams also mentioned that his anti-Masonic activities had helped wreck his reputation.[46]

[44] Binns to Sergeant, January 17, 1834, *Penn. Mag. Hist. and Biog.*, xxxi (1901), 499. See also, J. Robertson to W. Meredith, August 20, 1829, Meredith Mss, PHS.
[45] Lawrence to Clay, November 29, 1830, Clay Mss, LC.
[46] Adams to A. Everett, July 23, 1833, Adams Mss, LC.

Anti-Masonry cut sharply across the ranks of Federalism. In New York, where the fanatic sect had first sprung up, forces opposed to the Regency hoped that anti-Masonry could be brought into concert against Van Buren and Jackson. Encouraging moves in this direction were suddenly blasted when a group of Federalists committed to Henry Clay worked against the anti-Masonic gubernatorial candidate in 1830. "After every demonstration that could be made that the entire party of Anti-Masonics was in favor of the American system," a friend mourned to Clay, "Abraham Van Vecten, with many others avowedly opposed to the Jackson interest, gave their influence decidedly, openly and vigorously on the side of the Regency." Thus deceived, Clay's supporters doubted that they would ever get the support of anti-Masons.[47]

The anti-Masonic forces were as determined to avoid the taint of Federalism as they were not to accept Clay. Jacksonians had made a sustained effort in many states to check the cult's spread by linking it with the dreaded Federalists. William Wirt related to his friend Dabney Carr, that just after his nomination for president in 1831, a group of anti-Masonic leaders, headed by John Spencer of New York, took him aside for a private talk. They confided to their new candidate that some friends were hinting darkly that Wirt had not always "belonged to the Republican School of Mr. Jefferson." Wirt answered that he had taken his political principles

[47] B. Stoddard to Clay, November 8, 1830, Clay Mss, LC. Another of Clay's friends wrote him that the Patroon, Stephen Van Rensselaer, had called out his "numerous tenants" to vote against the anti-Masonic candidate, Francis Granger. W. Lawrence to Clay, November 8, 1830, Clay Mss, LC. Granger was so angry at Clay's Federalist friends that he wrote Edward Everett a nasty letter in the spring of 1831, answering Everett's suggestion that the anti-Masons and the National Republicans pull together against Jackson. Everett was so taken back by the tone of Granger's letter that he hesitated even to acknowledge it. Everett to Granger, November 10, 1831, Granger Mss, LC. See also, J. Willard to A. Flagg, August 20, 1830, Flagg Mss, NYPL, for evidence that "federalists opposed to Antimasonry" had already begun to act with the Regency in the summer of 1830.

from Jefferson and Monroe. The gentlemen pressed him for details. Wirt thereupon said that he just happened to have with him a letter written by Jefferson himself urging Wirt in 1808 to enter Congress in order to help support Madison's new Administration. Spencer and his friends broke into smiles as they read the letter. One exclaimed that the letter was worth "a cartload of gold" to them. Could they publish the letter at once? Wirt demurred until he could ask his confidant, Carr. The new candidate thought the idea a good one, but perhaps it would be well if Carr, who was writing a short campaign biography of Wirt, could "abate the federal prejudices" that would arise by mentioning some passages in Wirt's biography of Patrick Henry that would imply Wirt was not a strong party man.[48] Politics in these years was a demanding business!

Unhappy though they were with their Federalist allies, anti-Jackson Republicans did not in their campaign addresses try to disparage Jackson for his Federalist appointments or to dissociate themselves from such Federalists as wished to oust the Hero. The National Republican Convention, which nominated Clay and John Sergeant, pointed with pride in its official address to the heady draughts of nationalism which during Adams' Administration had blurred old party distinctions. Jackson, however, was blamed for once more dividing the country into hostile groups. The National Republicans praised Jackson's famous advice to Monroe but made no mention of his many Federalist appointees. Instead, they damned the Hero for not being charitable toward those who did not electioneer for him.[49] Local conventions of National Republicans continued to deplore Jacksonian claims to exclusivity and argued that the only meaningful issue in the early 1830's lay between following Jackson and preferring

[48] Wirt to Carr, September 30, 1831, Wirt Letterbook, LC.
[49] *Journal of the National Republican Convention . . . in the City of Baltimore, December 12, 1831 . . .* (Washington, 1831), 19.

justice and enlightenment. Political antecedents were adjudged to be irrelevant.[50] Why did the National Republicans choose to affect this posture? Perhaps the two most important reasons were that as a loose minority grouping they were forced to accept any aid they could find, Republican or not, and the fact that Federalists had by then crept into positions of power within the party structure. The many Federalists who had passed into the Jacksonian ranks were either true converts or, more frequently, were kept under the firm discipline of the Hero's astute lieutenants from the northern states. These men were able to impress upon their Federalist auxiliaries that Jackson was quite able to part with some of his support.

For thousands of Federalists the onset of Jacksonianism was deeply distressing. They did, however, find some comfort in the knowledge that most "respectable" men shared their despair. Variations on this theme were infinite. To some, their friends were "mostly quiet moral people—men of wealth and influence"; to others men of "moral weight & worth," or "the greater part of the intelligent and reading citizens." The most expressive word continued to be "respectable." A Jackson orator in Maryland took notice that a previous Adams meeting had been described as the most numerous and respectable ever held at that place. As he surveyed his audience the orator wryly observed that it would appear "numbers, and *some* respectability at least, is still left for Jackson."[51]

Respectable or not, Federalists by the early 1830's contested no elections, with one or two exceptions, under their ancient and honored name. Yet many Republicans still had not shaken off the subtle mixture of respect, envy, and awe

[50] See, for example, *An Address to the People of Maryland, from Their Delegates in the Late National Republican Convention* . . . (Baltimore, 1832), 7-10; and *Journal of the Proceedings of the National Republican Convention, Held at Worcester, October 11, 1832* (Boston, 1832), 19-20.

[51] *Speech of Thomas Kennedy . . . at the Jackson Meeting . . . in Hagers-Town . . . 1827* (Hagerstown, 1827), 1.

which had heightened their dislike of Federalists. They firmly believed that Hamiltonians still were able to exert an influence far out of proportion to their numbers. A life-long Republican, Ebenezer Sage, reflected this feeling when he wrote in 1831: "I know very well the Aristocracy, will finally prevail, & will show to the world a splendid Govt and a half starved, lousy population of white slaves, as in the case of the world. . . . The *Gentlemen* will be too cunning for the *Simple men.*" A Federalist could never become a Republican, Sage thought, "although the converse of the rule may, & often is the case."[52] A Republican physician in Connecticut bewailed the fact that in his county many theretofore firm Republicans had begun to act during the late 1820's with the old enemy. "When I see so many who are freemen, by our exertions when the word Democrat was a reproach," he sighed, "& against the strain of every federal nerve, voting with those their enemies, & preferring to act under Masters, I sometimes wonder that any intelligent men are left among our party & sometimes have a strong inclination to give up what are called the poorer class to their own destruction."[53]

Such dismal reflections were usually expressed in private, but another Connecticut Jacksonian, R. R. Heinman, chose to unburden himself at a local convention. He began by assuring his audience that those Republicans who stood with Adams had done so because they were "encouraged & flattered by the Federalists." He saw but little consolation in the fact that Republicans were not the first nor would they be the last "to share the fate of fallen Adam in the garden, by the weakness or treachery of our dearest friends." Comparing Webster's legions to the serpent, Heinman begged his friends not to succumb further. Amalgamation was a vicious trap which was all too alluring because, in the words of another "true" Republican, "many of the Democrats of Connt had

[52] Sage to J. Taylor, February 10, 1831, Taylor Mss, NYHS.
[53] S. Simons to G. Welles, February 25, 1829, Welles Mss, LC.

been so long under bondage to the federalists, that now while they have all the powers of the govt entirely in their hands, they could not pass a federalist, without dowsing their cap and exclaiming—*how do Massa.*" Heinman ended by exhorting the faithful to *"abandon Massa . . .* pause—consider—and unite—to support the great Republican family."⁵⁴ These passages go far to explain why Federalists and Federalism remained political issues of great moment long after there had been any real prospect that the party of Washington could win a national election. They help, too, to explain why so many Republicans wildly welcomed Jackson as a deliverer. Strength of character, firmness, determined action—even rashness—would all be necessary to turn back the ever-present enemy, whatever guise he wore. Under Monroe and Adams, Republicans had grown apprehensive and their self-confidence, built up so lovingly by Jefferson, had been sapped.

Reassertion of a two-party system during the 1830's marked the end of real conflict between Republicans and Federalists. Members of both old parties found their way into the new groupings, and new issues arose to ruffle the voters. Yet many of these issues were cast in terms that were only too familiar to those who had fought the battles of an earlier day. The name and aura of Federalism retained their strange and lingering power to evoke strong emotional response. A prominent New York Whig, Erastus Root, reported in 1840 that of the three surviving electors who had voted for Jefferson in 1800 and the nine surviving legislators who had voted for these electors, all but one was a Whig. Root wanted to name several of these men to the Harrison electoral slate. "I wish to present a ticket unequivocally of the Jefferson school," he concluded, "to repel effectively the charge of federalism too successfully made against us."⁵⁵

⁵⁴ Heinman to G. Welles, February 8, 1831, *ibid.*
⁵⁵ Root to J. Taylor, July 16, 1840, Taylor Mss, NYHS.

As year followed year some Federalists found only the glow of former glories to warm their hearts. The secretary of the Hartford Convention, Theodore Dwight, announced to Chancellor Kent as late as 1837 that he intended to write a book denouncing Jefferson. Dwight asked his venerable friend to comment upon a long list of particulars he had drawn up against Jefferson, because he had no opportunity to consult with "old Federalists," most of whom were dead, and he had found few among the younger ones from whom he could "derive any benefit."[56] A former Federalist governor of Connecticut could, in 1844, think of few ways to fling out against the powers of darkness. Only fond reveries remained. "I know not what may be your feelings," he rhapsodized to a friend: "but as to myself, I am prouder than ever of the name of *Federalist*; a name 'lovely and of good report,' associated with the halcyon days of Washington and Hamilton, commemorative of their patriotick and invaluable labours, and which in all future time will distinguish the first twelve years of our national government as the *Golden Age* of the American Republick."[57]

[56] Dwight to Kent, July 3, 1837, William Kent, *Memoirs and Letters of James Kent, LL.D.* (Boston, 1898), 219.

[57] J. Smith to "A Friend," December 21, 1844, William W. Andrews, *The Correspondence and Miscellanies of the Hon. John Cotton Smith, LL.D.* (New York, 1847), 183.

CHAPTER XIII

The Twilight of Federalism

T HOMAS JEFFERSON taught his followers thoroughly. They should always fear and distrust Federalists. To Jefferson and his disciples Federalism did not represent simply a complex of specific government policies. Rather did it symbolize a denial of the capacity of men generally to govern themselves or even to live successful and happy lives of their own. On this and other levels Federalists represented to Republicans all that from which they were consciously and even desperately trying to depart—strong government by the favored few, rigid class stratification, and wide differences in personal wealth. Often when troubles arose under Republican rule, Jeffersonians were tormented by half-doubts that perhaps the Federalists were right, that no successful society could ignore centuries of historical experience, be it that of eighteenth-century Great Britain or ancient Greece. The actual experience of government during the administrations of Jefferson and Madison, when Republicans were compelled to adopt many Federalist policies, tended to increase these doubts. So did the knowledge that tens of thousands of confirmed Federalists remained.

What sustained Jefferson's party, however, was the wide support received from "the people." This support added constantly to the almost mystical faith in, and gratitude to, the so-called average citizen. It led them on the one hand to extend the suffrage even further and on the other to fear divisions within their own party. How, they asked, could "the people" be served in other than the true Republican way. Republicans found continuing and real meaning in charges that their opponents were aristocrats or even monarchists who harbored contempt for most of the people. Such feelings, once planted firmly in Republican minds, were not easily erased, even by a series of political victories or the disappearance of sharp policy differences between the parties. Republicans believed Federalists to be ever dangerous as long as they continued to possess wealth, education, and resourcefulness. To keep them out of political life demanded constant vigilance, firm organization, and astute leadership. Popular government had not been obtained for so long, even in America, that men could simply shrug off charges that there lurked about men who would destroy democratic institutions. For many Republicans of little means and lowly estate there was an added impetus. Leadership of the Republican forces had come largely from men whose wealth and learning were characteristic of ruling classes throughout history. The ideological commitments of these leaders to democracy and republicanism were perhaps tenuous bases upon which simple folk could rest their hopes for a continuing democratization. Thus it behooved the Republican rank and file, as well as the leaders, to harry Federalism until it lay very, very still in its grave.

None could dispute that many Americans did doubt the capacity of most men to determine their government's policy. Federalists generally subscribed to the view that the passions governed actions by "the people," who, if given unchecked power, would tear down the temple of government. These men saw little in the first few years of Republican rule after 1801 to convince them that ignorance, poverty, and godlessness were not truly vicious threats to stable and correct government. The fundamental Federalist belief in an organic society was directly threatened by Republicans, not only in the specific area of government, but on all fronts. Individualism, wholesale migration, and a contempt for class distinctions, all seemed on the increase, spurred on by and indeed incorporated directly into Republicanism. The very foundations of civilized life were being washed away. Federalists, therefore, saw much

263

more involved in their struggle with the Republicans than was the case in ordinary political disputes.

In addition to being the manifestation of a basic view of human nature and society, Federalism was also a loose-knit and ill-organized political party which adhered to a set of specific policies. These policies, worked out largely by Alexander Hamilton, included the national bank, the funding schemes, a powerful military force, and a vigorous judiciary, all cemented together by a strong executive branch of the central government. But because Federalism *was* far more than a political party, it hung on grimly through a series of devastating political defeats and the seizure and adoption of most of its cherished policies.

If Jefferson had taught thoroughly, so had he wrought. The political party he helped to form in the 1790's swept all before it as the new century began. Rapid settlement of the western lands and the continued extension of suffrage swelled its ranks to such size that Federalist dreams seemed to vanish without trace and without hope. Americans could not, however, cultivate their chosen land by themselves. The great war in Europe moved inexorably across the ocean to involve American interests. Jefferson and Madison, hating every bit of it, tried desperately to keep it away. But war came in 1812. With it came a resuscitated Federalist party, strengthened by those who were disturbed by the course and effects of the war. Military stalemate and heavy taxes elected Federalists to office in increasing numbers. If Federalists could not contest with Jefferson under sunny skies, perhaps they could in the squally storm that was the War of 1812. Republicans rallied their forces under the ancient banners to meet this new thrust.

At the darkest hour a series of extraordinary events turned the enemy back. The Hartford Convention, favorable treaty terms, and the startling victory at New Orleans followed rapidly upon each other. Federalists watched their hope for national ascendancy crumple under a renewed burst of national pride and growth. The viciousness of Federalist attacks upon the war's conduct, coupled with threats of disunion, once again stimulated Republican fears. They would persist for many years. Whatever little chance had obtained during the previous fifteen years for Federalists to become one of two national political parties dissolved in pigheaded and spiteful Federalist conduct during the war.

Though hopes for national victory thus all but died after 1815, Federalists still remained a major political force in both the middle and New England states. Federalists in 1816 controlled the state governments of Maryland, Delaware, Connecticut, and Massachusetts. They cast between 40 and 50 per cent of the popular votes in New Jersey, New York, Rhode Island, New Hampshire, and Vermont. Their weakest position among these northern and eastern states was in Pennsylvania, where Federalists comprised just under 30 per cent of the electorate. Such wide support did not simply vanish at the onset of that unique period in our history, one of a dozen years in which no formal opposition faced the ruling party at Washington. The purpose of this study has been to uncover the role of this remaining core while the country awaited the slow re-emergence of a two-party system.

Wholesale adoption of the Federalist national program by Republicans during and after the war all but eliminated sharp policy divisions between the parties. Madison's Administration found to its sorrow that a strong navy could be most useful. The chaos of state banking systems after 1811, combined with the severe fiscal problems of the war, prompted a sharp turn away from what had been Republican dogma. The tariff and internal improvements issues had split both parties before the war and they continued to do so afterwards. By 1816 observers found it difficult to distinguish a consistent party position on any important facet of public policy. Staggered by the war's impact and by the new line of Republican policy, tens of thousands of Federalists, both leaders and supporters, struggled with an enormously difficult problem. What should they do? Should they try to keep a discrete party organization in the hope that new issues would arise and Republican governments founder? Or should they drop their party identity and try to break up the Republican party into factions which might welcome their support? Either choice was heart-rending.

The single most compelling motive for Federalists to engage in political activity after 1815 was the lure of public office, both for its own sake and because it meant that they would once again participate in the day-to-day actions of government. Federalists had always believed themselves peculiarly fitted to rule and their exclusion from office was perhaps more noxious to them than defeat on public issues. After Republicans had adopted most of the Federalist program, proscription was doubly agonizing. Until Jackson's Administration, Republicans appointed exceedingly few Federalists from the northern states to offices of consequence, either at the state or national levels. The devastating effects of proscription upon Federalists can be inferred from Edward Everett's poignant portrayal of the pre-eminence of public office in America. Everett, bred in Massachusetts Federalism, probed deeply into the nature of his society: "In this country, according to an ingenious remark of Mr. Canning, in one of his election-speeches at Liverpool, office is more important than in England. In England where families are hereditary, the hereditary family politics are of vast consideration. . . . Besides this, mere Rank is of vast consequence there, and fills the utmost ambition of many persons in a larger class of Society. Here it is unknown. Prodigious accumulations of fortune exist there, conferring of themselves very extensive influence and power, and making mere office a small thing with its possessors. The outgrown naval and military establishments open a career, in which the ambitions find scope for their talents. In place of all these, we have nothing, to which the ambitious can aspire, but office. I say nothing, because all the private walks of life are as Wide open in England as here, & afford, in that Country, as well as in this, occupation for much of the Active talent of the Community. But office here is family, rank, hereditary fortune, in Short, Everything, out of the range of private life. This links its possession with innate principles of our Nature; & truly incredible are the efforts Men are Willing to Make, the humiliations they will endure, to get it."[1] To attain office after 1815, Federalists had to pursue tortuous paths, to cleanse from at least their public utterances evidences of contempt for the lowly citizen, to learn the techniques of government in a democratic society, and to understand that they lived in a different age from that of Washington.

Proscription and constant Republican attacks upon them helped to keep Federalists a branded group standing apart long after they had ceased collectively to be a major party. That Federalists did gradually re-enter the mainstream of American political life can be traced in large part to their consuming desire for public office. Had they loftily held aloof as a bitter but powerful minority many serious effects might have resulted. The Republican party might have remained afraid to divide over real and important political issues for fear the Federalists might find some way to disrupt the government, either by cynically aiding one faction or by actually fomenting public disorder. The healthy expression of conflict through the two-party system might have been artificially and harmfully delayed even longer than it was. Federalists might have continued to be introverted and backward-looking with little incentive to adapt themselves to a rapidly changing social and political structure. A reservoir of sorely needed political talent could have been wasted. Lastly, the continued existence of a substantial non-participating minority, sullen and disaffected, could have destroyed the exhilarating claim of Americans that they had created a new society with a

[1] Everett to J. McLean, August 18, 1828, McLean Mss, LC.

267

system of government that was truly of, by, and for all its citizens.

The Republican party which James Monroe captained in 1817 was like an unnaturally swollen melon fast approaching soft maturity when it could be easily split open. Already it trembled from sharp factional quarrels within the states, quickening sectional animosities, and rude jockeying for claims to the succession. Monroe himself was curiously confused about his role as president. He was attracted to wistful fancies of a country unsullied by internal conflicts, yet he understood that he had assumed practical responsibilities as a party leader. He hoped that dissident Federalists could somehow be converted to Republicanism by kindly sentiments and friendly attention, yet he stubbornly refused to ignore what he called the legitimate and proper claims of his party. He hated political contention, yet he appears to have believed that some prominent Federalist leaders had once been monarchists. Over-all, Monroe's presidency presented the image of a syrupy overlay that covered endless frustrations and deepening hostilities. Federalists tried to pick their way back to political consequence while Republicans searched about for direction and purpose. All but the deluded knew that one-partyism was hopelessly artificial in America, but few could envision the new party groupings that must necessarily come forth. For Republicans the prospect of splitting their party aroused fears that ravening Federalists would somehow turn such a schism to their own advantage. Nevertheless, in several of the states Republicans quickly divided into factions and Federalists in turn offered their support in return for office and power.

Most Federalists sensed that Monroe's leadership was ineffectual; but they could not agree upon a single course of action to capitalize upon its ineffectiveness. If they retained their separate identity, Republicans could be rallied to unite against the old enemy; if they did not, they must either retire from the political field or else be swallowed up by Republican-ism in exchange for possible rewards that might be granted to individual Federalists. Monroe's policies met with general approval among Federalists and few had any wish to oppose the government at Washington. This decision was reinforced by the fatuous hope that Monroe would let down the barriers of proscription. In most of the states, on the other hand, Federalists wanted strongly to keep Republicans out of state and local offices, because there they honestly differed on policies. Their position, however, was seriously weakened by the lack of Federalist opposition to a Republican president. The result was that the Republicans inexorably toppled Fed-eralist administrations, one after the other, state by state and town by town.

Yet in spite of these victories, the disintegration of Jeffer-son's forces went on relentlessly. Two towering events both symbolized and promoted this disintegration. The Missouri debates and presidential campaign of 1824 opened great cracks in the Republican edifice. In each Federalists saw both a chance to break up the monolithic opposition and a stepping-stone to public prominence and office. Most Federal-ists in the North did not believe that the Missouri dispute alone would catapult their party into power. Rather did they view its political consequences in terms of forcing the Republi-cans to ask aid from the Federalists, and of creating sectional splinter parties which might be later manipulated and turned to advantage by Federalists. On the Compromise issue, too, individual Federalist leaders found an opportunity to regain prestige in their society by standing at the head of a powerful moral cause. Federalist leaders at Washington participated vigorously in the congressional debates, and all over the North Federalists joined with Republicans to organize protest meetings. Later on, Republican leaders, desperate as they were to bring an end to this divisive quarrel, fastened upon Federalism to further a solution. Thus they conjured up a

Federalist plot to account for both the onset of the Missouri question and for the profound differences of opinion that existed among Republicans themselves. But slavery was no more a false issue in 1820 than it was to be in future decades, however vigorously Federalism might be pushed forward as a scapegoat. Federalists were encouraged by the long-run implications of this controversy, but they could rejoice over few immediate benefits. The increasingly bitter presidential campaign promised more.

Each of the Republican candidates for the presidency in 1824 was aware from the beginning that the race would be close. Each, accordingly, was tempted by the lure of Federalist votes. It was dangerous business. To lose one's claims to Republican purity could be disastrous. Federalists themselves were well aware that a price might be paid for their support, a price to be measured, they hoped, in terms of public office and preferment. They also knew that Federalist support, if given generally to one man, would probably insure his defeat. For Republican candidates and Federalist leaders alike the campaign was marked by incredible deviousness, countless recriminations, and anguished soul-searching.

As the campaign wore on, various individual Federalists joined the cause of each candidate. Though personal and sectional allegiances did influence the course of some, Federalists could find remarkably little in the realm of public issues to distinguish the nominees. Their choices appeared to rest largely upon calculations of which candidate would most likely let down the bars of proscription. Thus Federalists were exceedingly eager to catch at any hint, however subtle, that a particular candidate would steer a new course. Adams' known dislike for violent partisanship, consequently, was a strong inducement for his Federalist admirers. Crawford's friends industriously circulated the promise that the Georgian's administration would be a "broad-bottomed" one. Calhoun held out the prospect that the election would bring about a new division of parties in which all could find a place. Lastly, the publication of Jackson's celebrated correspondence with Monroe in 1816 caused thousands of Federalist hearts to thump in joyful anticipation. Supporters of each candidate were able, with justice, to accuse the other hopefuls of pandering to Federalists. The chief beneficiary of these endless charges was probably the man whose Republicanism was most often called into question, the apostate Federalist John Quincy Adams. Just because he had been an apostate, Adams was rarely supported by Federalists with enthusiasm, and many Federalists saw little profit in backing him because the Republicans, still suspicious of Adams' conversion, would searchingly examine each of his appointees for signs of a Federalist taint.

Each of the candidates, then, had his train of Federalist auxiliaries when he went to the people for their suffrages. The desire of Federalists to re-enter public life in the wake of one or another of the candidates was matched by their candidate's lust for fresh support. Indecision at the polls threw the election into the House of Representatives. There Federalists joined in the melee with decisive results. Once again the critical point was the prospect of public office. Henry Clay's dramatic turn to Adams secured to the dour Bay Stater eleven states in all, some of them by the shaky vote of a single representative. Two more were needed. At this time Daniel Webster of Boston dropped his noncommittal course and set in motion a series of extraordinary moves involving the crucial votes of Federalist members from two states, New York and Maryland. Central to Webster's purpose was a private meeting with Adams a few days before the House vote. There Webster obtained a virtual promise that Adams would appoint to office at least one Federalist and probably others. This "pledge" in his pocket, and firm in his belief that Adams must necessarily be grateful for his services, Webster found the needed votes. Adams was elected president.

271

His term in office, however, would be haunted by highly-colored versions of the "pledge" story. Webster proved to be a faithful, not to say powerful, supporter of President Adams. Yet his adherence proved also to be a boomerang. To bring down Adams, Jacksonians worked tirelessly to weave the "pledge" story plus Webster's favored position among Adams' advisors into a heavy net that reeked of Federalism.

Jacksonians were helped immensely by political incompetence within the Adams Administration and by the personal conduct of Adams' Federalist friends. Some of the president's Republican intimates believed strongly that Adams must try to attract a wide support among Federalists, whereas others just as strongly argued against this plan. All the efforts to summon Federalist support were severely hampered by the fact that very few Federalists were ever actually appointed to valued offices. Of many reasons for this decision, perhaps the two most important were the prior claims of Adams Republicans and the threat of a renewed Jacksonian assault upon Adams' Republicanism. The Administration's relations with Federalists were never clear-cut, always vacillating. This fact both demoralized firm Republican adherents and provided prime ammunition for Jacksonian orators and presses.

Adams himself was anything but naïve about Federalists. He had lived too long among them. Yet he knew that there was no longer any possibility that Federalism would rise again or that its peculiar blend of self-designated class leadership could ever have a lasting place in the United States. Accordingly, he was often impatient with the lingering fears that prevailed among the mass of Republican voters. But his Federalist partisans, eager to use the Adams cause as a springboard to office, fanned these fears by pressing "amalgamation" upon the Adams Republicans. The strongest weapon of these Federalists was the plea that Jackson could be warded off only if all of Adams' friends worked together, sharing victory and defeat alike. Administration leaders, Adams among them, were neither astute enough nor tough enough (as Jackson's lieutenants were later to be) to make sure that these Federalists did not act as though they were members of an alliance rather than soldiers under a common flag. The Adams Administration was not a Federalist one, but it suffered terribly from the stamp of Federalism and its votaries.

Jackson's crushing victory in 1828 cleared the way for the re-emergence of two-party government in America. Along the way the Hero had secured the support of countless thousands of Federalists, or former Federalists as they preferred to be called. Their reasons for enlisting in his legions were many. None was more persuasive than the reasonable hope that the pride of Tennessee would generally disregard former party distinctions in forming his party leadership and making appointments. His correspondence with Monroe, his known loyalty to all those who supported him whatever their antecedents, and his residence in a state where Federalism had never counted in politics—all weighed heavily. Expectation turned to reality when Jackson, secure in his own glistening popularity, appointed numbers of former Federalists to the highest offices, indeed more than had been appointed by all his Republican predecessors combined. By 1830, men tutored in the tenets of Federalism had moved into the top leadership of both the Jacksonian party and the new National Republican party. Federalism still remained a political issue, but the creation of two new party groupings, with former Republicans and Federalists in each, signaled the opening of a new era. Federalists probably delayed this desirable event; they certainly played a major role in bringing about, albeit tardily, the new party alignment.

BIBLIOGRAPHY

THE MOST USEFUL SOURCES for such a study as this one are, of course, the private letters to and from the principal actors and the files of contemporary newspapers. Because Federalists found themselves in a Republican world after 1815, a world in which they had to find their way, the letters and newspapers of Republican worthies are almost as necessary as those of Federalists. Perhaps the three most useful of the available letter collections, published and unpublished, are those of Henry Clay, Rufus King, and Daniel Webster. Near these in importance is the correspondence of Simeon Baldwin, Vergil Maxcy, James Monroe, Timothy Pickering, John Taylor, and Martin Van Buren. No doubt many others of equal or greater value have escaped notice.

An articulate and politically-minded newspaper editor is always a joy to the researcher in nineteenth-century American history. Happily there were several of these gentlemen in the period 1815-1830. William Coleman of the *New York Post*, Robert Walsh of the *Philadelphia National Gazette*, and the young Federalist rebels headed by Charles King, who edited the *New York American*, have left us invaluable information and commentary. Just below these in value as newspaper sources are the *Boston Courier*, the *Connecticut Mirror*, *Niles Weekly Register*, and the *Portsmouth* (N.H.) *Gazette*. Once more it is necessary to say with sorrow that other files of consequence must have gone unread.

Though letters and newspapers are the chief mines of evidence the story could not be told without a mass of contemporary pamphlets, party addresses, the printed proceedings of both state constitutional and political party conventions, legislative debates and votes, and the diggings of scholars into the social and political history of America as it emerged from the War of 1812. Of special value in this latter category have been the writings of George Dangerfield and Philip Klein.

BIBLIOGRAPHY

Custom seems to demand, however unnecessary it may be to anyone who has tried to piece together a chapter of history, that a disclaimer be entered to the effect that this bibliographic listing is confined to the most important materials and that many other sources were consulted either for specific factual information or to swell the total of bitter-sweet disappointments that always attend research, whether in history or genetics.

LETTER COLLECTIONS

Library of Congress (LC)
John Q. Adams Mss
Nicholas Biddle Mss
Henry Clay Mss
William Darlington Mss
William Eustis Mss
Francis Granger Mss
Robert Harper Mss
James Heaton Mss
Robert Jarvis Mss
James Kent Mss
James Madison Mss
Vergil Maxcy Mss
John McLean Mss
James Monroe Mss
William Plumer Letterbook
William Plumer Mss
Samuel Smith Mss
Samuel Southard Mss
Martin Van Buren Mss
Daniel Webster Mss
Gideon Welles Mss
William Wirt Letterbook

Massachusetts Historical Society (MHS)
Miscellaneous Mss
Harrison Otis Mss
Timothy Pickering Mss

New York Historical Society (NYHS)
John Bailey Mss
William Coleman Mss

Charles Ingersoll Mss
Rufus King Mss
Charles Mercer Mss
Nathaniel Pendleton Mss
Henry Smith Mss
Henry Storrs Mss
John Taylor Mss
Gulian Verplanck Mss

New York Public Library (NYPL)
James Barbour Mss
Perry Childs Mss
Azariah Flagg Mss
Samuel Gouverneur Mss
Vergil Maxcy Mss
James Monroe Mss
Harrison Otis Mss
Caesar Rodney Mss
Winfield Scott Mss
John and Isaiah Townsend Mss

Pennsylvania Historical Society (PHS)
James Buchanan Mss
Lewis Coryell Mss
Alexander Dallas Mss
Dreer Collection
Gardiner Collection
Gratz Collection
James Johnston Mss
William Jones Mss
Thomas McKean Mss
William Meredith Mss

Richard Peters Mss

Robert Vaux Mss

William Woodhouse Mss

Springfield (Mass.) Public Library (SPL)

William Lathrop Mss

Yale University Library (YL)

Simeon Baldwin Mss

David Daggett Mss

NEWSPAPERS

Baltimore Federal Gazette

Baltimore Federal Republican

Baltimore Marylander

Boston Columbian Centinel

Boston Courier

Boston Jackson Republican

Boston Palladium

Boston Patriot

Connecticut Mirror

Hartford (Conn.) *Times*

New York American

New York National Advocate

New York Post

Niles Weekly Register

Philadelphia Franklin Gazette

Philadelphia National Gazette

Philadelphia U.S. Gazette

Philadelphia Union

Portsmouth (N.H.) *Gazette*

Providence Gazette

Rhode-Island American

Springfield (Mass.) *Republican*

Worcester (Mass.) *National Aegis*

PUBLISHED LETTER COLLECTIONS, DIARIES, AUTOBIOGRAPHIES, AND REMINISCENCES

Adams, Charles F., ed., *Memoirs of John Quincy Adams, Comprising Portions of His Diary from 1795 to 1848* (12 vols.; Philadelphia, 1874-77).

Adams, Charles F., ed., *The Works of John Adams* (10 vols.; Boston, 1850-56).

Adams, Henry, ed., *The Writings of Albert Gallatin* (3 vols.; Philadelphia, 1879).

Andrews, William W., ed., *The Correspondence of the Hon. John Cotton Smith, LL.D., Formerly Governor of Connecticut* (New York, 1847).

Barck, Dorothy C., ed., *Letters from John Pintard to His Daughter Eliza Noel Pintard Davidson* (4 vols.; New York, 1940-41).

Bassett, John S., ed., *Correspondence of Andrew Jackson* (7 vols.; Washington, 1926-35).

Beecher, Charles, ed., *Autobiography, Correspondence, Etc., of Lyman Beecher, D.D.* (2 vols.; New York, 1865).

Binns, John, *Recollections of the Life of John Binns* (Philadelphia, 1854).

Colton, Calvin, ed., *Works of Henry Clay* (7 vols.; New York, 1897).

Ellery, Harrison, ed., *The Memoirs of Gen. Joseph Gardner Swift, LL.D., U.S.A.* (Worcester, Mass., 1890).

Fitzpatrick, John C., ed., "The Autobiography of Martin Van Buren," *Annual Report of the American Historical Association for the Year 1918* (2 vols.; Washington, 1920), II.

Ford, Paul L., ed., *The Writings of Thomas Jefferson* (10 vols.; New York, 1904-05).

Ford, Worthington C., ed., *Writings of John Quincy Adams* (7 vols.; New York, 1913-17).

Hamilton, James A., *Men and Events, at Home and Abroad, During Three Quarters of a Century* (New York, 1869).

Hay, Thomas R., "John C. Calhoun and the Presidential Campaign of 1824. Some Unpublished Calhoun Letters," *American Historical Review*, XL (1934), 82-96.

Hilliard, George S., ed., *Memoir and Correspondence of Jeremiah Mason* (Cambridge, Mass., 1873).

Hunt, Gaillard, ed., *The First Forty Years of Washington Society* (New York, 1906).

Jameson, J. Franklin, ed., "Correspondence of John C. Calhoun," *Annual Report of the American Historical Association for the Year 1899* (2 vols.; Washington, 1900), II.

Johnston, Henry P., ed., *The Correspondence and Public Papers of John Jay* (4 vols.; New York, 1893).

Kent, William, ed., *Memoirs and Letters of James Kent, LL.D.* (Boston, 1898).

King, Charles R., ed., *The Life and Correspondence of Rufus King* (6 vols.; New York, 1894-1900).

Klein, Philip S., ed., "Memoirs of a Senator from Pennsylvania, Jonathan Roberts, 1771-1854," *The Pennsylvania Magazine of History and Biography*, LXII (1938), 361-409.

Lodge, Henry C., ed., "Letters of Hon. Elijah H. Mills," *Proceedings of the Massachusetts Historical Society*, XIX (1881-82), 12-53.

McGrane, Reginald C., ed., *The Correspondence of Nicholas Biddle Dealing with National Affairs: 1807-1844* (Boston/New York, 1919).

Moore, John B., ed., *The Works of James Buchanan* (12 vols.; Philadelphia/London, 1908-11).

Sargent, Nathan, *Public Men and Events* (2 vols.; Philadelphia, 1875).

Scudder, Henry E., ed., *Recollections of Samuel Breck with Passages from His Note-Books* (Philadelphia, 1877).

Story, William W., ed., *Life and Letters of Joseph Story* (2 vols.; Boston, 1851).

Tarbox, Increase N., ed., *Diary of Thomas Robbins, D.D., 1796-1854* (2 vols.; Boston, 1886).

Van Tyne, Charles H., ed., *The Letters of Daniel Webster* (New York, 1902).

Warren, Charles, ed., *Jacobin and Junto or Early American Politics as Viewed in the Diary of Dr. Nathaniel Ames: 1758-1822* (Cambridge, Mass., 1931).

Webster, Fletcher, ed., *The Writings and Speeches of Daniel Webster* (18 vols.; Boston, 1903).

Weed, Harriet A., ed., *Autobiography of Thurlow Weed* (Boston, 1883).

CONTEMPORARY PAMPHLETS, PARTY ADDRESSES, AND SPEECHES

Address of the Central Committee . . . Friendly to the Election of John Q. Adams . . . Held . . . in Boston, June 10, 1828 (Boston, 1828).

An Address to the People of Maryland, from Their Delegates in the Late National Republican Convention . . . (Baltimore, 1832).

Address of the Republican General Committee of Young Men of the City and County of New York, Friendly to the Election of Gen. Andrew Jackson to the Presidency, to the Republican Electors of the State of New York (New York, 1828).

The Presidential Question. To the Friends of Equal Rights (Philadelphia, 1828).

Republican Nomination for Governor and Lt. Governor. With an Address to the Electors of the State of New York (n.p., 1820).

Royalty of Federalism! Read, Try, Decide, on the Charge of Washington, That Leading Federalists are to Monarchy Devoted (Boston, [1816?]).

Sketches of Character; or Facts and Arguments Relative to the Presidential Election, 1828 (Philadelphia, 1828).

The Union Republican Ticket for 1820 (Hartford, 1820).

Who Shall be President? The Hero of New Orleans, or John the Second, of the House of Braintree. By a Republican of the Old School (Boston, 1828).

Speech of Thomas Kennedy, Esq. at the Jackson Meeting, Held at the Court-House in Hagers-Town (Md.), August 4th, 1827 (Hagerstown, 1827).

Speech of Thomas P. Moore, Esq., Delivered in the Court House in Harrodsburg (Ky.), June 3d, 1827 (Harrodsburg, 1827).

Speech of Mr. Plumer, of New Hampshire, on the Missouri Question, Delivered in the House of Representatives of the United States, February 21, 1820 (n.p., n.d.).

A Selection of Eulogies Pronounced in Honor of those Illustrious Patriots and Statesmen: John Adams and Thomas Jefferson (Hartford, 1826).

PROCEEDINGS OF PARTY OR STATE CONSTITUTIONAL CONVENTIONS, AND LEGISLATIVE BODIES

Annals of the Congress of the United States. Fourteenth Congress: First Session (Washington, 1854).

Debates of the Delaware Convention, for Revising the Constitution of the State, or Adopting a New One; Held at Dover, November 1831 (Wilmington, 1831).

The Debates and Journal of the Constitutional Convention of the State of Maine, 1819-20 (Augusta, 1894).

Journal of Debates and Proceedings in the Convention of Delegates Chosen to Revise the Constitution of Massachusetts, Begun and Holden at Boston, November 15, 1820 (Boston, 1853).

Journal of the Executive Proceedings of the Senate of the United States of America, III (Washington, 1829).

Journal of the National Republican Convention, which Assembled in the City of Baltimore, Dec. 12, 1831, for the Nominations of Candidates to Fill the Offices of President and Vice President (Washington, 1831).

Journal of the Proceedings of the National Republican Convention, Held at Worcester, October 11, 1832 (Boston, 1832).

Proceedings and Address of the Republican Young Men of the State of New York, Assembled at Utica, on the Twelfth Day of August, 1828 (New York, 1828).

Proceedings of the Administration Meeting in Baltimore County—June 1827 (Baltimore, 1827).

Proceedings of a Convention of the People of Maine Friendly to the Present Administration . . . Holden in . . . Portland . . . on the 23d of January, 1828 (Portland, 1828).

Proceedings of the Democratic Convention, Held at Harrisburg, Pennsylvania, January 8, 1828 (Harrisburg, 1828).

Proceedings of the Maryland Administration Convention, Delegated by the People, and Held in Baltimore, on Monday and Tuesday, July 23d and 24th, 1827 (Baltimore, 1827).

Proceedings of the New York State Convention Composed of Delegates Elected by Friends of the Present Administration of our National Government, Held at Albany on June 10 & 11, 1828 (Albany, 1828).

Proceedings of the National Republican Convention of Young Men, which Assembled in the City of Washington: May 7, 1832 (Washington, 1832).

Proceedings of the Pennsylvania Democratic Convention, Held at Harrisburg on January 4, 1828 (Harrisburg, 1828).

280

Proceedings of the State Convention of National Republican Young Men, Holden at Hartford, on Wednesday, October 17, 1832 (Hartford, 1832).

Reports of the Proceedings and Debates of the Convention of 1821, Assembled for the Purpose of Amending the Constitution of the State of New York . . . . (Albany, 1854).

Report of the Proceedings of the Town Meeting in the City of Philadelphia July 7th, 1828 (Philadelphia, 1828).

Summary of the Proceedings of a Convention . . . for the Purpose of Nominating a Candidate for the Office of Vice-President . . . Held at Baltimore . . . May, 1832 (Albany, 1832).

GENERAL HISTORIES, BIOGRAPHIES, JOURNAL ARTICLES, ETC.

Bemis, Samuel F., *John Quincy Adams and the Union* (New York, 1956).

Berthoff, Rowland, "The American Social Order; A Conservative Hypothesis," *American Historical Review*, LXV (April 1960), 495-514.

Bigelow, John, "DeWitt Clinton as a Politician," *Harper's New Monthly Magazine*, L (1874-75), 563-71.

Binney, Charles C., *The Life of Horace Binney* (Philadelphia/ London, 1903).

Bonney, Catharina V. R., *A Legacy of Historical Gleanings* (2 vols.; Albany, 1875).

Borden, Morton, *The Federalism of James A. Bayard* (New York, 1955).

Brown, Everett S., ed., *The Missouri Compromises and Presidential Politics: 1820-1825* (St. Louis, 1926).

Brown, Robert E., *Middle-Class Democracy and the Revolution in Massachusetts, 1691-1780* (Ithaca, N.Y., 1955).

Carroll, Eber M., "Politics During the Administration of John Quincy Adams," *South Atlantic Quarterly*, XXIII (1924), 141-54.

Curtis, George T., *Life of Daniel Webster* (2 vols.; New York, 1870).

Dangerfield, George, *The Era of Good Feelings* (New York, 1952).

Delaplaine, Edward S., *Francis Scott Key: Life and Times* (New York, 1937).

Dwight, Timothy, *Travels in New-England and New-York* (4 vols.; New Haven, 1821-22).

Emmet, Thomas A., *Memoir of Thomas Addis and Robert Emmet* (2 vols.; New York, 1915).

Fee, Walter R., *The Transition from Aristocracy to Democracy in New Jersey: 1789-1829* (Somerville, N.J., 1833).

Fuess, Claude M., *Daniel Webster* (2 vols.; Boston, 1930).

Hailperin, Herman, "Pro-Jackson Sentiment in Pennsylvania, 1820-1828," *The Pennsylvania Magazine of History and Biography*, L (1926), 193-240.

Hockett, Homer C., "Rufus King and the Missouri Compromise," *Missouri Historical Review*, II (1907-08), 211-20.

Hockett, Homer C., "Federalism and the West," *Essays in American History Dedicated to Frederick Jackson Turner* (New York, 1910), 113-35.

James, Marquis, *The Life of Andrew Jackson* (New York, 1938).

Klein, Philip S., *Pennsylvania Politics: 1817-1832. A Game Without Rules* (Philadelphia, 1940).

Klein, Philip S., "Early Lancaster County Politics," *Pennsylvania History*, III (1936), 98-114.

Konkle, Burton A., *Joseph Hopkinson* (Philadelphia, 1931).

McCormick, Richard P., "Suffrage Classes and Party Alignments: A Study in Voter Behavior," *Mississippi Valley Historical Review*, XLVI (December 1959), 397-410.

Meigs, William M., *The Life of Charles Jared Ingersoll* (Philadelphia, 1900).

Moore, Glover, *The Missouri Controversy: 1819-1821* (Lexington, Ky., 1953).

Morison, Samuel E., *The Life and Letters of Harrison Gray Otis* (2 vols.; Boston/New York, 1913).

Munroe, John A., *Federalist Delaware, 1775-1815* (New Brunswick, N.J., 1954).

Parton, James, *Life of Andrew Jackson* (3 vols.; New York, 1860).

Plumer, William, Jr., *Life of William Plumer* (Boston, 1857).

Quincy, Edmund, *Life of Josiah Quincy* (Boston, 1868).

Quincy, Josiah, *Memoir of the Life of John Quincy Adams* (Boston, 1858).

Remini, Robert V., *Martin Van Buren and the Making of the Democratic Party* (New York, 1959).

Richardson, Charles and Elizabeth M., *Charles Miner, A Pennsylvania Pioneer* (Wilkes-Barre, Pa., 1916).

Schauinger, Joseph H., *William Gaston, Carolinian* (Milwaukee, Wis., 1949).

Semmes, John E., *John H. B. Latrobe and His Times, 1803-1891* (Baltimore, 1917).

Shipp, James E. D., *Giant Days or the Life and Times of William H. Crawford* (Americus, Ga., 1909).

Steiner, Bernard C., *Life of Roger Brooke Taney* (Baltimore, 1922).

Steiner, Bernard C., "Van Buren's Maryland Correspondents," *Maryland Historical Magazine*, VIII (1913), 141-49.

Sullivan, William, *Familiar Letters on Public Characters, and Public Events, from the Peace of 1783, to the Peace of 1815* (Boston, 1834).

Tudor, William, *Letters on the Eastern States* (Boston, 1821).

Tyler, Samuel, *Memoir of Roger Brooke Taney, LL.D.* (Baltimore, 1872).

Upham, Charles W. and Octavius Pickering, *The Life of Timothy Pickering* (4 vols.; Boston, 1867-73).

Van Buren, Martin, *Inquiry into the Origin and Course of Political Parties in the United States* (New York, 1867).

Walters, Raymond, *Albert Gallatin: Jeffersonian Financier and Diplomat* (New York, 1957).

Weston, Florence, *The Presidential Election of 1828* (Washington, 1938).

Williamson, Chilton, *American Suffrage: From Property to Democracy, 1760-1860* (Princeton, N.J., 1960).

INDEX

Adams, John, 28, 31, 79
Adams, John Quincy, 270-72; appointment policy, 134, 185-86, 208-09; attacked by Jacksonians, 201; attacks Federalist leaders in 1828, 242-43; and John C. Calhoun, 152-53; election in 1825, 172-83; and Federalism, 20, 67; Federalist opposition to, 217-22; and Joseph Hopkinson, 211-13; Inaugural Address, 186; and internal improvements, 128; and Rufus King, 187-88; the Missouri Compromise, 90; and New Hampshire, 192; political abilities of, 199-200; presidential candidate in 1824, 136-46; public image as president, 197; role in "Webster Pledge" episode, 215-16; as secretary of state, 39
Albany Argus, 126
American Society for the Encouragement of American Manufactures, 64
Ames, Fisher, 8, 40, 142
Ames, Nathaniel, 55
Anti-Masonic Party, 256-57

Bailey, John, 139, 214
Baldwin, Ebenezer, 220
Baldwin, Henry, 92, 238, 247
Baldwin, Simeon, 129
Baltimore, 83
Baltimore Federal Republican, 19, 49, 56, 60-61, 102, 109, 123-26, 139
Bank of the United States (Second), 14, 17, 22-23, 64, 126, 250
Barbour, James, 66, 189, 252
Bayard, James, 60, 205, 239
Baylies, Francis, 229, 246
Beecher, Lyman, 80, 96
Bell, Samuel, 224-26
Berrien, John, 196, 213, 245
Biddle, Nicholas, 160
Binney, Horace, 128, 247
Binns, John, 160-62, 218, 236, 254
Blake, George, 49

Bleecker, Harmanus, 183-84
Bogardus, Robert, 159
Boston, 29, 48, 117
Boston Courier, 142, 147, 155, 166-67, 192n, 204-05
Boston Jackson Republican, 220, 229, 244
Boston Palladium, 18, 25, 40, 62
Boston Patriot, 49, 68, 192n, 227-29, 253
Boston Statesman, 205, 229
Bowles, Samuel, 192n, 228. *See also Springfield Republican*
Bowne, Walter, 38
Branch, John, 245
Breck, Samuel, 99, 128
Brooks, John, 35, 81, 117-18
Buchanan, James, 135, 152, 157, 196, 238

Calhoun, John C., 58, 132, 135, 172, 197, 221, 270; Federalist view toward in 1824 campaign, 151-54; Pennsylvania Republican support, 157-59; helps Federalist friends get appointments in 1829-1831, 246
Carey, Matthew, 34, 61, 92, 155
Carr, Dabney, 256-57
Carroll, Charles (of Carrollton), 61, 177, 240
caucus, 9, 66
Charleston Mercury, 110
Chester (Pa.) *Village Record*, 121, 155
Cheves, Langdon, 27n
Clay, Henry, 55-56, 132-33, 137, 180-81, 205-06, 245, 257, 271; attacked by Jacksonians, 172, 201-02; Federalist views toward, 51, 154-56; helps form opposition party after 1829, 251; political officer of Adams' administration, 197-99; praises Daniel Webster, 99; role in appointment of Joseph Hopkinson, 212-13; role in "Webster Pledge" episode, 214; tariff advocate, 17

285

291